High Praise for Naomi H. Rosenblatt and
WRESTLING WITH ANGELS

"Naomi Rosenblatt is a remarkably stimulating and charismatic teacher. Her Bible classes were a weekly source of inspiration for all of us who attended them here at the U.S. Senate. Her book will provide a new and warm understanding of the Bible in clear and illuminating prose."
—Howard Metzenbaum, United States senator

"Eloquently interconnecting holiness and dailiness, *Wrestling with Angels* illuminates the Bible's enduring relevance to our modern-day struggles and fears and profoundest yearnings."
—Judith Viorst, author of *Necessary Losses*

"Naomi vividly brings to life Jacob, Joseph, and other biblical characters to provide special insights into today's world problems."
—Arlen Specter, United States senator

"It is as if she [Naomi Rosenblatt] has orchestrated the sweetest of family reunions, one where we are reintroduced to the people who have shaped our lives, only to discover that, as adults, we more clearly understand their strengths and flaws."—*Publishers Weekly*

"Naomi Rosenblatt is an exceptionally gifted person with a sharp mind and a winning personality. For five years I had the privilege of being her student. These were among the most challenging and rewarding years of my life."—Marvin Kalb, director, Shorenstein Center on Press and Politics, Harvard University

"Naomi is a wonderful person, and I don't think I have ever sat under a more effective teacher than she."
—Reverend Richard C. Halverson, chaplain, U.S. Senate

For Laura,
All the
best,

WRESTLING
with
ANGELS

———

What Genesis Teaches Us About
Our Spiritual Identity, Sexuality,
and Personal Relationships

———

Naomi H. Rosenblatt
a n d
Joshua Horwitz

Delta
Trade Paperbacks

A Delta Book
Published by
Dell Publishing
a division of
Bantam Doubleday Dell Publishing Group, Inc.
1540 Broadway
New York, New York 10036

Genealogy chart on p. 88 reprinted by permission of:
The Jewish Theological Seminary of America, 5080
Broadway, New York, N.Y. 10027.

ISBN: 0-385-31333-0

Reprinted by arrangement with Delacorte Press

Manufactured in the United States of America
Published simultaneously in Canada

October 1996

10 9 8 7 6 5 4 3 2 1

BVG

To the loving memory of my parents,
Sara and Ephraim Harris.

—N.H.R.

To Ericka,
who renews my world every day.

—J. H.

Contents

PART ONE
PROLOGUE TO THE FIRST FAMILY:
THE BIRTH OF SPIRITUAL IDENTITY

PART TWO
ABRAHAM AND SARAH: FORGING COVENANTS WITH GOD AND FAMILY

PART THREE

JACOB BECOMES ISRAEL: WRESTLING WITH THE CHALLENGES OF FAMILY RELATIONSHIPS

PART FOUR
JOSEPH AND HIS BROTHERS:
A FAMILY'S JOURNEY FROM BETRAYAL
TO FORGIVENESS

Acknowledgments

This book owes its inception to two individuals: Gail Ross, our agent and friend, who urged us to get together and write a book about the Hebrew Bible, and Steve Ross, our editor, who carried a bright torch for this project from the first day he read our proposal. We thank both of them for the encouragement and care they have lavished on us and our book for the past two years.

We would also like to acknowledge and thank several people who read the manuscript in different drafts and generously shared their insights with us: Bill Allman, Professor Harold Brodsky, Elinor Horwitz, Nessa Rapoport, Stephen Tukel, Lori Weinstein, Tamara Weisberg, and Rita Wolfson. Many thanks are also due to Jacquie Miller for kind assistance.

Special thanks to my husband, Peter, who tolerated a perpetually cluttered dining room these past two years, and whose support and sharp editorial pen have been indispensable. And my thanks, also, to my children, Therese, Daniel, David, and my son-in-law Marshall who enrich my life so, and to whom I owe many of the observations contained in this book.

Finally and most profoundly, my gratitude goes to my Bible study teachers at Beth Sefer Reali, my school in Haifa, Israel, who filled me with love, respect, and awe for the eternal Book.

—N.H.R.

I'd like to thank my wife, Ericka, for her patience, support and encouragement during the writing of this book, which coincided with the birth and first year of life of our daughter Tanya.

—J.H.

GENESIS:
AN ANCIENT BOOK OF
MODERN WISDOM

Family relationships are inherently challenging and rife with conflict. Yet the family unit endures as the universal crucible in which we forge our identity. As microcosms of human interdependence, families embody our limitless capacity for love and competition, for betrayal and forgiveness. Novelists and playwrights have detailed the infinite variety of troubled families, and modern psychology has charted the obstacle course of the human soul that family relationships must navigate. But neither literature nor psychology has been able to satisfy our hunger for a spiritual identity and a system of values to guide our lives.

Three millennia before the writings of Tolstoy and Freud, the Book of Genesis chronicled one family's multigenerational struggle to come to terms with the eternal themes of meaning and purpose. By exploring this saga of the first family of the Bible, we can discover how their conflicts and transcendent spiritual vision reflect our own contemporary search for a purposeful life. What makes the first family of Genesis uniquely contemporary and compelling? How do the lives of these people speak to us today? How do their struggles illuminate our personal issues of identity, meaning, and purpose? There are no simple answers, no pat formulas for salvation. But what the Book of Genesis does offer is a comprehensive framework for exploring human nature and for embracing adult life with all its rewards and responsibilities.

Both the human condition and family dynamic have changed remarkably little since ancient times. The men and women of Genesis are very much like you and me—lusting for pleasure and power, dealing with sibling rivalry, and learning, by trial and error, how to be parents. They fail more often than they succeed. But it is through failing that they move forward, however painfully, in solving their problems. To the end, this family prevails by clinging to its faith in its spiritual identity. One generation is linked to the next by a shared commitment to a higher purpose that transcends the mundane aspects of its members' lives, offering a code of behavior that curbs their worst instincts and gives expression to their highest ideals of compassion, love, and justice.

My love affair with the Hebrew Bible—also known as the Old Testament—began when I was a six-year-old schoolgirl in Haifa, Israel. Biblical studies were a daily part of school life, my treasured window into the adult world. The stories of the Bible were not fairy tales to me, but vivid human dramas with larger-than-life personalities. I learned about adult passion from David and Bathsheba, about jealousy from Sarah, about tenacity and enduring faith from Abraham, and about depression from Saul. Their Hebrew language was the language of my daily life. The land they walked on was the land that I hiked over and lived in. Early on I concluded that if I studied and internalized this Book, I could understand everything there was to know about life without ever having to leave my neighborhood.

I was grateful for the Bible's total candor in portraying humanity with all its frailties and imperfections. Its characters embodied all the highest and lowest human drives—even the heroes, whom I learned to embrace without illusions and without feelings of personal inadequacy. As a teenager plagued by the usual array of adolescent insecurities, I was reassured by the knowledge that I, too, could err and still feel entitled to love and acceptance. In a very direct way, the Bible invited and empowered me to become an adult. By presenting life as it is, with all its contradictions and subtleties, the Bible guided me down the long, patient path of understanding and compassion. This path, which began with Bible study, eventually led me to my work as a psychotherapist.

Genesis tells the story of a people who believed in an abstract, transcendent God and embraced the concept of their creation in His image as fundamental to their identity. The horror of the Holocaust, which was the omnipresent backdrop to my adolescence and young adulthood, taught me how crucial a spiritual identity is to overcoming life's adversities. Many of my immediate neighbors were refugees from Germany and, later, survivors of the death camps. They came to Israel with only what they carried on their backs— and inside their souls. As I was growing up, I watched them rebuild their lives from the ground up, building on whatever inner core of identity had survived. I couldn't comprehend the horror of the Nazi death camps, and the Bible provided no absolute answers. But it gave me the courage at an early age to confront tough questions about human nature. The Bible demanded that I challenge both myself and my God for an explanation of evil and injustice in the world, as characters throughout the Bible do, from Abraham to Job.

Half a century later, and half a world away from Israel, the Bible is still the prism through which I view the world. The biblical characters and stories I first encountered as a child continue to shape my adult roles as psychotherapist, teacher, wife, mother, and friend.

While the Bible shows us that human nature has not changed since ancient times, the social framework of our lives is utterly transformed. The multigenerational family has virtually disappeared. And without it, we've become cut off from our cultural, moral, and spiritual roots. There has been much talk in recent years about family values, but little serious discussion about what family represents and why family values are worth preserving.

So much of modern life is devoid of human warmth or a sense of belonging. Ninety percent of what I do in my therapy practice involves helping my patients combat the alienation and anonymity they experience because of the breakup of old patterns of bonding in families and in the community. Every day I meet people adrift in the world without an inner compass—filled with self-doubt, empty of any sense of purpose. Many of them are successful professionally; some are very wealthy and powerful. I see them distanced from their families and with no real ties to their communities. Often their job descriptions have become the only anchors for their identities.

One way to counteract these feelings of anonymity is by going back and reading the Bible, beginning with the Book of Genesis. Enjoying it first of all, being entertained by it, and ultimately, being guided and enriched by the wisdom of this ancient text. Genesis offers us not only a realistic portrait of the human condition, but also a pragmatic, down-to-earth approach to leading a meaningful life. It shows how a family transmits its unique spiritual identity grounded in its faith from one generation to the next—and how that faith becomes a way of life. Not in the sense of an insurance policy against misfortune, but as a tool for overcoming fear, emptiness, loneliness, and cynicism.

For the past twenty years I've been teaching the Bible to groups seated around my dining room table, in the U.S. Senate, on Wall Street, and in a variety of other settings in Washington, DC, and New York. These groups are devoted to discussing the same Book over and over again. There is always more to uncover, in the Book and in ourselves. One of my classes has been meeting every Friday morning for twenty years. The same people, the same Book. But our lives are constantly changing, and so does our perspective on the Bible.

As the foundation of all Judeo-Christian theology and morality, the Bible has profoundly shaped who we are and how we view the world. Our country was founded on biblical values of equality and freedom, and our greatest leaders, from Lincoln to Martin Luther King, Jr., have harkened back to these biblical precepts to articulate their causes. But for the vast majority of secular Jews and Christians today, the Bible remains the great unread, undiscovered masterpiece of Western thought. The first goal of our book, then, is to retell the riveting story of the family of Genesis to a generation that has largely ignored or rejected the Bible.

As the first of the thirty-nine Books of the Hebrew Bible, Genesis offers an ideal starting point for an inquiry into who we are and what we can accomplish in life. Written in Hebrew over three thousand years ago, Genesis presents a remarkably contemporary overview of human character, personality, sexuality, and family relations. It offers us a comprehensive framework for exploring human nature and illuminates our own search for a purposeful life.

As its name implies, Genesis is a book of origins. Regardless of our religious orientation—secular or observant, Jew or Christian—the Bible speaks volumes to us about freedom, justice, and compassion. The Bible outlines a code of ethics, values, and spiritual reference points that are indispensable to a grounded existence. Without a map of moral and spiritual signposts, we walk through life at the mercy of every crisis, every human rejection, and every change in external circumstances.

Genesis is a survival story narrating humanity's tenuous triumph over its self-destructive nature. The key to that survival, the lifeboat for humankind in a sea of anonymity and despair, is the family. While Genesis narrates the story of a particular clan, it teaches universal lessons about the resilience of individuals and of the family unit. It encourages us to rebuild our identity from the inside out, beginning with ourselves and the people we are closest to: our family and our immediate community. Most important, Genesis gives us the tools to reknit the fabric of our families and to rediscover the power of these most personal relationships.

Genesis epitomizes the Bible's unique capacity to entertain while it instructs. It's a great read—as subtle and closely observed as a Russian novel, as compelling as the best Shakespearean drama. It is an earthy and often violent saga of love and betrayal, sex and murder, plagues and natural disasters, cruelty and compassion, visions and hallucinations, laws and lawlessness. It is definitely *not* a G-rated story conceived for children.

Neither is it the story of saints. Genesis is populated by surprisingly modern personalities living in the real world—imperfect human beings inspired by a lofty spiritual ideal, but whose feet of clay drag plaintively along the ground. They are husbands and wives, parents and children, constantly torn between their highest aspirations and their basest instincts. They are at once bold visionaries engaged in direct dialogue with God, and frail human beings trapped by their own self-destructive behavior. The greatest heroes of Genesis are often the most deeply conflicted, and the children of each generation, like our own, are obliged to work through the same personal problems that plagued their parents.

The resilience of the human spirit—which has continued to amaze and inspire me throughout my years of therapy practice—is perhaps nowhere better demonstrated than in Genesis, which offers a compelling case study in becoming and overcoming. As a family drama of conflict and resolution, Genesis remains a fundamentally optimistic story because it always offers the possibility of a new beginning. Every generation represents a new start in life, each new child is ripe with potential. Regardless of the obstacles set in their paths, the characters in Genesis find within themselves the strength to begin again, to rebuild and renew their lives.

Genesis teaches that being made in the image of God is a privilege that carries with it solemn obligations. In Genesis, God forgives human frailty, yet holds humans accountable for their actions. Like a wise parent, God leads the men and women of Genesis from the womblike Garden of Eden toward the adult realm of responsible free will. They become accountable adults whose actions are the ultimate expression of their characters.

I feel very strongly that many of the current crop of recovery books do readers a disservice by encouraging them to see themselves as victims. They may feel comforted in the short run, but ultimately a victim is powerless to gain control over his life and to function as an adult. I think the time has come to stop coddling the child within us and to begin championing the powerful adult waiting inside each of us to be born.

The story of Genesis empowers us with the confidence to become accountable for our lives and answerable to the people we love. The most heroic characters of Genesis are not warriors or prophets, but mothers and fathers who take responsibility for the emotional and spiritual nurture of their children.

Who are we at the core of our most essential selves? What is our purpose in life? For the humanist, the religious, the agnostic, or the merely inquisitive, the Book of Genesis is an open invitation to probe the mystery, the miracle, and the drama of adult life in an imperfect universe.

MEN AND WOMEN IN SEARCH OF GOD

God is the omnipresent force driving the biblical narrative, but for many of us schooled in a secular society, the very concept of a living God is a major stumbling block to our returning to the Bible as a source of guidance. One of the unexpected surprises one discovers in the Bible is that men and women have been challenging God's authority ever since their creation. Absolute trust in God is the rarest form of faith. Wherever you may find yourself on the spectrum of belief in or doubt about God, some character in the Bible has been there. In Genesis, God not only permits but encourages challenges from His human partners. Each character's relationship with Him is unique, but God remains a constant force—always available and responsive, never silent.

While we live in a largely secular age, in poll after poll a large majority of Americans claim they believe in God. If nothing else, this high quotient of "believers" speaks to our deep-seated wish to believe that there is design and meaning to our universe, rather than mere randomness.

The belief that we are created in God's image acknowledges that we humans are blessed with attributes that separate us from the purely instinct-driven creatures on earth: free will, imagination, creativity, compassion, conscience, self-awareness, and a sense of the future. By choosing to make our lives an expression of our best selves, our innately God-like nature, we reaffirm our connection to the Creator.

SPIRITUAL IDENTITY, ACCOUNTABILITY, AND PURPOSE

Genesis outlines a three-step approach to endowing our lives with meaning and direction:

1. *Spiritual Identity.* The Bible begins by offering the reader a spiritual identity that transcends the ups and downs of daily life. Everything flows from the concept of God creating man and woman in His own image. If we feel deep within that we have been created in the image of God, then no matter where we are or what we are going through we never feel alone. We are never anonymous. This is a powerful message for us to internalize, because the first lesson of Genesis—and one of the first truths we learn in life—is that we cannot make it alone. No one can.

2. *Accountability.* Armed with transcendent spiritual self-worth, we can embrace the serious responsibilities that come with intimate human relationships. Only when we respect ourselves can we hold ourselves accountable to a code of behavior expressed most succinctly by Rabbi Hillel's first-century directive: "Do not do unto others as you would not have them do unto you." Trust between people can only be achieved when we feel morally accountable to one another.

3. *Purpose.* Finally, Genesis illustrates that what counts in life is not so much our thoughts as our actions. Free will implies that we each have the potential for good and evil, and that a moral life is built on converting these conflicted drives into good acts and caring relationships. The choice and the responsibility are ours. Sexuality can be used to express love and tenderness, or to inflict violence. We can apply our unique human intelligence to creative or destructive ends. Our purpose, according to the Book of Genesis, is to preserve creation by making our lives an expression of the innately divine qualities that make us human.

DEALING WITH GENDER
ROLES IN GENESIS

Despite the decidedly patriarchal perspective of Genesis, both the highest and lowest human traits are equally distributed between its women and men. A series of fully developed female characters is absolutely crucial to the story's development—beginning with Eve. For each generation of patriarchs, there is a parallel matriarchy of wives, daughters, and consorts—strong women who play an indispensable role in advancing the historical and spiritual identity of the lineage. The matriarchs are as important as the patriarchs, though they often work behind the scenes to steer the destinies of their families.

The Bible clearly espouses many sexist attitudes toward women. But we need to view the gender roles it describes in the context of the times they were written, not as prescriptions for contemporary life. In this early agrarian, seminomadic society, women spent the majority of their mature years bearing and raising children—having fifteen offspring was not unusual—with all the inherent power and limitations of this role. Their domain was largely "in the tent," while the men tilled the soil, herded the animals, fought wars, and acted as the political leaders of the tribe.

Genesis stresses the interdependence of women and men. Relations between men and women today are in upheaval, often marked by distrust, confrontation, and hostility. In order to move forward we need to acknowledge our continuing interdependence in resolving these conflicts. Sexuality, fidelity, fertility, childbearing, and child raising were as central to the lives of couples in Genesis as they are today. What's most striking is how constant the issues between women and men have remained over the millennia. Today, as in biblical times, women and men continue to be irresistibly attracted to each other, even though their intrinsically different natures create ongoing problems in their relations. They still have to face the task of meeting each other's needs and the needs of their families. They still have to navigate a life together with all the uncertainties that accompany child raising, the vicissitudes of health, the ups and downs of careers and personal fortunes.

To those women who feel alienated from the Bible because of its sometimes inescapable sexism, or because of sexism in the liturgy that has grown out of it, I would like to say this: Keep an open mind. Don't let ideology—either yours or others'—deprive you of the enrichments of this Book and its basic affirmation of gender equality.

I have, of course, encountered my share of insensitivity toward women. As my father's only child, I expected to recite the *Kaddish*, the Jewish prayer for the dead, as he was being lowered into his grave. The rabbi presiding forbade me from doing so because I was a woman. My son stepped forward to say this traditional prayer for his grandfather in my stead, but I felt terribly upset and humiliated. Women within most faiths are seeking to reform ancient customs that still exclude them. But traditions take centuries to evolve, and we can't expect them to change overnight.

HOW THIS BOOK WAS WRITTEN

My co-author, Joshua Horwitz, is a writer, friend, and longtime student of my Bible classes. Writing this book together has been a dynamic learning process for both teacher and student. Although we are both Jews, we bring totally different perspectives to this project. Joshua grew up in the sixties in America, while I came of age in a newly independent Israel. While I have three grown children and three grandchildren, Joshua's first child was born during the writing of this book. I naturally bring a woman's sensibility to this story, while his reflects male concerns.

Like many of his generation who grew up in largely secular homes, Joshua was more conversant with the Hindu Upanishads and the Tibetan Book of the Dead than with the Bible. Fifteen years ago, after a Quaker high school education and the study of Eastern religions in college, Joshua found his way to a weekly Bible class I held in my home. As he approached the adult responsibilities of home owning and child rearing, he came to identify more readily with the domestic drama of Abraham, Sarah, and Isaac than with the cosmic combat of Vishnu, Shiva, and Brahma.

The Bible has endured through the ages because it speaks with a clear voice to every generation. The tradition of reinterpreting the Bible goes back generation by generation to ancient times. This book is a modest contribution to that tradition. It is informed by my decades of Bible study and teaching, by my experience as a psychotherapist in private practice, and by the accumulated life experience of my co-author and myself.

The Talmud counsels the Bible student, "Turn it and turn it. For everything is in it." Indeed, the Bible can and has been analyzed on countless levels: as literature, as history, as theology. The interpretation of Genesis in this book is based on a psychological and spiritual examination of the multigenerational family it chronicles. Specifically, this book will be looking at how an individual's spiritual identity is expressed in his relationships with his parents, children, spouses and siblings.

In narrating the story of Genesis I have followed the example of rabbis and poets of every generation who have added imagined narrative details to the original canon as a way of fleshing out its often sparse outlines. Part of the mystery of the Hebrew Bible springs from its enigmatic language and narrative, which reflect the biblical view that human and divine motivations are often inscrutable. Interpreting and imagining what is *not* written is as important as what is. Our embellishments to the original text of the stories are historically correct and reflect our understanding of the biblical authors' intent. The original text of Genesis is printed in italics to distinguish it from our paraphrases of and embellishments to the biblical narrative.

On the subject of personal pronouns: we will sometimes be referring to God as "He." After much consideration we have elected, in the interest of stylistic consistency, to use the same pronoun used by the Hebrew Bible. Neither this book nor the Hebrew Bible intends this usage to impute gender to God. God in Genesis is without form, gender, or other explicit human attributes.

Finally, a word about translations. The Book of Genesis, along with virtually all the Books of the Old Testament, was written in Hebrew. The English translations presented here, denoted by italicized text, are taken from various traditional and modern translations. In some instances I have used my own direct translations from the Hebrew. In the interest of readability and continuity, some parts of the biblical narrative have been left out in our retelling of the story. We encourage you to read along with whatever translation of the Bible you find most accessible and inspirational.

When reading Genesis, whether for the first time or the twentieth, I urge you to heed the advice of the great philosopher and theologian Martin Buber:

> Read the Bible as though it were something entirely unfamiliar, as though it had not been set before you ready-made. . . . Face the book with a new attitude as something new. . . . Let whatever may happen occur between yourself and it. You do not know which of its sayings and images will overwhelm and mold you . . . hold yourself open. Do not believe anything a priori; do not disbelieve anything a priori. Read aloud the words written in the book in front of you; hear the word you utter and let it reach you.

If we listen to this ancient Book of wisdom and faith with an open mind, its verses will speak to our hearts in a timeless voice of truth.

—Naomi Harris Rosenblatt

WRESTLING WITH ANGELS

Part One

Prologue to the First Family: The Birth of Spiritual Identity

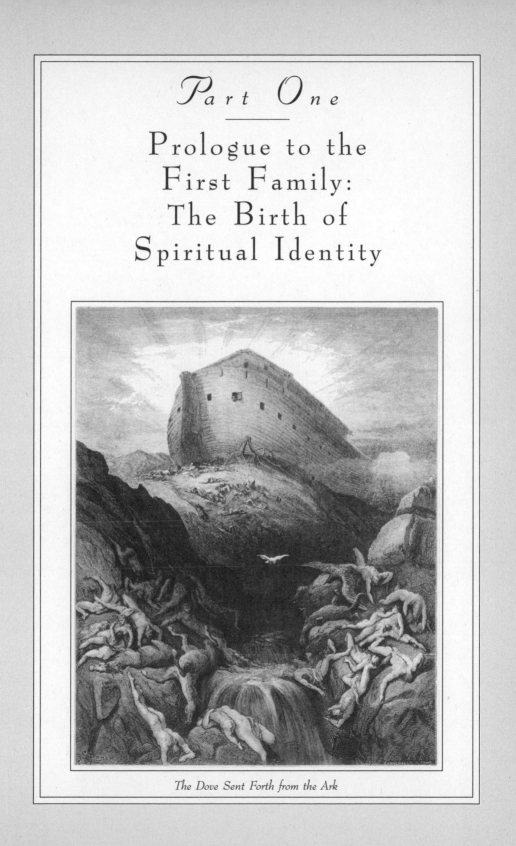

The Dove Sent Forth from the Ark

*M*any people who have waded through *Ulysses* or *Remembrance of Things Past* break out in hives at the prospect of tackling the Bible. How to start? Where to begin?

Genesis divides naturally into two parts: chapters 1–11 and chapters 12–50. The first eleven chapters of Genesis—Part One of *Wrestling with Angels*—trace the first twenty generations of humankind, from Creation through the world's near destruction during the Flood and its aftermath. This section lays out the universal building blocks of human nature and human development before the story narrows in focus to a specific family in Chapter Twelve.

These early stories, which serve as an extended prologue to God's covenant with Abraham, are myths largely derived from Mesopotamian culture. They depict primordial men and women adrift in the world without any moral bearings or spiritual destination. Humans roam aimlessly across the earth, at the mercy of each other's darkest impulses. Although they are created in the image of God, they have not yet integrated this spiritual identity into their lives. These early myths depict successive generations of humankind, beginning with Adam and Eve. But these early generations are not yet a family connected by a cohesive body of beliefs.

Genesis narrates the beginning of an extraordinary partnership between humankind and God. Part One of this story is actually a series of beginnings—false starts, if you will—as God and humankind proceed by trial and error to forge a spiritual alliance as Creator and caretakers of the world. It's a hit-and-miss affair. Humans fail to live up to the divine image in which they were created, while God wavers between disappointment and

3

acceptance of humans as they truly are: magnificently complex creatures capable of appalling evil and extraordinary compassion.

After failing to establish a workable partnership with the first disjointed generations of humans, God reaches out to a new Adam and Eve—Abraham and Sarah—to form an intergenerational covenant. The rest of Genesis then follows this "first family" for four generations, from Abraham and Sarah through their children, grandchildren, and great-grandchildren.

The English name for the first Book in the Bible is Genesis, which derives from the Greek word *geneseos*, meaning "origins." The original Hebrew title for Genesis, *Beresheet*, is taken from the first words of the Bible: "In the beginning."

Which is where our story commences. . . .

CREATION: BUILDING TREST THROUGH ORDER AND PREDICTABILITY

What is man, that Thou art mindful of him? For
Thou hast made him but little lower than the angels,
and hast crowned him with glory and honor.

—*Psalms 8:4–5*

Who are we? Why are we here? What makes us special as human beings?

These existential questions of identity and purpose are the starting point of all religious, philosophical, and psychological inquiry. The Bible addresses them head-on, in the very first chapter of its first Book, Genesis. The portrait of human identity painted in this first chapter—our spiritual potential, our limitations, our purpose—informs the entire narrative that follows.

Every time I read the first chapter of Genesis, I'm overwhelmed by its optimism, joy, and abundance. From the very beginning, this story places humans at the center of creation, elevating us above all other creatures. The creation story in Genesis endows us with a transcendent spiritual identity, beginning with the moment when God breathes life into the first human being. This momentary nexus of God and humankind remains the touchstone of an ongoing dialogue that continues throughout Genesis—and to the present day. What are the privileges of this gift of life and consciousness? And what are its obligations?

Our ongoing search for identity points us back toward the beginning of life. People in every era and in every corner of the planet have invented their own creation myths as a way of explaining and defining themselves to themselves. Creation in Genesis does not attempt a scientific description of the beginning of the world, because scientific speculation doesn't address our deepest questions about the origins of our human nature. Neither does history. Or literature. Or philosophy. We need a creation myth to express our greatest aspirations for ourselves, to measure our highest potential for becoming.

Why this myth? Because, for better or for worse, it's *our* story. This Judeo-Christian legend about our beginnings has shaped much of Western culture and our evolving view of ourselves. During the period of time that it was written—perhaps over three thousand years ago—Genesis's version of creation represented a concept of humanity, God, and the universe that radically differed from prevailing pagan assumptions. Today, when pagan cultures are in the dwindling minority, it remains an astoundingly contemporary description of our identity and our relation to the world around us. I personally experience it as the bedrock of my self-worth and self-respect. It reminds me that there are no limits to my spiritual potential, that despite the feelings of anonymity so prevalent in our urban society, I have a direct spiritual connection to the Creator and His creation.

In the twentieth century we humans have acquired the frightening power to manipulate life on a genetic level and to destroy ourselves and our planet. As we stand at this sobering threshold of knowledge and responsibility, it behooves us to revisit the dream of our beginning—of our spiritual birth and human potential. Thousands of years ago we fashioned a story about ourselves that begins with light and with goodness. In just thirty-four lines, the first chapter of Genesis details the creation of an entire universe, day by day, over the course of a week. From a single creative force emerges a complex ecosystem designed to support every life form in every habitat: from creatures of the deep, to birds of the air, to animals that creep upon the earth. And in a privileged position atop this pyramid of creation, charged with solemn obligations, are human beings. What can this ancient story teach us about our relationship to the rest of life on earth? What is our special responsibility, and how can we best discharge it?

As we read through this first chapter, try to clear your mind of every image you have of how life on earth began—or how your own consciousness was born. Think of the first lines of Genesis as the stage directions that precede the drama of life, detailing the outline of the set, the props, the sound effects, and the lighting design before the first character enters. As the curtain rises on Act One, there is no audience, not even a stage. There is only the formless void before imagination—and a creative spirit that sparks the drama to life. . . .

The First Day: Light out of darkness

In the beginning God created the heaven and the earth.

Like so many simple declarative statements in the Bible, this first line inspires a chain reaction of questions: What came before the beginning? What was God doing before He began creating? Who is He? Where did He come from and who created Him? Why is He called God anyway?

Genesis does not address these questions. Unlike pagan cosmologies depicting multiple deities battling for dominion over the universe, Genesis provides no "biography" of God, no elaborate background on how God came into being. The Bible accepts His existence as self-evident. We are introduced to God through His actions, which begin with bold strokes of creativity.

Now the earth was unformed and void, and darkness was upon the face of the deep; and the spirit of God hovered over the face of the waters.

And God said: "Let there be light." And there was light.

And God saw the light, that it was good; and God divided the light from the darkness. And God called the light Day, and the darkness He called Night.

And there was evening and there was morning, the first day.

THE IMPORTANCE OF ORDER

In this first creative burst, God displays all the loving concern of an ideal parent as He prepares the world for humanity's arrival. Establishing basic boundaries of order and predictability, He begins to build the safe and secure infrastructure that every infant must have to establish trust in her world. A child learns to trust through predictability and routine. As psychologist Erik Erikson pointed out, a newborn baby first learns trust through her own bodily systems. As she begins to breath and sleep and digest her mother's milk, the predictable functioning of her body becomes an analogue of the rhythms of the outside world—the days, the seasons, the tides. Day by day the child grows to trust in these consistent patterns in her life. Over time she begins to smile in recognition of the benignly predictable world around her.

To fulfill our potential as human beings we all need a modicum of order in our physical environment. The first thing a social worker tries to create in a troubled child's home is order and routine. Without a few fixed points in his daily life—dinnertime, bedtime, a parent at the breakfast table or waiting when he comes home from school—a child can't trust and learn and grow. Neither can an adult.

In the first day of creation, God creates order out of chaos. He creates light to balance the darkness. And He creates time by establishing a predictable progression from darkness to light, from evening to morning. This simple fact of life on earth—that the planet rotates regularly on its axis, that after every midnight there will be a dawn—gives order and stability to both our physical and spiritual existence. Every child who is frightened of the dark clings to this predictable truth. A Hebrew morning prayer praises God as "the One who renews creation every day." Each day's dawn renews our connection to the Creator and offers us the promise of a new beginning.

The Goodness and Optimism of Creation

God saw the light, that it was good establishes the first connection between creation and joy. This affirmation of "goodness" will be repeated six times in this chapter, at the end of virtually every creative day.

"Light" emerges as a source of both joy and truth. It nourishes plants and animals, defines the shapes and colors of the universe, and exalts the human spirit. Light illuminates truth as it banishes the darkness of ignorance. Significantly, the appearance of light in Genesis precedes the creation of the sun. As if to defy the sun worship that pervaded pagan cults, Genesis teaches us to revere not the sun, but the creative spirit that brought light into the world.

The goodness of light reminds us that our world was created by design, not by random accident. Unlike its pagan antecedents, the world of Genesis is not a capricious by-product of two gods making war or making love, but of one God who conceives and creates a good world for us to live in, and who finds joy and satisfaction in His creation. The entire creation is suffused with hope and optimism.

It's instructive to compare Genesis to the creation story of the dominant culture of its day: the Babylonian myth of Enuma Elish. Note the contrast between the gentle premeditation of creation in Genesis—

And the spirit of God hovered over the face of the waters. And God said: "Let there be light."

—and the bloody combat between the male and female gods of Babylonia:

So they came together—Tiamat and Marduk, sage of the gods. They advanced into conflict and joined forces in battle. Marduk shot an arrow; it pierced Tiamat's stomach, pierced her bowels and tore into her womb. At that he strangled her, made her life-breath ebb away, and cast her body to the ground. Standing over it in triumph, he slit her in two like a fish of the drying yards, the one half he positioned and secured as the sky. Therein traced he stars, star-groups and constellations. The great sun-gates he opened in both sides of her ribs. He made the moon to shine forth. He placed her head in position, heaped the mountains upon it, and made the Euphrates and Tigris to flow through her eyes.

The gentle and caring design by which God creates the world in Genesis is an important starting point for our identity. People who believe that they were conceived as unplanned accidents face an uphill struggle in building self-esteem. In order to love ourselves, we all need the feeling of having been wanted and planned for by those who created us. And as we will see, the creation of humans is the most deliberate and "hands-on" act of God's creation.

The Second, Third, and Fourth Days: Form out of void

In the course of the next three days God continues to bring order out of chaos, form out of shapeless void. Step-by-step He creates a secure cradle for life on earth: first by building a dome of sky over the waters . . .

And God said, "Let there be a firmament in the midst of the waters, and let it divide the waters from the waters." And it was so. And God called the firmament Sky.

And there was evening and there was morning, a second day.

. . . and then by separating the water from the land . . .

And God said, "Let the water below the sky be gathered into one area, that the dry land may appear." And it was so. God called the dry land Earth, and the gathering of the waters he called Seas. And God saw that it was good.

. . . and by planting seeds in the dry land where they can take root and grow into plants . . .

And God said, "Let the earth sprout vegetation: seed-bearing plants, fruit trees of every kind bearing fruit with the seed in it." And it was so. And God saw that it was good.

And there was evening and there was morning, a third day.

For plants to grow they need a regular pattern of sunlight and shade, so on the fourth day God arranges the sun, moon, and stars in the heavens as fixed points of light, each with its own orbit and dominion.

God said, "Let there be lights in the firmament of the sky to divide the day from the night. And let them serve as signs for the seasons and for the days and for the years; and they shall serve as lights in the expanse of the sky to shine upon the earth." And it was so. And God made the two great lights: the greater light to rule the day and the lesser light to rule the night; and the stars. And God set them in the firmament of the sky to shine upon the earth, to rule the day and the night, and to separate light from darkness. And God saw that it was good.

And there was evening and there was morning, a fourth day.

Fifth Day: Life appears in the sea and in the air

Finally the stage is set for the first life forms to emerge into the world. And significantly, it is only on this fifth day that we witness the first use of the word "create," as if this sublime expression has been reserved for the beginning of life. In a sequence that parallels evolution, life in Genesis begins in the dark, watery womb of the seas, then creeps up on land and soars through the skies. . . .

And God said, "Let the waters bring forth swarms of living creatures, and let birds fly above the earth in the open firmament of the sky." And God created the great sea-creatures, and all the living creatures of every kind that creep which the waters brought forth in swarms, and all the winged birds of every kind.

And God saw that it was good.

The animals arrive not in ones and twos, but in swarms multiplying into larger swarms until the skies and the seas are engorged with life.

And God blessed them, saying, "Be fruitful and multiply, and fill the waters in the seas, and let the birds multiply on the earth."

And there was evening and there was morning, a fifth day.

God's immediate reaction to the life forms He has created is to bless them and bid them multiply and fill His creation. The creation of life is the first blessed event, and reproduction quickly emerges as the driving life force in nature.

The Sixth Day: Life on earth

Once the seas and the skies are filled with life, God populates the land . . .

And God said, "Let the earth bring forth every kind of living creature: cattle, creeping things, and wild beasts of every kind." And it was so. God made wild beasts of every kind and cattle of every kind, and all kinds of creeping things of the earth.

And God saw that it was good.

Only after God surveys His creation with all its teeming life, and after He is satisfied with all its appointments, does He affix the jewel to His crown. God makes human beings in His own likeness to rule over the whole of creation.

And God said, "Let us make man in Our image, after Our likeness. Let him rule over the fish of the sea, the birds of the sky, the cattle, the whole earth, and all the creeping things that creep on earth."

God creates "man" in both genders, so they, too, can multiply . . .

A̲nd God created man in His image, in the image of God He created them; male and female He created them. God blessed them and God said to them, "Be fruitful and multiply, and replenish the earth and subdue it; and rule over the fish of the sea, the birds of the sky, and all the living things that creep on earth."

This last verse comprises a remarkable manifesto of human nature as described in Genesis. It lays out three major principles on which the rest of human history is predicated:

1. *Identity:* Our direct spiritual identity with God, who created us in His image.

2. *Equality:* The fundamental equality and interdependence of the sexes.

3. *Purpose: Preserving and replenishing God's creation.*

Identity: In the image of God

The idea of our being made in God's image is the fundamental paradox of the creation story—its most mysterious and empowering assertion. God is without form, without gender, without any tangible characteristics. How then can we be created in His image?

Being created in the image of an infinite God means that our spiritual potential for growth and transformation is limitless. If there is no ceiling on the concept of God, then we who are made in His image have infinite space to grow. We never reach the end of our potential. Never. Not in our marriages, not in our careers, not in our relationships with our children and our friends.

If we define ourselves as being made in the image of God, no one else can ever define us to ourselves. With this sense of spiritual identity firmly embedded within us, no one can ever usurp it or whittle it away—even when we are undergoing difficult life passages such as divorce, financial reversal, or the death of someone close to us.

If we don't have a sense of inner identity, we can feel lost and anonymous amid the billions of people with whom we share the planet. Being made in the image of God invests us with a portable spiritual center. No matter where we go, so long as we carry this core identity within us, we remain spiritually impervious to the ups and downs of external circumstances.

Biblical scholar Nahum M. Sarna points out how revolutionary this concept of being made in the image of God was in its day. In ancient Egypt and Mesopotamia, the pharaohs and kings were praised as being made in the image of gods. For instance, the name Tutankhamen meant "in the image of the god Khamen." Genesis marks a democratic innovation on this theme, proclaiming every human being a creation in the image of God—every man a king before his Creator. This is an important development because it guarantees each individual direct access to God. Every character in Genesis is entitled to a direct dialogue with God. Genesis extends this offer to us. We, too, can forge our own relationship with the Creator, wherever we locate Him or Her, on whatever frequency we can best communicate.

Equality: *Male and female He created them*

In this first chapter of Genesis, God creates man and woman in His own image: *In the image of God He created them; male and female He created them.* While Genesis later acknowledges and describes the fundamental differences between the genders, here it establishes beyond dispute that the source of their spiritual identity is the same genderless God. They are both endowed with free will and both bear the responsibility of exercising it for good rather than evil. This theme of the equal privilege and responsibility of men and women is developed further in Chapters Two and Three of Genesis.

Linked by our universal spiritual identity with God, we are self-evidently equal before God. We are all equally valuable as humans, regardless of our gender, race, or economic class, and we are all equally deserving of respect and dignity. Just as God has no gender, the first humans have no hint of race or creed. They are universal human beings, and the privileges and responsibilities assigned to the first man and woman apply universally to all humans.

Being made in the image of God is the common denominator uniting all humanity. And yet we are each unique, each custom-made in the likeness of an infinite God. None of us is a copy of another person. We are all destined to leave individual footprints as we make our journey through life.

Purpose: *"Be fruitful and multiply, and replenish the earth and subdue it"*

Armed with a spiritual identity, we can go forth into the world with a strong sense of purpose. But the empowering feeling of being created in God's image is only a starting point. With this gift comes the responsibility for ethical action in our daily lives. If we operate in a moral vacuum, feelings of empowerment become narcissistic— which is a great danger on any spiritual path.

Feeling good about ourselves may be a necessary beginning, but feeling good is not nearly as important as *doing* good. We can tell a child how wonderful she is all day long. But only when we give her a watering can and assign her the task of nurturing a plant will she begin to develop as a human being. Only by having a positive impact on the world around us do our lives assume meaning. And in the biblical view, the only true measure of a person's faith in God is his or her actions.

After the sixth day, God's work is done. But our job of continuing the work begun during creation has just started. The challenge for humanity is to make sense of God's command to "be fruitful and multiply," as distinct from the same command given to the animals, who are not expected to rise above sheer instinct. Unlike the animals, men and women are given the additional directive to "replenish the earth and subdue it." This special privilege and responsibility falls to us, the custodians of creation and God's partners in the ongoing task of creating and preserving life on earth.

"Replenish" and "subdue" are seemingly contradictory commands. But in fact, these opposing tasks give meaning to our purpose and our destiny on earth. We are given a mandate to subdue the earth, but only so long as we continue to preserve it and replenish whatever resources we consume. "Replenish the earth and subdue it" means when you cut down a tree for lumber to build a house, you plant a new tree in its place. After you harvest crops to feed your family, you let the field lay fallow and replenish itself. When you hunt for food, you cull the weakest animal from the herd.

There is a current belief in vogue that human beings are a blight on nature, that we can best heal the world by submerging ourselves in the rhythms of the universe. If only we could suppress our human nature and tap in to our hidden animal aspects, goes this line of reasoning, the world would return to a state of harmony and balance. But this naive world view belies the inescapable reality that humans are set apart from other creatures on earth. Being made in God's image is what separates us from the other animals and unites us as humans. Our separateness defines the inscrutable mystery of our nature. We humans are more than merely highly intelligent and social apes: we have unparalleled capacity for creativity and communication, for conceiving of the future, and for distinguishing between good and evil.

With these special talents comes a solemn obligation to exercise our free will to preserve, not destroy, the planet and its inhabitants. We have been appointed to ensure the safe passage of all creatures during our watch, as Noah had been commanded in his day.

The Talmud advises each of us to remind ourselves daily: "For me the world was created." Genesis's unabashedly anthrocentric view of creation is a gift for which we will always remain accountable. Whether we like it or not, the world is ours to replenish or to destroy. We are not here to worship nature—as our pagan antecedents did—but to enjoy it, harness it, and preserve it for future generations.

I find the ending of the sixth day very interesting. Before completing His creative week, God gives humans their first dietary directives. As with all dietary laws in the Bible, these first guidelines have less to do with nutrition and health than with our intended spiritual identity.

And God said, "Behold, I give you every seed-bearing plant that is upon all the earth, and every tree that has seed-

bearing fruit; they shall be yours for food. And to all the
animals on land, to all the birds of the sky, and to everything
that creeps on earth in which there is the breath of life, I
have given all the green plants for food." And it was so.

As if to remind us of our interdependent relation with animals, God states that all the fruits and plants of the earth were created for us to share with them. Humans are given the fruits of the earth as sustenance, and the animals are given the green plants. This vegetarian division of resources seems almost quaint, in light of what we now know about the carnivorous habits of humans and many animals. I believe that this verse reflects God's optimism at the outset of His creation. He envisioned a peaceable kingdom of lions lying down with lambs and of humans tending all the earth's animals as beneficent shepherds. As we will see, God very quickly amends this overly benign view of human appetites. By the time of the Flood, He will acknowledge the innate aggressiveness of human beings and will sanction the slaughter of animals for food. But for now:

God saw all that He had made, and found it very good.
And there was evening and there was morning, the sixth day.

At the end of the sixth day, during which God creates man, He looks on His work with evident satisfaction and deems it not simply good, as in the previous days' judgments, but *very* good.

The Seventh Day: Rest

On the seventh day, the frenzy of creation—the virtual orgy of new life sprouting and spawning—gives way to the calm of completion and rest.

And the heaven and the earth were finished, and all their
array. And on the seventh day God finished the work that
He had been doing, and He rested on the seventh day from

all the work He had done. And God blessed the seventh day and declared it holy, because on the seventh day God ceased from all the work of creation that He had done.

On the seventh day God ceased work on His creation. The Hebrew word *shabbat* means "to cease." We who are made in God's image remind ourselves of our direct connection to the Creator by ceasing from our labors on the Sabbath. A blessing recited on the Sabbath refers to this day of rest as "a memorial of the work of creation" when *God blessed the seventh day and declared it holy*.

The concept of the seventh-day Sabbath was probably borrowed—along with the seven-day literary framework of creation—from the Babylonians. According to Nahum M. Sarna, the Babylonian word *shappatu*, meaning "day of the quieting of the heart," referred to the full moon, which was believed to be a propitious day for appeasing the gods through sacrifice. All the other seventh days of the lunar month were designated as unlucky dates controlled by evil spirits during which fasts and rituals of atonement were prescribed. The weekly Sabbath of the Bible carries the opposite meaning: it is a day of freedom, joy, and contemplation—of direct communion between humanity and God.

Though clearly linked to the seventh day of creation, the biblical Sabbath is not institutionalized until the Book of Exodus, where its observance is mandated as the Fourth Commandment. Observance of the Sabbath has endured as a pillar of monotheism; Judaism celebrates its Sabbath on Saturday, Christianity on Sunday, and Islam has designated Friday as its day of rest and prayer.

THE SABBATH:
A WEEKLY SOURCE OF RENEWAL

The Sabbath is a day in which we reign over time, its master rather than its slave. It is our weekly sabbatical from routines, schedules, and clocks, a day when we tap in to the eternal and the internal. In the words of the twentieth-century theologian Abraham Joshua Heschel, "On the Sabbath we be, rather than do."

This sense of the Sabbath as a blessed oasis of calm from the rest of the working week took root in my life as a child growing up in Haifa, Israel. Each Friday afternoon around four o'clock, a hush would fall over the city. Men commuting home from work would pause at street corners to purchase gladiolus for the dinner table. By five o'clock I would stop by my next-door neighbors', the Ambachs, hoping they would invite me to join them for their Sabbath meal. My own family were secular Jews, early immigrants to Palestine who didn't observe the Sabbath. But for the Ambachs, Friday night was an evening of celebration and transformation.

Dr. and Mrs. Ambach, at one time middle-class Germans, had been forced to flee Berlin just ahead of deportation to the death camps. They arrived in Haifa with virtually no possessions. From the vantage point of the balcony adjoining theirs, I watched my neighbors rebuild their lives from the ground up, beginning with the observance of the Sabbath.

Despite their desperate circumstances, for the Ambachs Friday evenings were occasions of great dignity. Their children, who all week ran around like ragamuffins, were scrubbed clean and dressed in immaculate starched clothes. Mrs. Ambach wore her one remaining family heirloom, a gold watch on a necklace, and she laid the table with the single set of linen she had managed to bring with her to Israel. Dr. Ambach blessed the meal and wine from the head of the table, while his wife lit and blessed the Sabbath candles. It didn't matter that all through the week Mrs. Ambach was cleaning other people's houses and her husband, who had headed a hospital in Berlin, was reduced to selling pens and notions door-to-door. On Friday evening their family pride and self-respect were restored. By observing the Sabbath as a weekly infusion of spiritual renewal, these resilient human beings reaffirmed their enduring connection to God and to each other.

THE POWER OF A SPIRITUAL IDENTITY: FAITH OVER CIRCUMSTANCES

Many of my childhood neighbors had blue-green numbers tattooed on their forearms—a graphic reminder of how their captors had tried to strip them of their dignity and individuality. Nothing but the raw power of a deeply rooted spiritual identity enabled these people to survive the camps and reconstruct their lives from ashes. While most of us won't be tested by anything as brutal as a death camp, none of us escapes adversity and tragedy in our lives. Without a strong sense of personal identity we are helpless to confront hardships without feeling victimized. However, if we carry our sense of self deep within us, we can rise above almost anything.

The power of an internalized spiritual identity can even transcend circumstances beyond our control. We can't dictate what happens to us in life. We can't magically protect ourselves and those close to us from harm. But if we remember that we are created in the image of God, and are therefore endowed with free will, we *can* control how we interpret and respond to adversity. As the matriarchs and patriarchs in Genesis will demonstrate, faith in our spiritual identity is our best hope for triumphing over cynicism, despair, and defeatism.

A BUFFER AGAINST THE WINDS OF CHANGE

After living in Washington, DC, for several decades, I've witnessed countless examples of just how quickly the mighty can fall. Today's kingmaker is often tomorrow's has-been. I remember a friend who was voted out of office telling me: "The day after the election, the phone was quieter than a tombstone." The politicians I've known who have a strong sense of self that's independent of their external circumstances are adept at regrouping and rebuilding their lives. But those who embrace the trappings of power as the source of their self-worth are devastated when the winds of change turn against them.

A strong sense of identity is also indispensable for dealing with worldly success. My favorite example of a powerful man who never got a swollen head is Harry Truman. Even after he moved into the White House, President Truman is said to have washed out his own socks every night. This simple, humbling act was a daily reminder to him of his modest roots. He never wanted to forget where he had come from or where he was heading back to when his term in office ended. After eight years as president, he declined to run for reelection. The day he returned to Independence, Missouri, as a private citizen, Truman carried his own suitcases up to the third floor of his house and picked up his life where he had laid off eight years earlier.

MAN AND WOMAN IN THE GARDEN OF EDEN: LOVE ENTERS THE WORLD

My beloved is mine, and I am his.

—*Song of Songs 2:16*

I find the resentment and competitiveness so often expressed between women and men today disturbing. In our polarized and fragmented society, men and women are desperately looking for a true gender identity. Psychologist Theodor Reik has a perceptive diagnosis for this insecurity: "In our civilization," he writes, "men are afraid that they will not be men enough, and women are afraid that they might be considered only women."

Women and men struggle with the conflicts created by our intrinsically different natures. We communicate and express our emotions differently. Our sexual responses are not alike. But the basic equation of interdependence doesn't change: men and women continue to be irresistibly attracted to each other throughout their lives, from early adolescence well into old age. We need each other to overcome our essential aloneness and to realize our fullest human potential.

In *My Fair Lady*, Professor Higgins asks plaintively: "Why can't a woman be more like a man?" But it is precisely our differences that generate mutual attraction and define our interdependence. Our ability to create a harmonious relationship, despite our fundamental differences, best expresses what is human in us. To move forward together in an age of sexual equality, we must first acknowledge the differences between us in a spirit of appreciation, understanding, and respect.

How can we build bridges across the gender gap and transform our conflicts into opportunities for happiness and growth? By respecting each other's separateness. By systematically taking time to listen and attend to each other. By supporting and caring for the other's well-being, even before our own. By articulating our own needs. By committing to each other to the point where we don't bolt at the first sign of conflict or anger. By forging a sexual bond in which we trust the other enough to expose our most intimate selves. These are the ways we grow up and find fulfillment in our love relationships.

The story of Adam and Eve, the archetypal couple, underscores the fundamental interdependence of men and women. It teaches us that only by acknowledging our common needs can we harmonize our innate differences.

The first chapter of Genesis is the Creation writ large, banner headlines of an historic week of divine labor. Chapter Two is a close-up detail of the Creation, specifically the creation of the Garden of Eden as the first dwelling place of man and woman. If the Creator from Chapter One is a master architect, raising a dome of heaven in the sky and dividing dry earth from the seas, the Creator of Eden is the consummate landscape architect, constructing a garden of earthly delights as a verdant cradle for life on earth.

In the description of Creation we find in Chapter Two, man arrives ahead of the plants and animals, when the earth is still an arid desert, bereft of all life . . .

Such is the story of heaven and earth when they were created. No shrub of the field was yet on the earth, and no grasses of the field had yet sprouted, because the Lord God had not sent rain upon the earth and there was no man to till the soil.

And there was no man to till the soil suggests that God needs man as a partner before He can proceed with His creation and plant the Garden of Eden.

But there went up a mist from the earth and watered the whole face of the ground. Then the Lord God formed man from the dust of the earth and breathed into his nostrils the breath of life. And man became a living soul.

The first man, Adam, takes his name from the Hebrew word for the earth from which he is formed: *adamah.* Only after the first rains, when the dust becomes moist and malleable, can God form a man from earth. God's breath completes the chemistry of life: earth, water, and air, fired by creative energy. The gift of a living soul is conferred on man in an intimate face-to-face encounter, as the divine potter breathes life into His clay figure. This "mouth-to-mouth resuscitation" from inert dust is unique in Genesis. God subsequently forms the animals from the same soil, but in a comparatively impersonal fashion. Our body is merely a vessel that will someday return to the dust from which it was formed. But our spiritual identity—our soul—comes directly from God.

And the Lord God planted a garden eastward, in Eden, and placed there the man whom He had formed.

God plants Eden in the East, the place of newborn days and new beginnings. *Eden,* the Hebrew word for "delight," suggests a garden of earthly delights that God creates expressly for man's pleasure and nurture.

And from the ground the Lord God caused to grow every tree that was pleasing to the sight and good for food, with the tree of life in the middle of the Garden, and the tree of the knowledge of good and evil.

God designs the garden as an oasis of lush greenery where every tree is pleasing to look at and good to eat from. It is notable that the knowledge of good and the knowledge of evil grow from the same roots and bear fruit from the same tree. Why not a tree of good and a tree of evil? Because the knowledge of both good and evil is intertwined in the human heart.

And the Lord God took the man and placed him in the Garden of Eden, to till it and tend it.

The Hebrew word for "placed him," *va'yanichehu,* connotes great care on God's part. He sets man down in the Garden with tremendous delicacy, the way we might place a fragile and precious vase on a carefully laid table. God installs man as head grounds-keeper of the Garden and grants him a lifetime pass to His tropical paradise—so long as he observes a sole house rule:

And the Lord God commanded the man, saying, "Of every tree of the Garden you are free to eat, but as for the tree of knowledge of good and evil you must not eat of it; for the day you eat of it you shall surely die."

Adam lacks nothing in God's garden. He may eat from every tree to his heart's content—from all but the tree of knowledge. The clearly stated consequence for disobedience is that he become conscious of his mortality. Is God trying to protect man from the awesome knowledge of good and evil, or is He merely testing his obedience in the face of temptation?

Surveying His carefully cultivated garden, God perceives the essential isolation of man's existence, and He sets out to remedy it.

T he Lord God said, *"It is not good that man should be alone; I will make for him a helper who is his equal."*

Throughout the week of creation, God looked on His work and *saw that it was good.* Now, as He looks down on man, so lovingly positioned in the Garden, God sees something is amiss. *It is not good that man should be alone.* We humans are the most social creatures on the planet: we flourish in groups and perish alone. Our very survival—physical, emotional, and spiritual—depends on our interactions with others. Alone we stagnate. We can grow and mature only through our intimate relationships with other people. The dynamic between men and women is particularly challenging and rewarding, traversing the realms of companionship, intimacy, and love.

Before arriving at the concept of woman, God creates all the animals of the earth and presents them to Adam as possible companions.

A nd the Lord God formed out of the earth all the wild beasts and all the birds of the sky, and brought them to the man to see what he would call them; and whatever the man called each living creature, that would be its name. And the man gave names to all the cattle and to the birds of the sky and to all the wild beasts.

But for Adam no fitting companion was found.

No fitting companion was found for Adam among all the animals, because his nature was fundamentally different from theirs. We humans share 99 percent of our genes with our closest primate relative, the chimpanzee. But that 1 percent difference represents a gaping chasm of consciousness separating our species. Humans will always interact with animals, but never on an equal footing. And as this story emphasizes, we can transcend our aloneness only in a relationship between equals.

I often marvel at the bonds of companionship and devotion we can form with animals. Animals will never betray us, deceive us, or treat us cruelly. But animals will also never challenge our capacity for love, forgiveness, and growth the way a human being can. Neither can they share a good book, a good laugh, or a good cry.

It's relatively easy to befriend a dog or a horse. Loving another human being is a lot more challenging. As author and talk show host Dennis Prager points out, when a pet we love dies, we can get a replacement—and we often do. But imagine someone saying to you after the death of a beloved spouse or child: "Oh, I'm so sorry to hear that. Are you going to get another one?"

To create a fitting and equal companion for Adam, God must delve into man's own body, beside his beating heart. Thousands of years before the advent of reconstructive surgery, God anesthetizes Adam and builds a soul mate for him out of flesh and bone.

> *So the Lord cast a deep sleep upon man; and while he slept*
> *He took from his side and closed up the flesh at that spot.*
> *And the Lord God built the side that He had taken from the*
> *man into a woman; and He brought her to the man.*

The raw material for the first woman is commonly thought to be Adam's rib. But the literal translation of the Hebrew word *tzela* is "side"—as in the side of a ship. To me, this is a significant distinction. Woman being made from man's side implies that man and woman are two halves of a larger whole. Or in the words of the poet e. e. cummings: "One's not half of two, it's two that are halves of one."

Adam is utterly smitten by the appearance of his new human companion, his missing female half.

> *Then the man said:*
> > *This one at last*
> > *Is bone of my bones*
> > *And flesh of my flesh!*
> > *This one shall be called Woman,*
> > *For from man was she taken.*

The first love match in Genesis. There will be others—Abraham and Sarah, Isaac and Rebekah, Jacob and Rachel—but perhaps none so elemental as this. By creating Eve, God brings earthly love into the world, and the eternal flame of human attraction is ignited. Men and women are launched into a binary orbit of creation, their equality and interdependence established at the outset. Even the Hebrew words for man, *eesh*, and woman, *eesha*, confirm their common roots.

Now that male and female—the primordial halves of human identity—have been reunited, Genesis makes the following statement about the male-female relationship.

Therefore shall a man leave his father and mother and cleave to his wife, so that they become one flesh.

Becoming one flesh has both spiritual and sexual dimensions. Through our mates, we transcend the isolation of our bodies and souls. This mystical convergence, when we *become one flesh,* finds its most sublime expression when our bodies mesh in sexual union and our gene pools merge to create a single new life form.

In purely pragmatic terms Genesis is directing man to grow up and embrace the responsibility of setting up his own household with his wife. This does not mean cutting all emotional ties to his parents. But it does require severing the emotional umbilical cord and taking on a new set of adult commitments.

The last line of Chapter Two sets the stage for the drama to follow:

The two of them were naked, the man and his wife, yet they felt no shame.

Erik Erikson has written, "Shame supposes that one is completely exposed and conscious of being looked at: in one word, self-conscious." At this juncture in the story, man and woman are still as unself-conscious as children, stripped bare of any suspicion or shame. Totally innocent, altogether vulnerable.

Were the tale of Eden a children's garden of verse, the story could well end here, with man and woman living happily ever after, clinging to each other naked and unself-consciously in love.

But Genesis is a story about real life. This "happy ending" is only the starting point of Adam and Eve's evolution from childhood into adult experience.

ORDER VERSUS CHAOS
IN THE HUMAN SOUL

God has gone as far as He can with His Creation. He has brought order out of chaos and established a balanced ecosystem in which to house humanity. With the "building" of woman, God's creation is complete. He is now dependent on the humans, whom He has created in His own image, to till His garden and preserve His creation.

Like a Persian miniature, the Garden of Eden is a perfect closed system where all the elements are arrayed in artful relation to one another: the plants grouped around the trees of life and knowledge, a host of vegetarian beasts encircling man and woman, who sit side by side at the center of this tableau. For a fleeting moment, God can enjoy His peaceable kingdom. But what will happen when humans take control over their own destiny?

The first test of this closed system comes with God's command not to eat of the tree of knowledge. Will humans prove obedient, and the system stable? Or will chaos reassert itself in the form of human free will? God understands that He has endowed humans with the capacity to defy Him—otherwise He would not have warned of the consequences of disobedience. But what is God's intent for His garden-keepers? Does He want them to remain blissfully ignorant and perpetually childlike? Or is He using this temptation to nudge them, like a mother bird, to venture forth from their secure nest?

To me this ambivalence mirrors all parents' mixed emotions about their children's development. On one hand, we instinctively want to preserve our children's innocence for as long as possible, to protect them from the knowledge of good and evil in the world, from the complex passions of adult sexuality, and from the consciousness of their own mortality. But we also know that our job as parents is to prepare our young to face the challenges of adult life on their own. The paradox is that if we succeed in our job as good parents, the children we love so much will have acquired the independence to leave us when they become adults.

As the first "parent" in Genesis, God serves as a helpful role model for striking a balance between the extremes of child-rearing: between discipline and permissiveness, between asserting control and letting go, between unconditional love and clearly stated expectations.

THE GIFT OF SPEECH

While searching for a fitting companion for Adam, God bestows on him another gift that unites all humans and widens the gap between us and the animal world—speech. After naming each of the animals in creation and confirming that none of them can respond in kind, Adam concludes that there is no fit and equal companion for him among animals. Only woman can converse with him, exchange confidences and endearments. She alone can deliver him from his solitude.

Many animals communicate with each other through gestures and sounds, but only humans have the capacity to speak and comprehend complex languages. Only humans can sing, tell stories, write love letters, compose sonnets, and write novels. As Thomas Mann writes in *The Magic Mountain*, "Speech is civilization itself. The word, even the most fractious word, preserves contact—it is silence which isolates."

Throughout Genesis, speech is the key to communication. It is when we stop talking that communication breaks down and characters quarrel. Speech is bestowed on humans to draw them closer together, to connect them to each other and to God. Speech is what allows us to exchange ideas and to initiate intimacy by articulating our feelings. Speech gives us the language of prayer.

A *helper who is his equal*

Some feminists have problems with the way the Bible describes the creation of woman—from the side of man and as his helper. I frankly don't see any problem with woman's beginnings in Eden. Man is created from dust in a single verse. Woman is fashioned from flesh and bone over the course of six verses. Woman, like man, is created by God. And it is to God, rather than man, that woman remains accountable. As the feminist Bible scholar Phyliss Tribble writes:

> Man has no part in making woman. He exercises no control over her existence: He is neither participant nor spectator nor consultant at her birth. Like man, woman owes her life solely to God.

Woman's absence from Eden clearly signals its incompleteness to God. The writers of Genesis go out of their way to emphasize the improvement in man's existence after woman's appearance. Woman brings conversation, laughter, and sexuality into Adam's life. With the creation of woman, love enters the world.

So does companionship. It's important to note that the male-female relationship is introduced in Genesis under the banner of companionship—before either sexuality or procreation enters the picture. Sexual attraction comes and goes in cycles. But as this episode teaches us, the companionship we offer our mates is the single most enduring gift we bring to an intimate relationship. The more intimate the relationship, the more subtle and profound the companionship. No career, however important it may be, is as crucial to a man's or a woman's well-being as the richness and support found in intimacy.

Many of my female patients complain that they are most often the ones who take the time to maintain the emotional life of their intimate relationships. They understandably resent being the only ones to cultivate the emotional "garden" that both partners depend on and benefit from. My suggestion to women is to view this as an important leadership role within the life of a couple. Women's proclivity for intimacy is indispensable to the health and growth of a love relationship.

I like the term "helper," as in *a helper who is his equal,* so long as the help is mutual. Equality is a necessary condition of intimacy, but equality itself is not enough to sustain a couple. There is no substitute for the basic commitment of a couple to help and support each other.

What happens next is an oft-told tale—and reinterpreted by every generation as a mirror of its times. The apostle Paul read it and saw "original sin," observing that "by one man, sin entered the world." The poet John Milton saw an epic battle of Good versus Evil, a paradise lost as fallen angels tempted man into the free fall of the flesh. Madison Avenue saw a marketing opportunity—as it is wont to do—and invited us to feel deliciously wicked smoking Eve cigarettes and drinking After the Fall apple juice. Artists throughout the ages have recreated this scene in painting, sculpture, poetry, and drama. If there's any Bible story we know by heart, it's this one.

Or do we?

A host of surprises awaits the reader in this enchanted garden with its forbidden tree and talking serpent. We will find no mention of the word "sin" in the text of this story. No Satan. No fall. No apple. There is confusion and shame, but no tears of remorse. And in this same garden where God first breathes life into human nostrils, the mouths of man and woman will be filled with the fruits of His knowledge, and their eyes will be opened to the hidden world of human potential.

———

ADAM, EVE, AND THE FORBIDDEN FRUIT: AWAKENING SEXUALITY AND THE GETTING OF WISDOM

. . . *Cry out for insight and raise your voice for understanding, seek it like silver and search for it as for hidden treasure; then you will understand the fear of the Lord and find the knowledge of God.*

—*Proverbs 2:3–5*

Stolen waters are sweet, and bread eaten in secret is pleasant.

—*Proverbs 9:17*

What is the special genius of the story of the Garden of Eden? Why has this mysterious myth about a man, a woman, and a serpent endured in our collective imagination for over three millennia?

I believe it's because it views the male-female relationship and the human condition through the prism of sexuality. Sexuality is *the* common human denominator, extending across all ethnic, linguistic, geographic, and economic boundaries. In this story, the onset of sexual awareness represents Adam and Eve's passage from innocence into experience, as they assume the knowledge and responsibility that come with adulthood.

One way to decode the hidden meaning of this allegory is to return to the original Hebrew and uncover the word plays in the text. The story revolves around the tree of knowledge of good and evil that God has planted in Eden and forbidden the man and woman to eat from. I believe that it is no coincidence that the Hebrew word for "knowledge," *da'at*, refers both to knowledge about life and to sexual "knowledge." The term "to know" is a sublime biblical euphemism for the intimate and in-depth understanding that evolves over time in a sexual relationship.

How better to teach us about our human identity and the responsibility of free will than through this story of sexual awakening? Because of the intimate nature of sexual experience, it offers an early introduction to the moral choices and consequences facing us in personal relationships. After tasting of the fruit of the tree of knowledge, Adam and Eve's awakening sexuality becomes a direct corollary to their emerging sense of moral accountability. The tree of knowledge that stands at the center of the Garden fuses these two ways of knowing—sexual and moral—into one tantalizing "fruit." Eating this fruit of the tree of knowledge defines the universal human passage from childhood innocence into the world of adult experience.

When we last saw the man and the woman, they were as naked and unself-conscious as the animals—as oblivious as children.

The two of them were naked, the man and his wife, yet they
felt no shame.

Shame had not yet found a home in the Garden.

Now the serpent was the shrewdest of all the wild beasts
that the Lord God had made.

Enter the serpent. Who is he? What does he want?

As I see it, the serpent is a phallic symbol that represents
the sexual stirrings within the woman. The Hebrew word for
"shrewd," *arum*, also means "naked." No wonder that in ancient Near
Eastern mythology the serpent was the symbol of life and fertility. In the Garden of Eden the serpent lives among the branches
of the tree of knowledge, to which the woman is ineluctably
drawn.

What will happen when this most naked and shrewd of wild
beasts meets woman alone in the center of the Garden?

He said to the woman, "Did God really say: 'You shall not
eat of any tree of the garden'?"

Did the serpent speak those words, or was it only her heart's
murmuring? With so many other trees to eat from, why does this
tree of knowledge beckon so insistently to her?

The first seeds of doubt about God's words begin to take root
in the woman, the way a child inevitably begins to doubt her parents' rules. After struggling with the serpent's insinuations, the
woman repeats the one limit that God has set and makes it clear
that she understands the consequence of crossing that boundary—
namely, that she will become mortal.

The woman replied to the serpent, "We may eat of the fruit
of the trees of the Garden. It is only about fruit of the tree in

the middle of the Garden that God said: 'You shall not eat of it or touch it, lest you die.' "

The serpent keeps on prodding her.

A*nd the serpent said to the woman, "You are not going to die, but God knows that as soon as you eat of it your eyes will be opened, and you will be as God, knowing good and evil."*

Who can fault the woman for wanting to taste, to see, and to know good and evil? We all want to have our eyes opened to the unseen world, to know and understand what is hidden: who's doing what with whom, why the sky is blue and our blood red, who will live and who will die. Curiosity and imagination have kindled her hunger for knowledge.

But why should she listen to the serpent's sly words? She and Adam lack nothing—except what hangs upon those forbidden boughs. Perhaps she's grown restless and bored in their sultry garden, where everything she needs grows on trees. The gate at the far edge of the garden calls to her and bids her imagine what lies beyond.

We can picture the woman standing transfixed before the tree of knowledge, her senses alive and trained on its fruit. She's apprehensive and deliberate. Slowly she searches her heart and mind, weighing the risks and benefits of her next move.

A*nd when the woman saw that the tree was good for food and that it was a delight to the eyes, and that the tree was to be desired to make one wise, she took of its fruit and did eat.*

The fruit is indeed good for eating. A caress to all her senses.

She looks up into the tree, but the serpent is gone. Alone now at the center of the garden, the woman runs to share her newfound fruit with the man.

She also gave some to her husband, and he ate of it.

In this allegory of sexual awakening we can see what I perceive as the classic dichotomy of male and female response. Both have an appetite for the fruit, though they consume it differently. The woman ascends the staircase of sensual arousal slowly and cautiously, one step at a time. Only after she apprehends the wisdom hoarded inside the fruit and weighs the risks involved does she eat of it.

In contrast, the man needs no inducement. Once offered, he takes the fruit without compunction or inhibition. He swallows it whole and lies down to sleep.

But now he bolts awake—

Then the eyes of both of them were opened and they knew that they were naked; and they sewed together fig leaves and made themselves loincloths.

The serpent was right. Their eyes *have been* opened. And as he promised, they don't die—at least not then and there. What *does* expire is their blissful ignorance of their conflicted and divided natures. They suddenly feel so self-conscious . . . so exposed. . . .

Now that they've tasted of the fruit of knowledge, the man and the woman have to cope with what they see. And what they see is that they are naked—just like the other animals. As they gaze unblinking at each other's body, they have to admit that they look remarkably like animals. Less hairy, more upright. Bigger heads, perhaps. But they are undeniably endowed with the sexual organs of an animal. And like the other creatures in the Garden, they will someday die. What kind of hybrid creatures are they? Created in the image of God, they are endowed with transcendent souls—yet they must live in temporal bodies, contend with animal drives, and bear the consciousness of their own mortality.

In a poignant attempt to shield themselves from their newly

discovered self-knowledge, man and woman fashion the world's first loincloths out of fig leaves. This flimsy cover-up is doomed to failure. They cannot hope to camouflage the terrifying truth they have uncovered, either from themselves or from God.

And they heard the sound of the Lord God moving about in the Garden toward the cool of the day; and the man and his wife hid from the Lord God among the trees of the Garden.

The day is dying in the Garden, and the breeze now feels cool against their naked skin. Like frightened, guilty children, the man and the woman try to hide. But they are children no longer.

The Lord God called out to the man and said to him, "Where are you?"

"I heard the sound of You in the Garden, and I was afraid because I was naked, so I hid."

Then God asked, "Who told you that you were naked? Did you eat of the tree from which I had forbidden you to eat?"

That simple question—"Where are you?"—reverberates with innuendo. Where is man now, caught in a no-man's-land between innocence and experience, between his godlike self-image and his irrefutable animal form? How did he arrive at this predicament, crouched in a cold and darkening thicket of trees with only a fig leaf for cover?

The man and the woman are not yet ready to own up to their disobedience. They respond as so many of us do when confronted with our transgressions: they point fingers and assign blame—anything but accept responsibility.

The man said, "The woman You put at my side—she gave me of the tree, and I did eat."

And the Lord God said to the woman, "What is this you have done?"

The woman replied, "The serpent beguiled me, and I did eat."

Adam and the woman are about to learn that once we have crossed the borderline into adult experience, we can never again plead childlike innocence. As adults, we will be held to a higher standard of accountability.

Then the Lord God said to the serpent, "Because you did this, more cursed shall you be than all the cattle and all the wild beasts: On your belly shall you crawl and dirt shall you eat all the days of your life. I will put enmity between you and the woman, and between your offspring and hers; they shall strike at your head and you shall strike at their heel."

They shall strike at your head and you shall strike at their heel can be seen to diagram the ongoing struggle between humans and temptation. Eve's offspring, both men and women, will be under constant assault from the serpents of enticement that lurk in the underbrush and strike at their heels. Humans will stay busy staving off temptation with every fist and foot—though they will never stamp it out entirely.

Man and woman's gestation in the womb of Eden is now complete. But like every birth, their passage into the realm of adult responsibility will be traumatic.

And to the woman He said, "I will multiply your pain in childbearing. In pain shall you bring forth children; yet your desire shall be for your husband, and he shall rule over you."

The woman is the first to experience the mixed blessing of sexual maturity. A moment earlier, pain hadn't existed. Now she learns that the same instinct that gives such powerful pleasure—both physical and emotional—will also result in painful childbirth. Until very recently, childbearing was a life-threatening enterprise for women. One of the most beloved female characters in Genesis, Rachel, dies while giving birth. Throughout human history, death has cast a heavy shadow over the miracle of birth, and the drastic reduction in infant and maternal mortality stands as humankind's happiest success in "subduing nature." But despite all our medical advances, childbirth continues to inspire apprehension and awe.

"Yet your desire shall be for your husband" establishes that *despite* the pain and peril of childbirth, a woman will still desire sexual union with her husband and the new life it creates. The life force within her will win out over her fear of pain.

"And he [your husband] shall rule over you" is one of the most difficult lines in Genesis. Many have misinterpreted and misused it to justify male subjugation of women. In the context of this story we can infer that the Hebrew word for "rule over" also means "to protect." In biblical times, when birth control was nonexistent, a woman's fertile years were given over almost entirely to childbearing. During those periods when she was either pregnant, nursing, or rearing an infant, a woman and her children were entirely dependent on her husband's protection. Since the equation of male-female relationships throughout Genesis is not one of dominance and submission, but interdependence, I believe this line anticipates the woman's impending motherhood and assigns man the task of protecting her and their offspring. Here, as throughout Genesis, men are reminded of the solemn parenting responsibility that comes with "knowing" a woman.

As we have seen, Adam's transgression is not so much in defying God as in denying his personal accountability and projecting the blame onto his wife.

To man God said, *"Because you did as your wife said and ate of the tree about which I commanded you not to eat, cursed be the ground because of you; by toil shall you eat of*

*it all the days of your life: thorns and thistles shall it sprout
for you. But your food shall be the grasses of the field. By
the sweat of your brow shall you get bread to eat, until you
return to the ground—for from it were you taken. For dust
you are and to dust you shall return."*

When they are exiled from the Garden, man and woman must
both bear the burdens of adult life, sharing equally in its pain and
joy. While the woman will have painful labor in childbirth, man will
labor arduously to bring forth life from the soil.

As author William F. Allman explains in his book *The Stone Age
Present,* man's transition from the effortless fruit-picking of Eden to
the hardships of agriculture mirrors an historical shift in ancient
Near Eastern society. The evolution from a hunter-gatherer to an
agricultural society some 5,000 to 8,000 years ago wrought profound changes in human society. Food became more plentiful and
predictable, but humans were now totally reliant on the cycles of
the soil.

But the task of tilling the soil offers man tangible benefits. By
connecting him to the earth and all its life-giving mysteries, farming
serves as the male equivalent of childbirth. Through tilling the soil,
man participates in the creation of new life. By the sweat of his
brow, he sustains his family as surely as the mother who suckles her
children.

"For dust you are and to dust you shall return." How does
Adam react to the death sentence that awaits him after a lifetime of
sweat and toil? Does he beg for mercy? Does he curse God or
rebuke the woman? No. Adam turns out to be a man of character.
Instead of reviling his wife, he pays homage to her unique talent for
bringing forth new life from her body. Adam, whose name means
"earth," confers on his wife the name Eve, which in Hebrew—*Havah*
—connotes "life."

*The man named his wife Eve, because she was the mother
of all the living.*

God has compassion for the man and the woman. Before sending them out into the cold world to fend for themselves, God—like a concerned parent—tries to shield them from the elements.

And the Lord God made garments of skins for Adam and his wife, and clothed them.

This gesture is significant as an expression of God's mercy and love for humanity. Though He is banishing Adam and Eve from the temperate greenhouse of Eden, He does not desert them in their hour of need.

But God is determined to draw the line between human and divine identity. Human beings are destined to live as mortals in temporal bodies, not as gods. God bars their path to the tree of immortal life in order to establish the inviolable boundary between humans and God.

And the Lord God said, "Now that the man has become like one of us, knowing good and evil, what if he should stretch out his hand and take also from the tree of life and eat, and live forever?" So the Lord God banished him from the Garden of Eden, to till the soil from which he was taken.

We must never forget that though we are created in the image of God, we are not and will never be God. There is always a higher force than ourselves at work in the world. We are mortal and imperfect creatures who exert only limited control over our environment. No matter how much knowledge or power we accumulate, we are not entitled to wield God-like power over other humans. Our challenge is to acknowledge our imperfections—but aspire to overcome our human limitations.

He drove the man out, and stationed east of the Garden of Eden the cherubim and the fiery ever-turning sword, to guard the way to the tree of life.

God seems to conclude that Adam and Eve have outgrown the cradle of Eden He built for them, that adult sexuality may prove too uncontrollable a force in His carefully ordered garden. Like a parent with grown children, He sees that it's time for them to face life in the real world. God posts a sword-wielding sentry at the gate to the Garden to keep Adam and Eve from regressing to a childish life devoid of adult challenges and rewards. Once we lose our youthful innocence, there's no going back to the garden of childhood, much as we might yearn to.

Our hearts go out to Adam and Eve for their primal loss of innocence. But they also earn our admiration. As they leave the Garden arm in arm, we see a couple bound closer together by adversity. As Elie Wiesel writes in *Messengers of the Gods:*

> Rejected by God, [Adam] drew closer to Eve. Never were the two so united. . . . Expelled from paradise, Adam and Eve did not give in to resignation. In the face of death, they decide to fight by giving life, by conferring a meaning on life. . . . [Like Adam,] every one of us yearns to recapture some lost paradise, every one of us bears the mark of some violated, stolen innocence.

Adam and Eve's stoic exit from the Garden is a far cry from the tearful scene depicted in Renaissance paintings. They don't apologize or despair. Their perseverance defies the pessimistic "fall of man" interpretation of their expulsion from the Garden. With their departure, we witness instead the "rise of man" as the first man and woman forge a covenant of love and interdependence dedicated to their mutual survival and growth.

EVE REVISITED

As the consumer and purveyor of the forbidden fruit of the tree of knowledge, Eve has traditionally been portrayed as the instigator of man's "fall." She has also been cast as the culprit in humanity's banishment from the womblike Garden into the uncertainties of the world. Is she really a manipulative seductress, an agent of sin?

After countless readings, I've arrived at a different interpretation of this archetypal woman and this ancient tale of desire and the quest for knowledge. Rather than focusing on Eve's disobedience, I am drawn to her dynamic life force and the initiative she takes in exercising her God-given free will. Rather than a temptress, Eve acts as Adam's equal "helper," reaching out to him with the nourishing fruit of wisdom. She realizes that the sheltered greenhouse of Eden will never be conducive to intellectual or spiritual growth. I see Eve as a trailblazer who leads humanity from childlike innocence toward an adult life of challenge and responsibility.

Though Eve is not a developed personality, her basic character traits forecast many of the strengths of the women who will follow her in Genesis: Sarah, Rebekah, Leah, and Rachel. Like Eve, none of them is perfect. All of them, at a certain point in their lives, bravely take risks in pursuit of their families' ideals—and then must live with the consequences of their actions. They don't hesitate to act autonomously on behalf of their husbands and children. Like Eve, the women of Genesis emerge as strong matriarchs who exert profound influences over the course of their families' destinies.

In many respects I feel that Eve stands as a formidable role model for contemporary women. She is not content to blindly accept rules. When faced with the option, she relinquishes a world of safety and security for knowledge and experience. At some point in her life, every woman is an Eve: standing alone before the fruit of knowledge, carefully weighing its costs and benefits, and finally, deliberately, making her choice.

THE SEXUAL WAY OF KNOWLEDGE

Some people believe that the story of the Garden of Eden condemns sexuality as sinful. I feel that this negative interpretation clashes with both the text of this story and the spirit of the rest of the Hebrew Bible. Positive images of sexual passion appear throughout the Bible, the lushly sensual Song of Songs being only the most graphic example. In Genesis, the love relationships between the patriarchs and matriarchs are characterized by strong sexual and romantic bonds that often extend well into old age. From the very beginning of Genesis, the sexual chemistry between men and women emerges as a catalyst for intimacy and self-awareness.

However, Genesis is much too subtle to suggest that human sexuality is nothing but undiluted pleasure. Eve and Adam's initiation into adult sexuality is a bumpy passage at best. The story of Eden reminds us that our emerging sexuality introduces us to the lifelong connection between behavior and consequences, between pleasure and responsibility. Whether we are dealing with our sexual habits, drinking habits, driving habits, or eating habits, we adults must exercise a measure of self-restraint. If we refuse to accept any boundaries to our pleasure and passion, we risk causing irreparable harm to ourselves and the people we are closest to. Sex is the ultimate interpersonal act. How considerate we are of our partner's emotions is a telling measure of our maturity.

The most profound consequence of our sexual drive—and this is the inescapable subtext of Adam and Eve's story—is that a moment of pleasure may result in a lifetime of parental responsibility.

God's defining activity in Genesis is creation, and our sexuality is our most explicitly creative attribute and our most direct imitation of God. God's first directive to Adam and Eve is to *be fruitful and multiply*. Much of Genesis details the struggle of men and women to make sense of this command as distinct from the other creatures on earth. The biological consequences of reproduction carry a much heavier responsibility for humans than for any other species. Child-rearing is a protracted and demanding task that calls on all our adult faculties of caring, cooperation, and patience. But the command to "be fruitful and multiply" does not relate only to biological reproduction. It also means making our life a fruitful endeavor that benefits the world around us.

While at first glance Adam and Eve perceive their sexuality as an animal attribute, closer examination reveals profound differences in the way, respectively, humans and animals perform sex. Unlike most animals, whose sexual activity is relegated to set mating seasons, men and women are sexually receptive continually. We make love when we are simply feeling romantic or lustful, regardless of whether or not we are fertile, or even of childbearing age.

This ongoing sexual attraction between men and women helps maintain monogamous relationships over extended periods of time, promoting stability that benefits both the partners and their off-spring. And nonprocreative sex nourishes intimacy and attachment in couples well into old age. While there is a decrease in sexual activity with age, there are also compensations. Most of the couples I've worked with have found that the longer they know each other, the richer the sexual relationship. Men often become more patient and attentive lovers with age. And many women find that the cumulative trust, intimacy, and commitment of a long-term relationship makes them freer and more open with their partners.

CARING AND COOPERATION BENEATH THE TREE OF KNOWLEDGE

Compatibility between the sexes doesn't come ready-made. We have to work at it. In order to make love—as opposed to merely having sex—a man and a woman need to take the time and have the patience to harmonize the fundamental differences between their sexual natures. Sexual intercourse is a trial-by-error training ground for cooperation between the sexes.

The story of the Garden of Eden shows us how dependent men and women are on cooperation. God sees that it is not good for man to be alone—stuck in his infant stage of development—so He gives him woman as a catalyst for growth. While there is only one human in the Garden, life is simple and orderly. But as soon as God adds a second person, of the opposite sex, to the mix, a synergistic process is set in motion that propels humans out of the Garden and into the wider world. Freud pointed out that sexual curiosity is a distinctly human trait. Our instinctual impulses—looking, touching, showing —are learning tools that we direct toward self-discovery. When Eve sees that the fruit of the tree of knowledge is good not only for eating but *was to be desired to make one wise,* she tastes it—and immediately passes her discovery on to Adam. Not to corrupt him, but to reach out and share knowledge with him—the first act of cooperation. As a woman in one of my classes once remarked, to peals of appreciative female laughter: "If Eve hadn't offered Adam the fruit, he'd still be sitting around waiting for his dinner."

The first act of cooperation between Adam and Eve—sharing the fruit of "knowledge"—also implies sexual intercourse and the conception of a child. It takes a fleeting moment to create a baby, and a lifetime of cooperation to raise that child.

DEDICATION TO LIFE, NOT IMMORTALITY

The most sobering information that Adam and Eve glean from the tree of knowledge is their mortality. We are not gods. Our tenure on earth is limited by the life span of our bodies. The lesson of this story of banishment from a garden of eternal life is clear: our goal is not to escape death, but to embrace life and savor its challenges and its gifts.

Mortality is *not* God's punishment for eating of the tree of knowledge. As human beings, Adam and Eve are destined to be mortal; they simply have to find it out for themselves. Each of us, as children, bumps up against the immovable reality of our mortality, and we spend the better part of our adult lives grappling with its implications. Death is what endows life with meaning and a measure of urgency. With the awareness of death comes an understanding of just how finite and precious each day of our life is.

Freud posited two opposing instincts in our psyches: Eros, the sexual life drive named for the Greek god of love, and Thanatos, the Greek word for "death." These primordial instincts compete for dominance as each individual life moves inexorably toward death. Respect for the dynamic tension between life and death is something we can teach our children by example. As Erik Erikson noted: "Healthy children will not fear life so long as their parents have integrity enough not to fear death." As we'll see later in Genesis, the patriarchs and matriarchs are remarkably matter-of-fact in the face of their mortality. "Dust to dust" is accepted as an inescapable reality rather than as a tragic consequence of life.

This emphasis in Genesis on mortality represents a significant departure from the dominant pagan cultures of biblical times—Babylonian and Egyptian—which were fixated on the lure of eternal life. In their mythologies, the highest goal was to cross over the chasm of mortality, become a god, and reside forever in a deathless realm. A favored few were rewarded by the gods with membership in the fraternity of immortal beings. But these cults of eternal life betrayed an obsessive fear of death.

The cosmology described in the Garden of Eden affirms that there is only one immortal God and that the focus of human endeavors should be life, not death. The serpent was a Mesopotamian god of eternal life who was reborn every time he shed his skin. The serpent's fate in Eden—*"more cursed shall you be than all the cattle and all the wild beasts: On your belly shall you crawl and dirt shall you eat all the days of your life"*—is a clear rebuke of the cult of immortality the serpent symbolized.

The sexual drive within each of us—the God-like power to create new life and to transcend the isolation of our physical bodies—is our ultimate response to the knowledge of death. Absolute immortality is beyond human reach. But our sexuality connects us—both genetically and spiritually—to our ancestors and our progeny. The art and culture we create during our life, the children we bear, and the memories we leave behind constitute our inalienable bridge to the future.

GROWING UP AND LEAVING HOME

On the level of psychological development, the story of Adam and Eve narrates the universal human voyage out of the family nest. It's a story about growing up and leaving home, about severing the umbilical cord to our parents, establishing intimate bonds outside the family, and creating our own nucleus.

We all begin our lives as children in the Garden of Eden, although some children's Gardens are more paradisiacal than others. Then we grow up. Some people don't want to grow up, because it means leaving our childishness behind. It means renouncing the innocence of childhood and taking on the responsibilities that come with adulthood. We have no choice about aging, but we each have to choose whether or not to behave like an adult. The world is full of middle-aged children who have chosen not to grow up—who drink and drive, who gamble with rent money, who don't pay their child support.

In this story God can be seen as the ambivalent parent who simultaneously wants to protect His children from worldly knowledge and prepare them to meet the challenges of the outside world —who wants to shield them from the confusion and vulnerability of their emerging sexuality while wishing for them all the fulfillment of intimate relationships. Adam and Eve are every boy and girl who are drawn irrevocably through the awkward passage of adolescence. They are attached to the safety and security of their home, but attracted to the stimulus of the wider world as personified by the opposite gender. Sexual maturity speeds the younger generation's exit from the household and into the wider world.

Once we cross the boundary of childhood innocence, we are forever wandering abroad in the world of experience. This going forth in search of knowledge is the narrative and spiritual framework for all of Genesis. Man must *leave his mother and father and cleave to his wife.* Then he and the woman must exit the Garden altogether. Noah sets forth in an ark to begin the world anew. And the patriarchs and matriarchs will later go forth from their homelands in pursuit of a promised land.

The lesson of all this restless wandering in Genesis is that the getting of wisdom demands that we constantly voyage forth beyond established boundaries. Whether we travel inside the structure of the human cell, to the depths of the ocean, or to the outer reaches of space, we are always pushed by our appetite for knowledge beyond geographic and intellectual borders, driven to "open our eyes" to the farthest reaches of the creation.

Columbus set out across uncharted waters toward a New World, though not the one he sought. The Hubble space telescope is only our latest and most literal attempt to see outside our world, to expand our field of vision to the cosmos beyond. Humankind's eternal journey toward knowledge mirrors the direction of the universe, expanding outward since the "big bang" of its beginning.

In the Garden of Eden, Eve emerges as the catalyst for change. She is the pioneer who moves humanity away from a life of yawning passivity, who parlays the security of innocence for knowledge. She grasps her free will with both hands and, along with Adam, forces open the gates of experience, out of the Garden and into the world.

Given the choice, who of us would want to turn back?

CAIN AND ABEL: CONFRONTING THE BEAST OF RAGE WITHIN

Who is the hero? He who conquers his own urges.

—*The Talmud*

As author and psychoanalyst Willard Gaylin has noted with stark clarity, "Anger thrives on intimacy." It's the people we love most who can drive us into the worst paroxysms of fury.

Why is this? Why are love and rage so closely linked in our intimate relationships—particularly in the family? How can we tame the beast of domestic violence that crouches just outside the doors to our homes?

The family is an inevitable breeding ground for feelings of hurt, resentment, anger, and rage. The more we love—whether the object of our affections is a parent, a sibling, or a spouse—the more we need that love returned in kind. When our love isn't reciprocated, we convert our humiliation into anger. Unless we have the maturity, humility, and courage to confront the pain we are experiencing, our frustration can explode into emotional and even physical violence toward the people we are closest to. The process of controlling our aggressive impulses requires discipline, introspection, and honesty—in other words, all the ingredients of adult love.

We all cherish the winning qualities of children: their spontaneity, openness, and creativity. But children are unable to control their impulses because they don't have the tools to deal with frustration. One brother hits another when he takes his truck, instead of negotiating its return. Many of us as adults still resolve our interpersonal conflicts in this childish way, with impulsive hostility, verbal abuse, or violence. When it comes to exerting control over our actions and taking responsibility for how we behave toward others, we should aim to subdue, rather than elevate, the child within us.

When Cain fails to master his jealous rage, Abel becomes the first sacrificial lamb on the altar of human jealousy. The tragedy of Cain and Abel is narrated in sixteen concise lines, but the specter of sibling rivalry will continue to haunt every generation of their family—and every generation of the human family to this day. As we will see, this story of two young brothers is about sibling rivalry fueled by the hurt and rage they feel when their gifts of love are not returned in kind.

Now the man knew his wife Eve, and she conceived and bore Cain, saying, "I have gained a male child with the help of the Lord." She then bore his brother Abel.

With the path back to the innocence of everlasting childhood blocked to them forever, Adam and Eve have nowhere to go but forward, out into the world of adult experience. To their credit, they don't surrender to recrimination, fear, or despair. They begin to cultivate their own garden and to build a family.

As soon as Adam and Eve leave the Garden, Adam "knows" Eve, and she conceives a child *"with the help of the Lord."* Even though they have been expelled from Eden, Adam and Eve have not been abandoned by God. Eve acknowledges God's role in helping her conceive, and throughout Genesis the mysterious gift of conception will be linked to God's blessing. Every child's birth marks a new beginning for the human family, and God infuses every new soul with His spiritual likeness as it enters the world.

But the fruit of sexual knowledge—childbearing and child-rearing—is bittersweet. We are about to witness the hidden meaning behind God's prophecy to Eve, *"In pain shall you bring forth children."*

Cain and Abel's story begins on a deceptively hopeful note of pious gratitude—the brothers thanking the Lord for sharing His bounty with them. What makes this tale so tragic is that it begins in piety and ends in bloodshed.

Abel became a keeper of sheep, and Cain was a tiller of the soil: In the course of time, Cain brought an offering to the Lord of the fruit of the soil; and Abel, for his part, brought the firstlings of his flock.

As in many families, the sons' rivalry is established from the outset by their competing professions. Like many a first son, Cain goes into the "family business" of farming, while the second son stakes out his own turf in a new field of endeavor—in this case, becoming the first shepherd. Younger siblings often make lifestyle choices—clothes, social circles, recreation—to distinguish themselves from older siblings and attract their own share of parental attention.

And the Lord paid heed to Abel and his offering, but to Cain and his offering He paid no heed. And Cain was very angry, and his countenance fell.

This first human offering to God underscores a sobering lesson in the art of giving: when we give, we should not expect to get. Of course, when we feel we are giving our love, it's impossible not to want that gift reciprocated. And when this doesn't happen, the spirit of our offering can quickly turn from love to resentment to anger. It's unclear why God prefers Abel's offering over Cain's. Perhaps He is testing Cain's motives: Was Cain actually offering thanks to God, or was he fishing for approval?

When God—whom we can interpret in this story as a surrogate parent—does not acknowledge his offering, Cain is driven into a jealous rage. We all yearn for mutuality and reciprocity in our intimate relationships. And a child like Cain wants not only requited but exclusive love from his "parent."

And the Lord said to Cain, "Why are you angry, and why is your countenance fallen?"

Like a good parent, God takes note of Cain's distress and steps in to try to train him away from the dark thoughts already telegraphed by his face. He intercedes and admonishes Cain to locate the source of his anger before it spirals out of control. Today, when a child begins to have a tantrum, child therapists advise parents to intervene and urge the child to "use your talking voice" as a way to express his anger verbally rather than physically. By recognizing the therapeutic value of identifying and naming our pain, the Bible anticipated Freud's groundbreaking "talking cure" by several millennia.

"If you do right, shall you not be accepted? And if you do not right, sin crouches at the door. And to you shall be its desire, and yet you may rule over it."

Sin finally makes its entry in the Bible—a full generation after Adam and Eve—portrayed here as a wild animal that crouches at the door of our souls, waiting for a moment of weakness to force its way into our lives. God sees Cain's unhappiness, understands the evil urges stirring in his heart, and warns him that there is yet time to subdue them. *"Yet you may rule over it"* affirms that our hostile impulses can be conquered. While this story acknowledges that sin is seductive—*"And to you shall be its desire"*—we are not slaves to our darkest impulses. Our human free will grants us the ability and the responsibility to choose the right action over the wrong one.

But Cain turns a deaf ear to God's admonition. No sooner does God finish warning Cain to rule over his sinful urge than Cain surrenders to it:

And Cain said to Abel his brother, "Come, let us go into the field." And Cain rose up against Abel his brother, and slew him.

Sin claims its first victims, and the immediate gratification of a violent impulse snuffs out a human life.

Tragically, Cain can't even bring himself to respond to God's entreaties. Talking to an all-powerful parent about our anger is simply too threatening a prospect to most of us. It's much easier to take Cain's path of redirecting our rage toward a defenseless younger sibling. This episode underscores a recurrent lesson in Genesis: sibling rivalry has less to do with direct conflict between brothers or sisters than with competition for their parents' attention.

And the Lord said to Cain, "Where is Abel your brother?" And he said, "I know not. Am I my brother's keeper?"

Like his parents before him—and like most of us when confronted with our shameful acts—Cain's first line of defense is self-righteous denial. It's human nature to deny guilt, even in the face of overwhelming evidence. Children are well-known for their ability to flatly deny blame, even when literally caught with their hands in the cookie jar. So are public figures, when their hands are caught in the till. And when we don't have the character to admit our wrongdoings, we often go on the attack, as Cain does with his belligerent rejoinder: *Am I my brother's keeper?*

Cain's timeless question *Am I my brother's keeper?* continues to reverberate to this day. Though God does not respond to Cain's rhetorical question, the answer is self-evident: Yes, we *are* our brother's keeper. We *are* accountable for how we behave and how those actions affect others.

We need to keep posing this question because the answer is so central to our highest moral challenge. We must constantly remind ourselves that we are our brother's keeper precisely because sibling rivalry is so ingrained in the family dynamic. We can also extrapolate this lesson of moral accountability to the extended family of man. Because we humans are so prone to anger and aggression, we need this story to remind us that all murders are fratricide within the human family—that we are all brothers and are ultimately consigned to each other's safekeeping.

By failing to take the time to examine and master his dark rage, Cain forfeits control over his future. By succumbing to a moment's violent impulse, he earns a lifetime of anguish.

And God said, "What have you done? The voice of your brother's blood cries out to Me from the ground. Now you are cursed from the earth, which has opened her mouth to receive your brother's blood from your hand. When you till the ground, it shall no longer yield her strength to you. A fugitive and a wanderer shall you be on earth."

In the Bible, a person's blood is directly connected to his soul. Here, in a chilling image, Abel's blood *cries out* from the ground, which is personified as opening her mouth to swallow Abel's blood. Once he has defiled the earth with his brother's blood, the soil *shall no longer yield her strength* to Cain. Because of his unbridled rage, the soil he tills becomes barren and Cain the farmer becomes alienated from the source of his sustenance and nurture.

When we allow the beast of emotional or physical violence to force its way into our lives, we poison our most intimate relationships, until they too *no longer yield [their] strength* to us. We banish ourselves from the relationships that nurture us most.

And Cain said to the Lord, "My punishment is greater than I can bear! Behold, You have driven me out this day

from the face of the earth, and from Your face shall I be
hidden. I shall be a fugitive and a wanderer in the earth, and
whoever finds me shall kill me."

Even at this point, Cain is reluctant to take responsibility for
his actions. *"Behold, You have driven me out,"* he cries, casting
himself as a victim of God's wrath rather than of his own reckless
rage. In actuality, Cain has brought his banishment on himself. And
like many of us, Cain projects his own lack of impulse control onto
others. Because he is a violent person, he views the outside world as
hostile and threatening, peopled by murderers. Consumed more by
self-pity than by remorse, Cain feels emotionally orphaned: banished from the face of the earth—the mother—and the face of God
—the father.

T*he Lord said to him, "I promise, if anyone kills Cain,*
sevenfold vengeance shall be taken on him." And the Lord
put a mark on Cain, lest anyone meeting him should kill
him. And Cain left the presence of the Lord and settled in
the land of Nod, east of Eden.

In Genesis, God's judgment is always leavened by mercy, and
the sanctity of human life emerges as His highest teaching. God
responds to Cain's despairing cry by reassuring him that He will not
abandon him. In the same way that God makes clothing for Adam
and Eve before evicting them from Eden, God now confers on Cain
the proverbial "mark"—which is commonly misunderstood as a
curse—to signify that Cain remains under God's protection.

The *land of Nod* to which Cain is exiled is more a spiritual
than a geographical domain. *Nod* is the Hebrew word for wandering, and it is the bleak landscape of Cain's guilty conscience that
defines the parameters of his future life. Peace of mind will always
elude this fugitive wanderer who, as a moral being, will forever be in
flight from his crime of passion. Stained by his brother's blood,
Cain's soul is indelibly "marked" by grief, guilt, and shame.

EMBRACING THE POWER
OF FREE WILL

Despite the tragic resolution of Cain and Abel's story, it carries an empowering lesson: we have the capacity—indeed the obligation—to rein in our anger and destructive drives. This moral imperative is a distinctly human task. Animals aren't subject to any such expectation. We don't expect compassion or understanding from lions and tigers. But as human beings created in the image of God, we are granted moral autonomy. Once we know the difference between right and wrong, we are obliged to act on our best instincts and restrain our worst ones. Our modern criminal justice system is based on this same biblical credo of moral responsibility. Children, the mentally retarded, and the insane do not have the moral judgment to distinguish right from wrong, and are therefore not held accountable for their actions.

Like Cain, we have a right to be upset when we feel spurned by the ones we love. In the family paradigm, conflict is inevitable. Parents can't possibly be altogether consistent in the proportion of attention they give, and children feel stung by this emotional injustice. (Even today, when I visit my three grown children in New York City, I am acutely aware of how carefully and equally I need to divide my time among them.) But the inequalities inherent to family life don't release us from our obligation to behave responsibly. It's up to each of us to help heal the wounds that are inescapable in the family arena. This is our highest calling, our greatest challenge.

Genesis makes a crucial distinction between a dark thought and a dark deed. We all have evil urges, but that does not entitle us to commit evil acts. In the end we are judged by our actions, not our thoughts. As Immanuel Kant remarked centuries after Genesis, action is the only reliable measure of morality. This applies to good and evil actions alike. Merely feeling love for someone is not enough. Only when we *behave* lovingly do we best express our humanity.

The Talmud observes, "Who is the hero? He who can subdue his urges." I want to be clear about the distinction between subduing our destructive impulses and repressing them. Repressing urges means blocking them out even before we become aware that they exist—and before we have the opportunity to examine them. Subduing urges requires acknowledging our desires, then testing those desires against our values and against the consequences of acting on those urges. This is the path of hard-won maturity and self-respect.

Freud once posited that "civilization is sublimation." Our ability to subdue our destructive urges and channel them into constructive and creative outlets is what makes us distinctly human. Freud identified sublimation as the wellspring of our most lofty accomplishments in the arts and sciences. The postscript to the story of Cain and Abel suggests that sublimation offers Cain redemption from his violent nature: chastened by his tragic surrender to violence and his banishment to Nod, Cain marries, fathers a son, and sows the seeds of our original civilization by building the first city.

TAMING THE BEAST THAT CROUCHES AT THE DOOR

The Book of Ecclesiastes observes that *there is nothing new under the sun*. Sadly, there is nothing new about the violence spawned by family passions. As in this first biblical clash of sibling rivals, the majority of today's assaults and murders are crimes of passion committed between close acquaintances or family members. The statistics of wife beating, child abuse, and other forms of domestic violence are numbing. And for each murder or assault, there are countless acts of psychological violence. The Bible refuses to gloss over the harsh reality of domestic violence. Genesis forces us to confront the roots of our destructive passions and exhorts us to stand guard against the *sin [that] crouches at the door* of the family, waiting like a calculating predator to pounce on its prey.

What can we do to dissolve the links between love and rage in our most intimate relationships? There is a brief window of time when we can stop ourselves from striking out, emotionally or physically, in anger. But the task of unlearning ingrained patterns of behavior requires a serious commitment of time, will, and emotional energy. In the course of my therapy practice I've worked with many families trying to break the same cycle of hurt, frustration, and resulting anger that doomed Cain and Abel. These families, in which anger builds and builds and finally explodes into either hurtful words or acts, or into actual physical violence, are "murdering" trust and intimacy at home.

Here are the steps I've found most helpful in dealing with these destructive patterns:

Acknowledging the problem:

We are all imperfect, and our modes of communication are imperfect. It's inevitable in intimate relationships that we get our feelings hurt and we hurt other people. When we love or feel close, we are at our most vulnerable. But while it's perfectly human to occasionally behave thoughtlessly in our close relationships, it's enormously difficult to accept this same thoughtless behavior in those we love.

For instance, one of the difficult thresholds to cross in psychotherapy is facing the fact that we feel our parents may not have met each and every one of our emotional needs. A patient of mine began one of our sessions by railing against an emotionally remote father. But when I simply restated his complaint—"I hear you saying that you felt your father seemed more involved in his law practice than in raising you"—the patient leapt to his father's defense, explaining what a good provider and husband he was.

It's hard to acknowledge that people we love and depend on may let us down. But confronting this truth is absolutely essential to our emotional health. Facing our feelings of hurt head-on helps us deal with our anger cleanly so that we can leave it behind us.

Accepting the risks of intimacy:

When we don't get what we want in intimate relationships, we despair. Many times we feel ashamed to acknowledge our need for others to reciprocate our feelings. So instead of assuming responsibility for those feelings of hurt—and accepting them as a normal part of intimate relationships—we become angry. Feeling anger toward someone we love can be confusing and troubling because we associate anger with the absence of love. That confusion produces guilt, which only increases our anger.

The more intimate we are with someone, the more vulnerable we become. That intimacy and vulnerability are good and desirable, even if emotionally frightening. Accepting our deep emotional bonds with those we love is often the first step toward diffusing the anger that dependency can engender.

Giving voice to our anger:

Communicating with each other about our pain and resentment is the single best way to diffuse anger. This may sound simplistic, but it emerges as one of the most fundamental lessons of Genesis. Again and again we will see that when communication breaks down, family discord erupts into physical or emotional violence. And as a therapist I constantly witness an inverse relationship between communication and conflict—whether between husband and wife, parent and child, or siblings.

In Genesis, a person's ability to engage in dialogue with God becomes a barometer of his character. Because Cain can't respond to God's questions, he falls victim to his own darkest impulses. Later in Genesis, Abraham will distinguish himself as a moral leader when he elevates his dialogue with God to a new level of openness and intimacy.

Holding ourselves to our highest standards of behavior:

When we allow our anger to escalate into unbridled rage and retaliation, we hurt the person we lash out at—whether emotionally or physically—and we usually punish ourselves with remorse and guilt. I try to remind families I work with that it is a lot easier to destroy trust and intimacy than to build it back up.

We must accept our human limitations, but constantly endeavor to stretch those limits upward and outward to embody our highest expectations for ourselves. Therein lies our best hope of loving and respecting ourselves and sharing that love and respect with others. Every day we face choices, large and small, about which aspects of our nature to express and which to restrain. As humans we are destined to err, but perfection is not the object. Our goal is to keep moving closer to reflecting our noblest self-image— the image of God in which we were created.

THE NEXUS OF PSYCHOLOGY AND MORALITY

Psychotherapy is an invaluable tool for personal growth. But the Bible offers us a model for human transformation that transcends the limits of psychotherapy—namely, a moral standard of behavior. While we humans universally possess the power to choose how we respond to situations, we need a moral compass by which to guide those choices.

Genesis astutely introduces the theme of moral choice along a very clear divide: murder is unacceptable, a boundary that cannot be crossed without severe consequences. From this basic principle other moral imperatives emerge: each individual human life is precious; human dignity must not be violated by the "little murders" we commit every day. Though few of us express our hostility by wielding a club or a knife in anger, we are all capable of "killing" with a look, a word, a gesture.

I am very troubled by the degree to which the nonjudgmental ethic of psychotherapy has spilled out of the therapy room and swamped our lives and popular culture. An attitude of total acceptance that may be appropriate in the therapy room can be disastrous if transferred to the outside world. When a patient enters my office, all judgments are suspended for fifty minutes. My total acceptance and nonjudgment of my patient is necessary to promote the trust that allows for uncensored communication. But my relationship with patients is professional, not personal. When the boundaries of the therapy setting are extended and the same lack of censorship and judgment is applied to our intimate relationships, people often feel entitled to act irresponsibly and hurtfully. And when judgmental immunity invades TV talk shows, all behavior is presented as potentially acceptable and negotiable. Even more troubling is the increasing reluctance of the criminal justice system to apply moral, or even legal, standards to defendants who offer psychological justifications for immoral and illegal acts.

The genius of the biblical narrative is that rather than consigning morality to a murky realm of abstraction, it teaches morality through action. The story of Cain and Abel goes beyond analysis of the psychology of impulse control to the specific issue of moral behavior. To the degree that we can teach moral behavior to our children, it is a task we need to begin at home and at an early age. If a child grows up watching one parent humiliating the other, he accepts that as normal behavior and is likely to repeat it in his own marriage. Conversely, if a parent demonstrates integrity in his or her life, the child will absorb that as a high moral standard against which to measure himself.

We parents must do all we can to transmit love and values to our growing offspring. However, once our children are adults they become responsible for their own lives. Regardless of our best intentions and highest hopes as parents, grown children are autonomous beings who make their own choices in their lives. If God can't control the behavior of the creatures He created in His own image, who are we to think we can or should control the conduct of our grown children? As a parent, I've always drawn comfort from this lesson, which also underlies many episodes in Genesis.

As a society, we seem to be institutionalizing parent-bashing as a way of justifying our misconduct. It strengthens our tendency to see ourselves as victims rather than as autonomous adults. If we don't eventually release our parents from blame and take responsibility for our own lives, we are doomed to remain children. In order to grow up we need to subdue the petulant child within us and call forth the powerful adult persona to emerge.

———

The Flood: Building an Ark in a World Awash with Violence

He *who saves a single life, saves the whole world.*

—*The Talmud*

Why does the story of the Flood hold such enduring fascination for us? And why is it one of the first Bible stories we traditionally share with children? After all, this is not what we'd usually think of as a children's story: human violence spiraling out of control, a natural cataclysm that destroys the entire earth and virtually all the animals and people who inhabit it.

I think there are several reasons why children like having this story of near disaster and deliverance read to them. As Bruno Bettelheim explains in his book *The Uses of Enchantment,* frightening folk and fairy tales offer a child the opportunity to work through deep-seated anxieties:

> They speak about his severe inner pressures in a way that the child unconsciously understands, and offer examples of both temporary and permanent solutions. . . . [Fairy tales teach him] that a struggle against severe difficulties in life is unavoidable, is an intrinsic part of human existence—but that if one does not shy away, but steadfastly meets unexpected and often unjust hardships, one masters all obstacles and at the end emerges victorious.

Or as the German poet Schiller wrote: "Deeper meaning resides in the fairy tales told me in my childhood than in the truth that is taught by life."

As with other scary tales—from Little Red Riding Hood to Hansel and Gretel—hearing the story of the Flood lets children act out their primal fears of chaos and destruction. Children crave the security of an orderly domestic routine. What better metaphor for safety and security amid chaos than the sanctuary of Noah's ark in the storm? An entire universe is preserved and recreated from an orderly procession of creatures marching up the ramp, two by two. In this peaceable kingdom at sea, the lamb literally lies down with the lion. No matter how fiercely the winds and rains rage outside, the ark is always warm, safe, and dry. An unsinkable and portable home, the ark will always find its way back to dry land.

Children also find this story reassuring—and we feel empowered by telling it—because it promises that their parents will always protect them. Children identify with Noah, the obedient child, delivered from the floodwaters by an omnipotent and merciful parent, God. They also identify with the animals, all equal before God, each species equally deserving of space on the ark—the spider as welcome as the elephant. This floating menagerie of creatures of every kind is also a child's first lesson in biodiversity—a complex but intricately designed web of life where every animal has its place and its mate.

But what is the lesson of the Flood for adults? As the biblical narrative moves from the fraternal violence between Cain and Abel to the worldwide stage, its message is clear: if we do not take steps

to contain the swelling tide of human violence in our communities
and in the world at large, we will surely all drown in it.

The generations that descended from Cain charted a down-
ward spiral into violence and lawlessness, as if Cain's murder of
Abel had unleashed brutality on the world. God's grand experiment with free will now lay in ruins. Without a guiding vision
for their lives, humans ran amok, choosing brutish violence
over peaceful coexistence. The strong preyed on the weak,
men violated women, and humankind despoiled the earth that
God had commanded them to protect. By abusing God's gift of
free will, man abdicated his right to rule over the earth he had
stained with blood.

Ten generations after creating Adam and Eve in His own
image, God surveyed His creation and was filled with despair.

The Lord saw how great was man's wickedness on earth,
and how every plan devised by his mind was nothing but evil
all the time. And the Lord grieved that He had made man on
earth, and His heart was saddened.

He had given man so much—a Garden of earthly delights, a female companion equal to himself, dominion over the
animals, free will. And man had sacrificed it all on an altar of
violence. Created in God's image, only to become a wild beast!
The Lord decided to undo the work of His creation.

"I will blot out from the earth the men who I created—
men together with beasts, creeping things, and birds of the
sky—for I regret that I made them."

Then, against this landscape of darkness, God found a ray
of light.

But Noah found favor with the Lord. Noah was a righ-
teous man; he was blameless in his generation; Noah walked
with God.

Somehow, amidst all the lawlessness and violence, a single
man had survived with his humanity intact: the Lord's last hu-

man partner on earth and a possible ambassador to His next creation. God addressed Noah directly:

"I have decided to put an end to all flesh, for the earth is filled with violence. I am about to destroy them with the earth."

Noah didn't flinch, didn't speak or question. Since his fate still hung in the balance, he decided that silence was the best response. Were he and his family doomed to perish along with everyone else?

God commanded him in a firm voice:

"Make yourself an ark of gopher wood; make it an ark with compartments, and cover it inside and out with pitch."

Strange and mysterious words were these. Noah was practiced in righteousness, not carpentry. But it seems that God knew His man. Noah was born to carry out orders, so long as they were clearly given.

"This is how you shall make it: the length of the ark shall be three hundred cubits, its width fifty cubits, and its height thirty cubits. Make an opening for daylight in the ark, and terminate it within a cubit of the top. Put the entrance to the ark in its side; make it with bottom, second and third decks."

An immense vessel—more than four hundred feet long, seventy feet wide, and two stories high!

"For My part, I am about to bring the floodwaters upon the earth to destroy all flesh under the sky in which there is a breath of life; everything on earth shall perish."

But Noah knew nothing of seafaring. He was a tiller of the soil. Surely he, too, would perish in such a flood. God read the anxiety in Noah's face and hastened to reassure him.

"But I will establish my covenant with you, and you will enter the ark with your sons, your wife, and your sons' wives. And of all that lives you shall take two of each into the ark

to keep alive with you; they shall be male and female. From birds of every kind, cattle of every kind, every kind of creeping thing on earth, two of each shall come with you to stay alive.''

He would be saved! He and his wife and his sons and their wives. And he would be a rescuer to every kind of animal on earth.

God instructed him further:

"For your part, take everything that is eaten and store it away, to serve as food for you and for them." Noah did so; just as God commanded him, so he did.

Noah set to work with his three sons: Shem, Ham, and Japheth. Shem was a decent carpenter, and Ham was strong enough to load hay into the hold all day with no complaint. But without Japheth's special way with animals, all would have been lost. He was uncannily skilled at soothing the wildest beast and charming the most venomous snake. And he could discern the gender of any creature, no matter how strange or obscure. Within a fortnight, all the animals were gathered in pairs in a corral that Japheth had built outside the ark.

Then the Lord said to Noah, "Go into the ark, with all your household, for you alone have I found righteous before Me in this generation. And of every animal you shall take two into the ark, one male and one female, to keep their seed alive upon all the earth."

Getting all the animals on board was a chore in itself. Some were stubborn and had to be whipped; others were skittish and required gentle coaxing. Japheth had to blindfold the horses and calm them with whispered words just to lead them up the ramp to the second deck of the ark where the rest of the hoofed beasts were housed. The rabbits and squirrels had to be carried aboard, then counted again once they were stowed inside. Noah kept a careful inventory of every beast that was brought aboard.

And the Lord told Noah:

*"In seven days' time I will make it rain upon the earth,
forty days and forty nights, and I will blot out from the earth
all existence that I created." And Noah did just as the Lord
commanded him. And on the seventh day all the fountains of
the great deep burst apart, and the floodgates of the sky
broke open.*

This was a storm like no other. The waters of the heavens
and the waters of earth gushed forth at once. From the sky,
from the rivers—even from mouths of wells—the waters
poured forth. Noah and his sons raced through the ark, securing every hatch and shutter, while the women comforted the
animals in their fright.

*The Flood continued forty days on earth, and the waters
increased and raised the ark so that it rose above the earth.
The waters swelled and increased greatly upon the earth, and
the ark drifted upon the waters.*

The ark had no rudder or sail, yet it moved like a great
leviathan through the waters! What a remarkable silhouette it
made on the horizon: a small point of light on a darkened sea,
with two giraffes' necks sprouting like trees through the top
deck. More a house than a boat, the ark sliced through the
raging waves, as if guided by celestial navigation.

*When the waters had swelled much more upon the earth,
all the highest mountains everywhere under the sky were covered. And all flesh that stirred on earth perished—birds, cattle, beasts, and all the things that swarmed upon the earth,
and all mankind. All in whose nostrils was the merest breath
of life, all that was on dry land, died. All existence on earth
was blotted out. Only Noah was left, and those with him in
the ark.*

Now came the quiet days, the eerie silent time. Even the
animals seemed hushed as the ark drifted aimlessly in the
deathly calm after the storm. In every direction there was noth-

ing but a boundless gray expanse of sea and sky. All space and time were consumed by the steady pitch and roll of the ark, rocking like a cradle on a watery grave.

And when the waters swelled on the earth one hundred and fifty days, God remembered Noah and all the beasts and all the cattle that were with him in the ark, and God caused a wind to blow across the earth, and the waters subsided.

After forty days more, Noah sent out a raven—a faithful compass to ancient mariners—and the raven went to and fro across the top of the water. But it found no dry land.

Then Noah sent out a dove. At first *the dove found no rest for the sole of her foot, and she returned to the ark because the water was over all the earth.* Seven days later he sent her out again, and this time the dove returned, *and there in her bill was a plucked-off olive leaf!* This peace offering from God was a signal that life had sprouted again on earth. After another seven days, Noah sent the dove forth again, and this time *she did not return to him anymore,* so he knew that the waters had subsided.

The top of the tallest mountain showed above the waters, and the ark came to rest there. Then the tops of the other mountains rose into view. *And when Noah removed the covering of the ark, he saw that the surface of the ground was drying. And in the second month on the twenty-seventh day of the month, the earth was dry.*

Then the Lord told Noah to come out of the ark and release the animals and *let them swarm on the earth and be fruitful and multiply.*

The soil was soft underfoot as Noah led his family off the ark. They couldn't stand from dizziness. The animals were dazed after so long a journey at sea and had to be led gently off the ark. They exited two by two—the camels and the donkeys, the cheetahs and the bears.

In the morning Japheth chased the animals away. From among those that remained behind, Noah made a burnt offering to the Lord.

God was finally ready to make peace with His flawed human creation. He took a long, hard look at the creature He had created in His own image. Noah was a righteous man, but he was human and therefore imperfect. Like a beleaguered parent who eventually accepts his beloved but delinquent child with all his limitations, God resolved to Himself:

"Never again will I doom the earth because of man, since the imaginings of man's mind are evil from his youth; nor will I ever destroy every living thing, as I have done.

So long as the earth endures, seedtime and harvest,

Cold and heat, summer and winter,

Day and night shall not cease."

By recognizing that man's imagination often leads to evil in his youth, God hoped that man's imagination would also be used for good. God was ready to create once again, to replant the earth and watch it flower. Perhaps this time things would turn out better. After the destruction of the Flood, God restored order, stability, and continuity to the world. Then God blessed Noah, his servant, and Noah's sons, saying:

"Be fruitful and multiply, and fill the earth. Every creature that lives shall be yours to eat; as with the green grasses, I give you all these."

It seems that this was still the Lord's fondest desire—that the earth should teem with life, and that man should rule over the earth and preserve it. But by now, God had seen enough of man to know he was not the vegetarian creature God had wished him to be in the Garden. He was a hunter and a predator. So God gave the animals to man for food, hoping to satisfy his lust for blood and save the lives of other men.

God made one unequivocal demand of human beings: that they not murder the creatures He had created in His own image.

"Whosoever sheds the blood of man,

By man shall his blood be shed;

For in His image
Did God make man."

God hoped that this time things would turn out better.
But then again, why should Noah be any different from Adam?
Or Shem and Ham prove any less violent than Cain and Abel?
Better to accept man as he was, a mixture of good and evil.
Regardless of man's conduct, God would never again unite the
waters of destruction that He parted at creation.

God offered this unconditional commitment to Noah, His
second Adam:

"I now establish My covenant with you and your off-
spring to come, and with every living thing that is with you
—birds, cattle, and every wild beast as well. Never again
shall there be flood to destroy the earth."

At that moment a rainbow appeared in the sky, a luminous
bridge connecting heaven and earth. And God proclaimed:

"I have set My bow in the clouds, and it shall serve as
a sign of the covenant between Me and the earth. When I
bring clouds over the earth, and the bow appears in the
clouds, I will remember My covenant between Me and you
and every living creature, so that the waters shall never again
become a flood to destroy all flesh."

The rainbow of peace hung in the sky, a prism for the
light of heaven to shine through. This protective shield against
the devastating floodwaters of the clouds was a symbol of a
covenant of everlasting life between God and His creation.
This umbrella of trust was God's unconditional vow to preserve
the earth—and His command to man to do the same.

So Noah, the tiller of the soil, was the first to plant a
vineyard. He harvested the grapes and pressed them into
wine. It was the color of blood, and it smelled of brambles and
earth. That night Noah drank alone in his tent. He began to
hear the voices of the dead calling to him from below the dark
waters. Noah drank more deeply, amazed at how the wine

helped drown out the sights and sounds of death he had witnessed.

The next morning Noah's sons discovered him naked and unconscious in his tent. Embarrassed to see him so exposed, *they took a cloth, placed it against their backs and, walking backwards, they covered their father's nakedness.* But they knew not the dread that seized their father while in the grasp of the bloodred wine. And they knew not the sorrow that he had carried with him into this new world.

THE FLOOD IN ANCIENT MYTHOLOGY

According to paleontologists, during the last period of global warming, about 10,000 years ago, the sea rose as much as 500 feet, submerging most low-lying human settlements. For people in the ancient world, flood stories were a way to sublimate their terror of total annihilation, either from overflowing rivers or other natural disasters. To understand the lesson of this Flood story, it's useful to look at how it differs from the traditional mythology from which it sprang. Virtually every Near Eastern culture has a myth of a deluge, but in none is it so closely tied to a moral tale of human behavior and consequences as it is in the biblical version.

The closest antecedent to the biblical Flood is the Mesopotamian Epic of Gilgamesh written in the third century B.C.E.* The locale of both stories was probably the flat, alluvial plain that was subject to periodic inundations from the Tigris and Euphrates rivers. As in Genesis, the flood in the Epic of Gilgamesh occurs when man's behavior angers the gods. The two stories share many of the same characters: a favored man is designated to survive the flood and repopulate the earth. There is a raven and a dove. In both stories a man is commanded to build a boat and take aboard animals of every species. But the main concern of the Epic of Gilgamesh is the inevitability of death and the futility of man's trying to escape it.

---

* B.C.E., standing for Before the Common Era, is an alternative designation to B.C.

The Epic of Gilgamesh has no moral underpinnings or causality. Biblical scholar Nahum M. Sarna speculates that in the Gilgamesh story there "is no more exalted motivation for the flood than that the sleep of the gods was disturbed" by men. The Bible's Flood story, on the other hand, is a morality tale about our human potential for self-destruction and redemption. As Sarna summarizes the lesson of the biblical Flood: "Man cannot undermine the moral basis of society without endangering the very existence of civilization."

NOAH THE ANTIHERO

Though Noah is described as *a righteous man in his generation*, biblical interpreters have never accorded him the honored status of the later patriarchs. Noah obeys God's directions and preserves the animals and his own family for the future. But he never pleads with God on behalf of the wicked of the earth who are condemned to die, as Abraham will later plead for the citizens of Sodom and Gomorrah. *Noah walks with God*, but he lacks the courage and compassion to be a leader of men.

I've always found Noah's relative mediocrity the most compelling detail of this story. He is not a hero or a visionary. He makes no speeches, asks no existential questions—he speaks not at all. He's the world's first drunkard. But when he is called upon to respond to a crisis, this ordinary man becomes an extraordinary force for salvation. What does this tell us about our own potential for having a lifesaving impact on the world around us?

When I think about Noah, the ordinary man-turned-hero, I am often reminded of the war profiteer-turned-rescuer Oscar Schindler. A shady businessman and philandering husband, he transformed his self-absorbed life into a mission of mercy during World War II. In the shadow of the Holocaust, he put his own fortune and life at risk to save a small community of forgotten souls. After the war he reverted to his ne'er-do-well habits. But by opening his heart to a cruel injustice in his midst, he redeemed his own life while saving hundreds of others.

EMERGING FROM A CULTURE OF VIOLENCE

We all find it difficult to acknowledge how deeply ingrained violence is in our culture. How do we account for our concurrent fear of violence and insatiable appetite for it? We will cross the street to avoid a threatening person leaning against a lamppost—and then stop at the corner video store to pick up our nightly ration of slickly packaged violence. Do we really believe that television would be so clogged with tales of violence—real and fictional—if something within us didn't clamor for them so insistently?

Humankind has made many impressive advances in the millennia since the biblical era. We've cured diseases, lowered infant mortality, and more than doubled the average human life span. But the deadliest affliction of humankind—violence—has only grown worse with the passage of time. From our city streets to outer space, the entire planet bristles with armaments. The very survival of the earth hangs in the balance. To quote the Reverend Martin Luther King, Jr.: "It is no longer a choice between violence and nonviolence in this world; it's nonviolence or nonexistence."

The story of the Flood sounds an urgent alarm at the fragility of the earth, and it reminds us of our individual responsibility and potential for becoming an island of rescue in a sea of violence. The child in us would like to believe that the protective powers of a rainbow will shield us from our violent nature. But an adult reading of the Flood commands us to subdue the violence in our midst. The Flood should not be read as a story of natural calamity or the wrath of God. Rather, it tells us that human violence and lawlessness, if allowed to continue unabated, will eventually drown us all. We need only look back to the 1940s to find a time when virtually the whole world was submerged in violence. And in every decade since then, whole countries have been buried beneath uncontrolled spasms of self-destruction.

The Bible takes a very realistic view of humankind's violent nature. At the end of the Flood story, God comes to a sobering realization about the human beings He created in His own image. Even the best of them will always embody a mixture of good and evil impulses. He accepts this inescapable truth while acknowledging that humans remain the only partners He has, His only hope to repair and preserve His creation. The world will survive or be destroyed according to their deeds.

But Genesis resists pessimism by encouraging us to recognize evil in the world and in ourselves and to use our God-given free will to subdue it. After the Flood has subsided, God renews His call for humankind to preserve His creation and offers the rainbow as a symbol of the eternal covenant of preservation between God and humanity.

Any one of us can take a stand against violence and destruction wherever we find it in our daily lives. Whether we choose to defend the environment against despoliation, endangered animals against extinction, or a single child against the brutality of poverty, we each have the power to preserve our own tiny corner of creation. The story of the Flood speaks to each of us with a clear voice today: Make your own life a small ark of hope in a world awash with violence.

Though it narrates the destruction of virtually all human and animal life on earth, the story of the Flood remains a hopeful tale of rebirth and renewal. It's a terrifying and wonderful drama—born of despair, drenched in destruction, and finally redeemed by the promise of a rainbow.

———

THE TOWER OF BABEL:
THE FOLLY OF
SPIRITUAL
MATERIALISM

Pride goeth before destruction and a haughty
spirit before a fall.

—*Proverbs 16:18*

I started my psychotherapy practice twenty-two years ago. In terms of current technology, that was the Stone Age. We had no fax or phone answering machines, no voice mail. Our homes weren't wired for cable and the only people I knew who worked with computers were mathematicians.

Although these amazing innovations have altered the way many of us live and work, the fundamental issues in my patients' personal lives have not changed.

To judge from my younger patients, technology has en-croached on what little leisure time modern life allots them. They are constantly on call via their voice mail and E-mail. They even work in their cars, formerly the last refuge of solitary contemplation and privacy.

Admittedly, advanced technology has its merits. All of us benefit from cheaper long-distance phone rates, and computer technology has given us continual access to information. The creativity of the human mind is truly awe-inspiring. However, this new technology has not and never will nourish our souls or teach us compassion. We can fill our schools wall-to-wall with computers, but unless responsible parents and teachers join together to transmit a love of learning and respect for academic disciplines, the most sophisticated technology will prove useless.

The Tower of Babel is a story about a technological breakthrough three thousand years ago, as important as the microprocessor in our day: the invention of the brick. The Tower of Babel is also the beginning of the Bible's polemic against idolatry—namely humanity's penchant for worshipping its own handiwork. When we believe that through our inventions we will become like God, in total control of our lives, we will have lost touch with our own humanity.

The story of the Flood ends with God promising eternal allegiance to mankind in the form of the rainbow—a celestial bridge between heaven and earth. God appoints Noah as His new Adam and directs him to *"be fruitful and multiply and replenish the earth."* But only a few generations later, humankind loses sight of its God-given mission and concentrates instead on *"[making] a name for ourselves."* The Tower of Babel with *"its top in the sky"* subverts the concept of the rainbow bridge into a literal ladder to heaven made of brick and mortar, reducing man's spiritual connection with God to a material plane.

This tale is told in nine short verses. But it speaks volumes about our tendency to grasp at the surface of our lives rather than cultivating our spiritual center.

All the earth had the same language and the same words. And as men migrated from the east, they came upon a valley in the land of Shinar and settled there.

They said to one another, "Come, let us make bricks and burn them hard." Brick served them as stone, and bitumen served them as mortar. And they said, "Come, let us build a city, and a tower with its top in the sky, to make a name for ourselves; else we shall be scattered all over the world."

The Lord came down to look at the city and tower which man had built, and the Lord said, "If, as one people with one language for all, this is how they have begun to act, then nothing that they may propose to do will be out of their reach. Come, let Us then go down and confound their speech, so that they shall not understand one another's speech."

Thus the Lord scattered them over the face of the whole earth; and they stopped building the city. That is why it was called Babel, because there the Lord confounded the speech of the whole earth; and from there the Lord scattered them over the face of the earth.

A GREAT LEAP FORWARD IN TECHNOLOGY

Despite its brevity—or perhaps because of it—the Tower of Babel is a difficult story to decode. It's much more subtle than the humorous children's story of tower builders who are suddenly thrown into disarray and argument when they begin speaking different languages. The lesson of this story has less to do with language than with the human drive toward self-aggrandizement. A brief look at Babel's historical context helps us understand this enigmatic fable.

The Tower of Babel is the first biblical story that we can connect with an historical location. *Babel* is the biblical name for the ancient city of Babylon, called *Babilim* by the Mesopotamians. Babel is also a play on the Hebrew word *bilbool,* meaning "confusion," which applies equally to confusion of language and Babel's stunted spiritual values. In some respects Babylon was a precursor of our own culture of materialism. The throne of Mesopotamian power and luxury from about 2000 B.C.E. to 500 B.C.E., Babylon was renowned for its hanging gardens and tall towers. It was located on the shores of the Euphrates River, not far from the city of Abraham's origin, Ur. The *valley in the land of Shinar,* where the story is set, refers to Sumeria, a region of Mesopotamia located in present-day Iraq.

When the Greek historian Herodotus visited Babylon in the fifth century B.C.E., he described a famous tower that rose three hundred feet with seven narrowing stories. Babylon had five of these towers—or ziggurats, as they are called. Their sole function was the worship of their local patron god, Marduk. In the cosmology of the day, height was identified with heaven, and the mountains dotting the flat plain of Mesopotamia were considered holy places. Ziggurats were conceived as man-made mountains, symbolically connecting heaven and earth.

They said to one another, "Come, let us make bricks and burn them hard." Brick served them as stone, and bitumen served them as mortar.

The emergence of the towered cities of Mesopotamia would not have been possible in the absence of a simple but profound technological advance: the invention of the brick. Before 3000 B.C.E. man had learned to fashion crude bricks from mud and straw dried in the sun. But this material, similar to the adobe used in the American Southwest, could only support structures of one or two stories. Building multistoried towers like the ziggurats of Babylon required the innovation of oven-baking to produce much harder bricks. With the addition of locally available bitumen as mortar, colossal architectural structures were born.

Every Generation Builds Its Towers

God was clearly distressed by how this self-aggrandizing construction project distorted the values of the people of Babel. According to one rabbinical embellishment on this story, mud and mortar became more precious in Babel than human life. When a brick fell to the ground and broke, the people wept aloud. But when a worker fell from the tower and died, no one paid any attention. Just as Adam and Eve wished to eat forbidden fruit and become "as gods," the men of Babel overreached their human limits when they tried to reach the heavens by building a tower *"with its top in the sky."* God had to intervene to remind them that human endeavors should be rooted in the earth and serve the people who live there. Though the Babylonians viewed the ziggurat as an umbilical cord connecting man to heaven—the so-called *axis mundi,* or "navel of the earth" —this story reminds us that we are linked to God by good deeds, not by brick and mortar.

The builders of the tower of Babel succeeded in "subduing nature" by baking a soft brick into a hard one. But with this simple technological advance came overweening pride in their own creations—the beginning of idolatry. Architecture became an object of worship rather than a tool for serving human needs.

Architecture and technology are inherently neither good nor evil. We can apply our human ingenuity to either constructive or destructive ends, as we choose. We can build shelters for the homeless or monuments to our egos—*"to make a name for ourselves."* Friedrich Nietzsche commented on the peculiar temptations of architecture in his book *Twilight of the Idols:* "In architecture the pride of man, his triumph over gravitation, his will to power, assume a visible form. Architecture is a sort of oratory of power by means of forms."

Every generation builds its own towers. Anyone who has ever watched a child in a sandbox can attest to the deep-seated human drive to build. But why have people in every generation from ancient times till today wanted to build a tower that reaches the sky? I believe that we build as a response to our own mortality and our relative insignificance in the universe. The pyramids, for example, were the Egyptian pharaohs' way of thumbing their noses at death and securing their own immortality. Modern stadiums are still modeled on innovative designs developed by Roman architects over two thousand years ago. But Roman coliseums were the site of the most brutal forms of entertainment—contests to the death between gladiators, or between wild beasts and unarmed humans. In every corner of the globe, and during every stage of human history, vainglorious monarchs have impoverished their people to fund construction of gold-encrusted palaces and tombs.

While the fascination with monumental architecture was common to many ancient cultures, the urge to build towers to the heavens has found its most extravagant expression in the twentieth century. Even the names of these modern-day towers of power—the World Trade Towers, the Empire State Building—bespeak man's desire to dominate his landscape. The greatest concentration of tall towers in Manhattan is downtown, where the headquarters of the giants of the financial world literally scrape the sky.

A variation on Mesopotamian idol worship is explicitly reenacted at every year's Academy Awards ceremonies, when a parade of actors, directors, and producers are given gold statuettes of a man named Oscar. As each winner mounts the dais to accept his statuette, he gleefully holds his Oscar aloft, stroking and kissing it for the benefit of the assembled press. Forever after, the Oscar idol will adorn the winner's office or home, an enduring icon of fame and fortune that visitors may or may not suppress the urge to touch.

Perhaps the most graphic example of the folly of human vanity is the stretch limousine, an absurdly distorted automobile that serves no purpose but to draw attention to itself and the unseen passenger sequestered behind its darkened glass. In fact, limousines are explicitly designed *not* to function as transportation. The more they tie up traffic and the more attention they attract, the better.

LIVING WITH BALANCE IN THE MATERIAL WORLD

All that really distinguishes our society from ancient Babel is the degree to which we have refined materialism. We have developed endless ways to display our socioeconomic status through our lifestyles: in the food we buy, the schools we attend, the recreation we pursue. And no matter how much we elevate our standard of living, there is always a higher stratum to achieve: a bigger house, a more luxurious car, a greater array of expensive toys for our children.

I am not suggesting that the only way to preserve our spiritual identity is to divest ourselves of all material possessions or take vows of poverty. We are entitled to enjoy the fruits of our labor, and the material plane provides many of the blessings of life on earth. The problem arises when we define ourselves and our sense of self-worth by lifeless objects—as our consumer society constantly encourages us to do. And while we may achieve a short-term sense of security by driving the "right" car or wearing this season's fashions, they will not sustain us through inevitable periods of loneliness, sadness, and pain. Only by believing in our transcendent spiritual identity with God do we achieve an enduring sense of self-worth that is immune to the vicissitudes of life.

IDEOLOGY AS IDOLATRY

Even abstract values, if taken to an extreme, can become idols. Whether it's communism or capitalism, liberalism or conservatism, any ideology that becomes an end in itself can quickly devolve into idolatry. Even religion, when it turns God into a commodity, can be idolatrous. One of the things I most admire about Sigmund Freud is how he kept revising his ideas until the end of his life to keep them dynamic and alive. He always remained vigilant against the danger that his theories would become enshrined as ideologies.

Idolatry is the human compulsion to bring spiritual ideals down to a tangible level—to turn human qualities into commodities by compartmentalizing, externalizing, and worshipping them. For instance, when we become overly attached to the idea of our child getting an Ivy League diploma, a high-status education becomes a commodity and the lifelong value of education can easily become obscured.

In his book *You Shall Be as Gods*, Eric Fromm points out that man is always on the verge of regressing to the worship of the tangible products of his own hands. The acknowledgment of God in the Hebrew Bible is fundamentally a negation of idols. Fromm argues that only by accepting God's authority is man guaranteed independence from human authority.

Our story is about to veer away from the idol-worship of Mesopotamia. A single man, inspired by God, will set forth from this idolatrous culture in search of a more meaningful life. God will light the way through the wilderness, but only His human partner can choose to take the first step.

Part Two

Abraham and Sarah: Forging Covenants with God and Family

Hagar and Ishmael in the Wilderness

THE FIRST FAMILY OF GENESIS

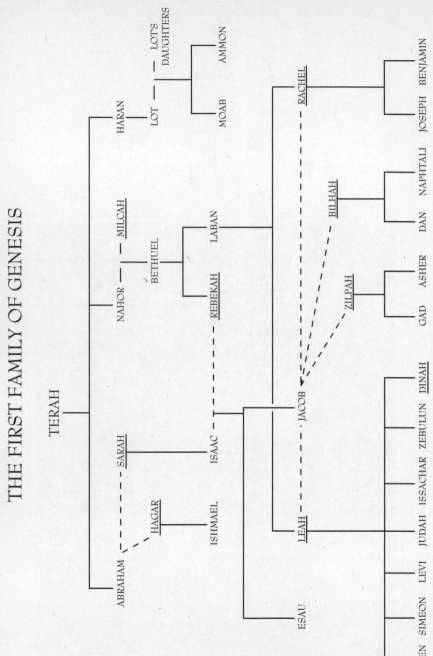

*T*heologian Abraham Joshua Heschel once suggested, "All human history as described in the Bible may be summarized in one phrase: God in search of man." With the next generation of men and women in Genesis we witness a radical innovation in God's search for a working relationship with humankind.

In the twenty generations since Creation, humans have confounded God's best intentions for their development. Instead of preserving the earth, they've despoiled it. Instead of using their free will to subdue their destructive impulses, they've indulged every opportunity to exploit each other for personal gain. Ten generations earlier, God had tried to erase His Creation with the Flood and populate it afresh with the descendants of Noah. But the evil urges within man soon reemerged and plunged the world back into violence and lawlessness.

At this point God hopes to heal the world of its ills by planting a new garden of righteousness—a chosen family—in its midst. Instead of ruling by fiat, as He did earlier, God now actively recruits a human partner to help Him repair His Creation. Rather than commanding humanity to obey Him, God initiates a dialogue with one family that will develop into an interdependent covenant. Under the terms of this covenant, God and the successive generations of this family will work together and become a blessing to the world.

The narrative focus now narrows to a single couple— Abraham and Sarah—who will give birth to a new family in a promised land. The rest of the Book of Genesis will recount the first four generations of this family, who lay the foundation for Judaism and, later on, for Christianity and Islam—as well as providing the ethical underpinnings of Western civilization.

The personalities in the earlier chapters of Genesis are stick figures who illustrate fundamental human qualities. But with Abraham and Sarah, we are introduced to naturalistic personalities—people like ourselves who inhabit recognizable real-life situations where the boundaries of ethical behavior are not so simply drawn. Genesis now enters the gray zones of life where the tough decisions and timeless moral dilemmas lie.

Abraham and Sarah's clan becomes a test case for the development of archetypal family relationships. Embodying all that is best and worst in our natures—our most loving and self-sacrificing selves, as well as our most competitive, rebellious, and hostile aspects—the family unit emerges as the crucible of human character. Genesis is unflinchingly realistic about the tensions inherent in family relations. But it also recognizes that a tightly woven, multigenerational family is the key to the survival and growth of the human race.

As the first generation of a new family line, Abraham and Sarah blaze a trail through the wilderness for their children and grandchildren to follow. Their story is set in an historical period with cultural conventions that may strike us as archaic—particularly its preoccupation with sons and rigid gender roles. But their family endures as a role model for us today because it embodies values that transcend time and place, values we desperately need to reclaim: fidelity between husbands and wives, a shared commitment by parents to raise their children in a spiritual path, a willingness to make sacrifices for future generations.

Despite marital strife and sibling rivalry, this family perseveres. In the course of their journey toward a promised land, the members of this family constantly run up against obstacles beyond their control. But their faith in their covenant with God triumphs over adverse circumstances.

God can't give this family their faith ready-made. But He *can* provide the touchstones we all need to build faith in our special destiny: a geographic and historical destination, rituals to anchor our spiritual identity, and a feeling of being blessed. This family's covenant with God is a constant reminder of the privileges and responsibilities of being made in His image. And it offers those who lose their way a beacon back to His path.

THE MOVEMENT FROM MYTH TOWARD HISTORY

The patriarchs and matriarchs of Genesis, according to some scholars, appeared on the stage of history during the Middle Bronze Age between the twentieth and nineteenth centuries B.C.E. It was a period of economic and political turmoil with masses of people migrating from Mesopotamia toward the Mediterranean— which might explain this family's departure for Canaan. Once they set forth from Mesopotamia, Abraham and Sarah's clans were believed to have been seminomadic tent dwellers who traveled between the major urban centers of their day, with donkeys and beasts of burden as their mode of transport. Generally, they kept to the sparsely populated hill country on the periphery of the Canaanite towns and cities. Over the course of the four generations described in Genesis, the family wanders through Syria and Canaan, eventually settling in Egypt. (See map, page 389.)

But Genesis is a spiritual as well as historical drama. In the first act Adam and Eve set out from the Garden of Eden to make a life for themselves in the real world. The introduction of Abraham and Sarah marks a new beginning in the evolving partnership between God and humanity. A middle-aged couple goes forth into the wilderness armed only with a promise. Their journey of self-discovery, begun four thousand years ago, continues to this day. You and I are the heirs to their ongoing process of becoming, their ever-unfolding tale of character and deed that each of us authors in his own life and time. As we read their story, we join them as they embark on their journey toward an unnamed land and an unknown future.

———

ABRAHAM GOES FORTH:
FOLLOWING A
PERSONAL VISION

Where there is no vision, the people perish.

—Proverbs 29:18

My patients have one trait in common. They enter therapy when their lives become so painful that change is no longer an option—it's imperative. But even in desperate circumstances, change remains an intimidating choice requiring courage. It means abandoning the familiar for the unknown, and therefore carries with it unforeseen risks and consequences. As the French novelist Anatole France wrote, "All changes, even the most longed for, are melancholy. For what we leave behind us is a part of ourselves. We must die to one life before we can enter another."

The tension between the desire for change and the fear of it can be painful. What is it that allows some people to transform their lives while others only imagine personal change?

We can embark on a new beginning only when we have enough confidence in our vision for the future to overcome our anxieties about change. But to do so, we first need to achieve a measure of clarity about the leap we are making.

My patients often find it helpful to walk through the following steps:

First, identifying the source of our pain and dissatisfaction. This isn't as obvious a step as it may sound. It's often easier for us to deny the causes of our unhappiness than to face them head-on. Because once we locate the source of our pain, we're called upon to take action to remedy it.

Second, articulating a vision for the future. A personal vision emerges from an amalgam of our imagination, hopes, and values. But we have to take the first step. We can't sit passively by and wait for a personal vision to appear to us. We have to articulate the changes we want in our lives and decide which choices we are ready to commit to.

Third, building faith in our vision and in ourselves. Since there are always unpredictable consequences to change, we need to have enough confidence in ourselves to embark on the long journey toward realizing our dream. We have to be willing to take on risks, to overcome obstacles, and to view the inevitable setbacks as necessary detours on the winding road of change and growth.

We are the only ones who can bring about change in our lives. No hero from literature, the movies, or the Bible can do it for us. But by witnessing the risks that others have had the courage to take on, we can strengthen our own faith in the rewards of change.

Like so many of us, Abraham sits down at the banquet of life and comes away hungry. But unlike most of us, Abraham demonstrates both the vision and the courage to go forth in search of a more fulfilling life.

Ten generations after the Flood, God once again despaired of the course of human development. People clustered together in cities where violence and injustice reigned supreme, where men prayed to gods of gold and built monuments to their own greed.

But after the Flood God had promised never again to destroy the world. If He now hoped to repair His creation and rescue humans from their own worst instincts, God would have to turn to human beings for help. God looked to the great metropolises of the day for a partner in this new venture. He wanted someone who had lived among men and had proven his mettle, a mature and seasoned householder. Not a Noah, who was merely an obedient follower of God's command, but a leader of men who could see beyond his own life to the generations that would follow.

God surveyed the human settlements from one end of the fertile crescent to the other. To the north and the east were the cities on the Tigris and Euphrates rivers—Babylon and the moon-worshipping centers of Ur and Haran. To the south, across a semiarid plain and desert wilderness, lay the sun-cult Egyptian capitals along the Nile. These were the cradles of civilization where, four thousand years ago, men learned to mint currency, beat weapons out of bronze, and inscribe their histories on clay tablets and papyrus scrolls. They constructed temples, towers, and law courts. And they worshipped gods of every stripe: gods of the sun and moon, of the stars, of the seasons. Gods of fertility, of war, of gold.

In the Sumerian port of Ur, five days downriver from Babel, an itinerant clan of merchants—the family of Terah—caught God's attention.

Now this is the line of Terah: Terah begot Abram, Nahor and Haran; and Haran begot Lot. Haran died in the lifetime of his father Terah, in his native land, Ur of the Chaldeans. Abram and Nahor took to themselves wives, the name of Abram's wife being Sarai* and that of Nahor's wife Milcah.

Now Sarai was barren, she had no child.

Though it had long been one of the cultural capitals of

---

* Abram and Sarai will later be renamed Abraham and Sarah. We will refer to them as Abram and Sarai in the narrative portion of the text until their name change, and as Abraham and Sarah within the commentary.

Mesopotamia, Ur was now a city in decline, under continual attack by invading armies. The harbor was filling up with silt from the delta, and there was no money to dredge new channels. The citizens of Ur looked to their gods to reverse their fortunes, but Terah understood that the port of Ur was doomed, that his family's future lay beyond this place.

Terah took his son Abram, his grandson Lot, and his daughter-in-law Sarai, the wife of his son Abram, and they set out together from Ur of the Chaldeans for the land of Canaan. But when they had come as far as Haran, they settled there.

God watched over the tribe of Terah, and they prospered in the cultic center of Haran where the people prayed for protection from Sin, the god of the moon. *Haran* means "crossroads," and for once among this family, Haran would prove a momentous turning point. Abram had turned his face away from the man-made idols of fear and towers of greed. The greater his family's fortunes grew, the more starved his spirit became. Abram hungered for a new direction, but his life was soon to change course in a way he could not foresee.

And Terah died in Haran.

After his father died, Abram became afraid for the first time in his seventy-five years.* He awoke in the middle of every night now feeling alone in his bed of fear, though his wife Sarai lay beside him, still lovely to him after all their years together.

Sarai's womb was barren of life. And though many had urged him to take second and third wives—as was the custom —Abram had never seriously considered it. His heart was entwined with hers, and she knew the byways of his soul as no other could. Their love had grown with every passing decade, while their hopes for children slipped away. Now that Sarai was beyond the time of childbearing, the two of them drew even closer together.

---

* Ages in Genesis might not corrolate with the way we now count years. We do know that Sarai was beyond childbearing age and that Abram was ten years older than she.

Abram rose from his bed and roamed through the rooms of their house, one of the finest in all Haran. But for him it had come to feel like a mausoleum. Ever since his father had died, Abram sensed his own mortality hovering before him like a darkened vault. It wasn't the end of life that frightened him so much as the hollowness of all that he had acquired: a grand house, servants, livestock—in short, everything a man of means could desire. But what did all these possessions, these things, have to do with him? Abram hungered to leave behind him something larger and more alive than the mere *things* he claimed as his own.

Awake before dawn in his sleeping household, Abram felt terribly alone in his life. Gazing upward from his courtyard at the blank gray sky above, Abram strained to see, to hear something, anything that would lead him out of this pit he had dug for himself in the world. He heard a dog whimpering with hunger in the street . . . a gong sounding dimly from a far-off temple . . . the rumble of cart wheels on cobblestones.

The Lord saw Abram, lost in his life, and He spoke to him.

The Lord said to Abram, "Go forth from your native land and from your father's house to the land that I will show you.

"I will make of you a great people
And I will bless you.
I will make your name great
And you shall be a blessing;
I will bless those who bless you
And curse him that curses you,
And the families of the earth
Shall bless themselves by you."

Abram stood motionless, yearning to hear more. But now there were only the domestic sounds of his household stirring awake in the new day.

Sarai listened patiently as her husband repeated and repeated the promise he had heard, as if to ratify the pledge by giving it voice. *"I will make of you a great people, and I will bless you. The families of the earth shall bless themselves by you."*

That evening Abram was still going on about the voice he had heard. *"Go forth from your native land and from your father's house to a land that I will show you."* He didn't seem the least bit troubled by the vagueness of the promise. Abram spoke boldly about the great future that suddenly lay before them: the wondrous journey they would make, the new horizons that would open on their lives. They would be a blessing to the entire world Listening to her husband, Sarai could sense the hope growing in him. And she felt it taking root in herself like some long-buried, half-forgotten seed stirring in the earth.

He was intensely focused, making lists of things to take, dispatching servants in search of maps of every charted territory from the Euphrates to the Nile. She hadn't seen him this alive with purpose since their courtship. It was contagious.

"Toward where exactly," she asked her husband, "are we to go forth?"

"To a promised place. We will be shown the way."

Abram was pleased to hear that his nephew, Lot, was eager to join him. When Abram's brother died back in Ur, Abram had promised to watch over his only child. In the years since then, Lot had become almost like a son to him, the closest to an heir that he had on this earth. Together they could begin to build a new future.

They wasted no time in making preparations, and within a fortnight they were ready to head off. The day Abram and his people departed, the citizens of Haran scaled the city walls to watch them go. At the city gate Abram paused to take in the wilderness before him. As far as he could see, there was nothing but a blank expanse of sand and stone.

Abram went forth as the Lord had commanded him, and Lot went with him. Abram was seventy-five years old when he left Haran. Abram took his wife Sarai and his brother's son Lot, and all the wealth that they had amassed, and the persons that they had acquired in Haran, and they set out for the land of Canaan.

If he hoped to find a homeland outside of Mesopotamia, Abram had only one direction open to him: south along the trade routes toward Damascus. The journey was difficult for his caravan of men, women, children, and herds. The sun hung so low in the sky they almost had to duck their heads to pass beneath. When the wind blew, the sand became a torment, scratching their eyes and covering the ancient footpaths for days at a time. When they lost their way, they would move to the hilltop trails where the high ground gave broader views— and a wider berth to other travelers.

When they arrived in the land of Canaan, Abram passed through the land as far as the site of Shechem, at the terebinth of Moreh. The Canaanites were then in the land.

Abram had heard tales of the terebinth at Moreh, the sacred oracle of the tree-worshipping Canaanites. Towering more than forty feet above the desert, this tree was visible on the horizon from a day's journey off, and the shade it cast could shelter an entire tribe at midday. Abram camped by a nearby stream to water his herds, and he pitched his own tent beneath the terebinth tree. Opening his tent flaps to the branches above, he lay beside Sarai in the night air and listened to the leaves whisper each to each.

The Lord appeared to Abram and said, "I will give this land to your offspring."

At these wondrous words, Abram looked out from the base of the great tree. The dawn revealed a stark and stony landscape, but it was not without water and grass. As he gazed into the future of the land, Abram envisioned an oasis in the wilderness. And he saw that God had blessed this land with promise. His offspring would grow strong in this place, sink deep roots into its soil and be a blessing—like the great terebinth—to all who dwelt there.

And Abram built an altar to the Lord who had appeared to him.

Throughout the heat of the day he piled stone upon stone, refusing all offers of aid from his men. At sundown, just as Abram had completed the altar, a procession of Canaanite priests and fivescore Canaanite pilgrims approached to consult the oracular tree. This land, so filled with strangers and their strange ways, could not yet be his home. For now it was enough that God had shown Abram the face of the future. So Abram moved his camp from Moreh.

From there he moved on to the hill country east of Bethel and pitched his tent, with Bethel on the west and Ai on the east. And he built there an altar to the Lord and invoked the Lord by name. Then Abram journeyed by stages to the Negev in the south.

THE POWER OF A BLESSING

In this short chapter of the Bible, the word "blessing" appears five times. God's hope is that by blessing the men and women of this family, they in turn will become a blessing to the earth. But first, they must *feel* blessed.

What does it mean to feel blessed?

In simplest terms, a blessing is the unconditional love that a parent can confer on a child. It is a way for the parent to envelop the child with a sense of safety and care. We need the blessing of our parents' love in order to feel whole, protected, and connected. We need this feeling of being blessed in order to go forth into the world with a sense of purpose and responsibility. If we feel truly blessed with love, our human potential multiplies exponentially. Feeling blessed allows us to love and to lead, to inspire by example or to walk alone when necessary.

When we are endowed with our parents' blessing, we internalize that feeling of being cared for and protected. We can then become receptive to and grateful for the myriad blessings of our life: the joy of being alive, the beauty of nature, the miracle of human creativity in all its manifestations. Only then, when we are fully appreciative of our blessings, can we become a blessing to the world by sharing our bounty with others.

God's blessing of Abraham initiates a tradition of each generation conferring a blessing on the next. God will also bless each generation as an affirmation of the covenant and a sign of His continuous care and protection. God's blessing is not merely a feel-good experience that descends from the heavens. It's a reminder to Abraham's descendants that they are created in His image and obliged to live up to their highest human potential. To be blessed by God carries a solemn responsibility to share that blessing with others. For Abraham and Sarah, becoming a "great people" and a blessing to the world entails a commitment to endow their actions with a significance that transcends their own lifetimes.

THE FIRST FAMILY

While the first eleven chapters of Genesis chart the foundations of human character, the rest of the book portrays the building blocks of an archetypal family. In the course of the next four generations we watch this family forge an identity, embrace a purposeful vision of its future, and, finally, become accountable to each other—and to God—for their progress toward that destination.

God initiates His covenant with this family by reconnecting with an individual—His first direct communication with a human since Noah. God blesses Abraham with the promise of a future, and that promise immediately connects God not just to Abraham, but to his wife and their family to come.

Abraham and Sarah have already built a committed relationship by the time God selects them as the first patriarch and matriarch. Their relationship embodies much that will make this family strong—love, emotional accountability, trust, respect, and fidelity. When they go forth from Haran, Abraham and Sarah are seeking a future not just for themselves but for the offspring they hope to produce. Their willingness to work toward and make sacrifices for a future they will never see makes them ideal leaders of a family of destiny.

By choosing a childless couple, God underscores the importance of the future of their family. Beginning with the double obstacle of Sarah being both barren *and* too old to bear children, the story focuses relentlessly on God's promise to give them a new beginning at building a family and becoming "a great people." The significance of their promised offspring is as a symbol of this family's future and its continuing covenant with God. Without a future, their covenant with God would end in their lifetime. But through a child, Abraham and Sarah will be linked in an endless chain with their ancestors and their progeny. The hoped-for birth of a child will mark a new beginning for Abraham and Sarah, a starting point from which to infuse their line with a renewed sense of purpose.

The Unending Journey Toward a Promised Land

The corollary to the promised child is the promised land. In this chapter of Genesis, and at every subsequent meeting, God will promise Abraham the land of Canaan as a possession for his offspring at some unspecified time in the future. As with the promised child, the promise of land confronts Abraham with a double test of faith. First, this land grant from God is postdated until well after Abraham's death. Abraham has no guarantee that God will make good on His promise. And second, the land promised to his offspring is currently inhabited by a variety of tribes who worship other gods.

On one level, the promised land is a spiritual domain, a realm of the future where Abraham's clan will dwell under God's everlasting protection and blessing. The promised land lies always on the horizon, the destination of a continuous journey. And like all promises, its fulfillment dwells in the future. Yet the promised land in Genesis is a spiritual ideal that is rooted in a specific geographic location, an actual piece of real estate. We all need a home, even if it's only a tent we pitch each night on a different hillside. Even a homeless person living on the street needs a sense of place, of personal boundaries—be it a cardboard box or a square of sidewalk.

It may seem ironic that Abraham, who has turned his back on a material culture, should need something as concrete as a parcel of land. But that's precisely why God gives him this future homeland: in recognition of the human need to build faith from the ground up. In order to realize spiritual goals, we need to live in the world with our feet planted firmly on the ground. The promised land is not a blank canvas empty of human life, because a new community or a new nation isn't built in a vacuum. We have to work within the existing political realities. Though Abraham is a spiritual pioneer, he understands that he must navigate in the real world.

Which is why Abraham and Sarah remain such fitting role models for us today. They were born to a Babylonian culture not unlike our own—one that worships materialism and neglects the life of the spirit. But having exhausted the limits of materialism and rejected it for a more meaningful spiritual life, Abraham and Sarah do not take vows of poverty and asceticism. When they go forth from the towered cities to build a new life for their people, Abraham and Sarah take their worldly goods with them: *Abram took his wife Sarai and his brother's son Lot, and all the wealth that they had amassed, and the persons that they had acquired in Haran, and they set out for the land of Canaan.* Because they are unencumbered by the baggage of materialism, they are free to integrate their spiritual aspirations into a worldly life. Because they have a clear vision of where they are going, they can reclaim the barren desert of Canaan and make it blossom with the promise of the future.

What God gives this first family of Genesis is a vision of the future they can journey toward. When God expelled Adam and Eve from the Garden of Eden, He gave them no direction or destination. Cain became an aimless wanderer in the land of Nod. God told Noah to build an ark and fill it with animals. But once the ark was set adrift on the floodwaters, it had no star to steer by, no port of call to navigate toward. In this chapter of Genesis, God decides to become a less remote, more hands-on presence in the lives of humans. Like a concerned parent who resolves to spend fewer hours at the office and invest more "quality time" at home, God pledges to be an ongoing source of inspiration, reassurance, and guidance to His chosen family.

And most important, He gives this family both a physical and spiritual direction—in short, a sense of purpose. Like any good parent, God understands that it is not enough to love a child. We must also give a child a sense of personal responsibility and purpose. By giving this family a mission in life—to be a great people, a blessing by example to the other families of the world—God helps them forge an identity they can transmit to future generations.

A vision is not the same as a plan. In fact, we often plan our lives obsessively so as to deny that we have no overall vision of why and toward what goals we are working. We plan our careers, our vacations, our retirements. We renovate our houses, change our lifestyles, and switch partners. But how often do we seriously assess where we are going in our lives, what values we want our lives to embody, or what we are willing to sacrifice for those values?

For Abraham, that reassessment comes relatively late in life, after he has secured for himself everything that life in cosmopolitan Mesopotamia has to offer—and found it wanting. Only when he finally allows himself to dream of a world beyond the boundaries of his daily routine—when he heeds the voice that commands him, "Go forth"— does Abraham's life begin anew. Until then he has lived both literally and figuratively "in his father's house." He has not yet made his life his own. It has been said that our life isn't really our own until our parents die. Many scholars have speculated about why the Bible provides so little biographical detail about Abraham's life before he hears God's call in middle age. One reason is that his story, and to some degree his life, does not truly begin until after his father Terah dies. Only then can he hear God's call to *"Go forth from your native land and from your father's house to the land that I will show you."*

ABRAHAM AS AN ADULT RISK-TAKER

Like all the patriarchs of Genesis, Abraham is a seeker. He is also a risk-taker. But it is Abraham's distinctly adult persona that sets him apart from the classical seeker after wisdom. Unlike the mythological heroes of other cultures, Abraham is not a young man setting out to seek his fortune, draw a sword from a stone, rescue a princess, or capture the golden fleece. He is a man in late middle age who has none of the advantages of youth: physical vigor, illusions of invulnerability, naïveté, innocence. What he does have is the maturity to seek a higher goal than romance, adventure, and personal glory. Having already learned the ways of the world, he has the perspective to see beyond his own life and to understand the importance of making sacrifices for future generations. His essential role is not as a son, but as a future father and head of a clan. Abraham has the maturity to conduct an ongoing dialogue with God while continuing to tend to the needs of his family and tribe.

Abraham's advanced age is what makes his leap of faith so impressive. His midlife crisis is a familiar phenomenon, but his response to it is not. Most of us gripe about our lives and fantasize about making a radical change. But how many among us actually heed our soul's call to "go forth"? Most of us conclude we are better off bearing whatever disappointments we may harbor in our lives. By the time we reach middle age we have too much at stake to make bold course corrections. We have our reputations to worry about, assets to protect, bills to pay, children to feed and educate. Rather than take a blind leap into the unknown, we usually settle for buying a new car or taking up a new hobby. Abraham remains an inspirational role model because he demonstrates the power of faith to overcome cynicism, despair, and defeatism at any age.

FAITH IN THE FUTURE

Faith in the future is—in all of our lives—constantly at war with fear of the future. The playwright Tennessee Williams captured our ambivalence about the future when he wrote, "The future is called 'perhaps,' which is the only possible thing to call the future. And the important thing is not to let that scare you." Overcoming the innate human fear of the future is Abraham's greatest achievement. When God tells him to "go forth," He doesn't tell him how or where or for how long. He merely promises that there is a future worth exchanging his present for. Though Abraham's fear never vanishes completely, God remains at his side to help conquer it. Abraham's faith in the future demonstrates that it's never too late in life to make a new beginning, and it is never too early to overcome spiritual inertia and give substance to our personal dreams.

Our ability to conceive of a future beyond our own lifetime, and to plan for that future, is what separates us from other animals and unites us with God. God conceived a plan for the universe and invited humankind to collaborate in its implementation. To the degree that we can conceive of the future as tangible—and act on that vision—we imitate God, in whose image we're created.

If we believe in the future, every choice we make today matters. Whether to plant a tree or pollute a stream, whether to build more schools or more prisons, whether to make peace or make war —none of these choices matters unless we feel responsible to the generations that follow us. But viewed through the lens of the future, the impact of everything we do today is magnified tenfold.

Any new venture—be it a marriage, a family, a business, or a voyage into the unknown—requires faith in the future. In this regard, Abraham is a prototypical immigrant, his journey fueled more by hope for the future than by any tangible assurances. When the Pilgrims journeyed to the New World, they had no concrete image of what awaited them at Plymouth Rock. All they knew was that if they could find a land where they would be free to worship their God, everything else would take care of itself. The Pilgrims were among the first, and perhaps the boldest, to emigrate to these shores. But every region of America was settled by trailblazers. When the pioneers headed west in wagon trains, they were guided by primitive maps and fragmentary anecdotes of what lay beyond the last settlement. But their journey into the wilderness was driven by a deep-seated hunger for a place of their own, a promised land in the New World.

My maternal grandfather, Moses Abrahamson, was a lifelong sojourner in search of a homeland. At age seventeen he fled religious discrimination in Lithuania for the streets of London. For a while the freedom and tolerance of Victorian England was intoxicating. But when he was in his early thirties, the Crown offered free land to anyone willing to homestead in western Canada. He felt that England was too homogeneous a country to ever truly accept a Russian Jewish immigrant, so he moved his family to Winnipeg, Manitoba, where he became a respected and involved member of his community.

In 1917, when my grandfather was fifty-seven years old, England's foreign minister Lord Balfour declared Palestine the future Jewish homeland. My grandfather loved Canada, and Palestine was a place he had visited only in his imagination or while studying the Bible. But my grandfather immediately announced to his family that he was ready to answer the call to rebuild Zion. When he and his wife and three grown daughters boarded the train for New York, where they would catch the first of a series of boats to Haifa, the small Jewish community of Winnipeg came to the station to see them off. *"Moishe, vu gaist du?"* they asked in Yiddish. "Moses, where are you going?" Though his red beard and handlebar mustache were now streaked with gray, he answered in the voice of a young man, *"Ich gai aheim."* "I'm going home."

SAYING "NO" TO THE STATUS QUO

As the first dissident of the Bible, Abraham stands as a symbol of the power of a courageous individual to change the course of history. Abraham said "no" to the polytheistic culture surrounding him and began a tradition of monotheism that shaped Western civilization. Throughout time, individual men and women have demonstrated that simply by saying "no" to ignorance or injustice in their midst they can alter the tide of human events. When Sigmund Freud said "no" to the repressive Victorian culture of his day, humans made a quantum leap in the way they viewed themselves and the world around them. When Gandhi said "no" to colonial subjugation and "yes" to the idea of nonviolent disobedience, the British empire was shaken to its foundations. And when Rosa Parks said, "No, I won't be made to sit in the back of the bus because of the color of my skin," generations of pent-up demand for racial justice was unleashed in this country. If we, like Abraham, have the courage to walk alone and forge a path for others to follow, we each have the potential to become a leader in our own life, family, and community.

On a more personal level, saying "no" to the status quo is the first step toward personal change and growth. Like Abraham, most of us don't embrace change in our lives until our current situation becomes untenable. Until our lives become unbearably frustrating or meaningless—until our loudest inner voice shouts "No" to the pain and emptiness in our lives—it is usually less frightening to stumble onward than to alter the direction of our life path.

In my practice, I have used Abraham's experience as my own guide to locating a starting point and a destination in the therapeutic process. I begin with new patients by asking them what they are saying "no" to in their own lives. Where does it hurt? What is it that they find so frustrating, so painful, so unsatisfying? What do they want to change about themselves? Once we locate their current psychological coordinates, I ask them to articulate a vision of where they want to arrive in their inner lives. What is their personal promised land? Where lie their hopes and aspirations for the future? Then I warn them that we are heading off into the wilderness together—and we launch into our voyage of exploration and discovery.

That journey, from our dissatisfied present to a promised destination in the future, defines the process of spiritual growth. It's a journey that begins in adolescence and continues throughout our lives. Whether we choose to be or not, we are all travelers toward the frontier of the future. The Bible can provide a map and a compass for the journey, but we must each go forth to discover our individual destiny.

————

SARAH IN PHARAOH'S COURT: SURVIVING THROUGH SACRIFICE

A *woman of valor, who will find?*

—*Proverbs 31*

𝓘n our highly individualistic society, we are raised on the myth that we can exert total control over our lives, that we have absolute choice about its direction and course. We have turned the concept of choice into an idol and the pursuit of happiness into a religion.

The truth is that we aren't always free to choose. Reality—illness, war, financial reversal, emotional crisis—sometimes dictates what we must do to survive.

How we deal with these circumstances beyond our control is the ultimate test of our character. Our culture is so devoted to the concept of individual choice that we rarely feel obligated to make sacrifices for something larger than ourselves. Today, our feeling of entitlement usually wins out over our sense of obligation.

Many marriages today are breaking up because we are not willing to take on the obligations of a binding covenant—particularly when reality collides with our romantic fantasies. Over the course of a long relationship, bad things inevitably happen. We might not be able to conceive children according to a set plan. One spouse may become seriously ill, requiring personal and professional sacrifices on the part of the other. Couples clash over goals: a wife may prefer to work instead of staying home with the children, or a husband may choose not to be as ambitious or financially productive as his wife might prefer.

The first test of a partnership—whether we're partners in marriage or partners in a business—is our resiliency in the face of disappointments. The final challenge to all of us is to deal with the inevitable setbacks in life without becoming embittered or cynical. Painful as they may be, these obstacles are an inseparable part of any long-term relationship. Prevailing over these disillusioning experiences is vital to our spiritual and psychological growth.

We first meet Abraham as a dissatisfied dreamer and seeker. He abandons a life of material ease to pursue a more spiritual future for himself and his family. But personal goals are not actualized in a moment of revelation. The path toward a promised land is long and circuitous. For Abraham, the harsh realities of survival follow immediately on the heels of God's call to "go forth." The trials of the next several episodes will test not only Abraham's faith in his vision, but his wisdom as a husband, uncle, and tribal leader.

There was a famine in the land, and Abram went down to Egypt to sojourn there, for the famine was severe in the land.

No sooner had Abram and his people arrived in the land of promise, than the earth dried up and became barren. There was no rain, and no grass on which to graze his flocks and herds. His sheep and cattle, raised on the abundant water and grass of Mesopotamia, were ill-prepared for the parched wilderness. One by one they died, and Abram's caravan butchered and ate them as they dropped. But the animals were so emaciated that they gave little nourishment.

Abram bought sheep from other tribes, but they were sickly also. Eventually there was neither grain nor animals to buy throughout the land of Canaan. Abram ceased moving his tents and his people began to die. Had he gone forth from Haran in vain, simply to perish here in the wilderness? He knew that in the Nile delta there was grain, even in times of famine. So he left the land of promise and headed south for Egypt.

Abram was not happy about returning to a land of false gods like the one he left in Haran. In Egypt men worshipped a man, Pharaoh, as if he were a god on earth. This Pharaoh owned all that entered into his realm, and he was known to lust after beautiful women and to possess one of the largest harems in all the world.

However, Egypt had strict rules governing the sanctity of marriage. Even the Pharaoh was forbidden to take another man's wife as his own. But there was no law against Pharaoh killing a man first, and then taking his widow. Abram faced a terrible choice. If he did not go down into Egypt, he and his people would die of hunger. If he went down to Egypt and Pharaoh wanted his wife for his own, Abram would be powerless to protect Sarai. He would be killed and God's promise would remain unfulfilled. His entire clan would vanish in the sands.

The night before his tribe was to cross into Egypt, Abram left the men at his campfire and took Sarai aside. He could put off speaking to her no longer. But now that they were alone together, he couldn't find the words to begin.

Sarai could tell that something weighed heavily on his mind. "Fear not," she said to him. "Soon our cattle will water at the shores of the Nile, and our people will be fed."

Abram shook his head and spoke before he lost his nerve.

He said to Sarai his wife, "I know that you are a

beautiful woman to look upon. If the Egyptians see you and think, 'She is his wife,' they will kill me, and let you live."

Sarai had to smile. She was well past her prime, hardly the kind of woman men killed for. But it moved her that her husband still saw the beauty running deep within.

Abram feared that Pharaoh would want to possess Sarai, the woman he had chosen above all others. And he knew that only with Sarai's help could their people hope for a future in the land of Canaan.

"Please say that you are my sister, that it may go well with me on your account, and my soul shall live because of you."

Sarai sat in silence and considered the paths that lay before them. If Abram was right, and Pharaoh took her for his harem, then there was no hope for her. She would never again see the outside of Pharaoh's palace. But if Abraham was killed, neither of them would ever see God's promise fulfilled. The dream they had left Haran for would evaporate. She must do whatever she could to keep their dream alive. If need be, God would provide Abram another woman with whom to build a future for his people.

She nodded that yes, she would travel into Egypt as his "sister." They leaned forward and touched foreheads, their hands clasped between them.

And it came to pass, that when Abram entered Egypt, the Egyptians saw how beautiful the woman was. Pharaoh's courtiers saw her and praised her to Pharaoh, and she was taken into Pharaoh's palace. And Pharaoh treated Abram well for her sake. He acquired sheep, and oxen, and male asses, and menservants, and maidservants, and female asses, and camels.

It was almost too much for Abram to bear. Not only had he disavowed his wife and surrendered her to another man, but he was enriched on account of her. He lay alone inside his tent, tormented by the thought of Sarai inside Pharaoh's palace.

Once Sarai had been separated from her husband, she abandoned all hope. She had never let herself think beyond the idea of saving Abram. Now she was in the palace, surrounded by beautiful women from around the world who eyed their latest rival with suspicion. Pharaoh had sent word that he wanted her that night, and all day a flock of handmaidens had hurriedly prepared her for her rendezvous with their "immortal" ruler. They filed down the calluses on her feet, repaired her ragged nails, bathed and massaged her body with perfumed oils, painted her face with black and red dyes, and plaited golden beads into her hair.

As she waited for the sun to set and Pharaoh to arrive, Sarai considered her fate. If she submitted to Pharaoh, as countless others before her had, what would it matter? She knew he was no god, but a man with desires like other men. There was nothing he could do to her that was worse than what he had already done in stealing her life and her future. She and Abram would never again lie in their tent beneath the stars, never again dream of raising a family together—never even know when the other ceased to live. Her life was over.

Sarai looked down from the window to the courtyard four stories below. If she hurled herself over the balcony, she could end her torment. But life was not something to cast away like a broken vase, even a life as wretched as hers. She and Abram had chosen the path of life, not of death. Sarai whispered in her heart to the God who had promised her husband so much. She vowed that if God would remember Abram, remember His promise to bless him throughout the days of his life, then she would accept her fate without bitterness.

After the sun set and the night torches had been lit, Pharaoh appeared at her chamber door. On his shoulders hung a magnificent cape stitched from gold thread, and his head was adorned by a golden crown emblazoned with brightly colored jewels. He seemed to Sarai like a dreamlike bird of prey—and she the cornered rabbit. But as he stepped inside the chamber, Pharaoh's body doubled over in pain. His headdress clattered to the floor, and he lurched forward onto his hands and knees, prostrate before her. Sweating and retching violently, he pawed frantically at the floor. Pharaoh looked up at Sarai, his eyes pleading for help.

And the Lord afflicted Pharaoh and his household with great plagues on account of Sarai, Abram's wife.

None of the palace sorcerers could banish the sickness from Pharaoh's palace. One by one, the members of his household—his women and children, his ministers and slaves —were all stricken. Only Sarai remained unafflicted. When Pharaoh heard that in all the palace only Sarai was healthy, he had her summoned to his sickbed. She looked down on his contorted body, his sweat-stained tunic. He was indeed only a man, a man in great pain and full of fear.

Now Sarai was unafraid, because she saw that God had remembered His promise to bless Abram and curse his enemies. "It is the God of my husband, Abram, who has afflicted your house," she said to Pharaoh. "For you have sickened Abram's heart by taking his chosen wife from him. Now He has become my God and my protector also."

And Pharaoh sent for Abram, and said, "What is this that you have done to me? Why did you not tell me that she was your wife? Why did you say, 'She is my sister,' so I took her as my wife?"

Abram replied, "Because I was a man too much in love with life and too much afraid to die. Now return her to me, so that you, too, may live."

Pharaoh had Sarai brought to them. Abram didn't even recognize her behind her painted mask and gold-plaited hair. But when she walked straight to him and took his hand, Abram remembered Sarai's touch.

"Now, here is your wife. Take her, and begone!"

And Pharaoh put men in charge of him, and they sent him away with his wife and all that he possessed.

Pharaoh's men escorted Abram and his caravan to the

border. Though they had entered the land with hungry eyes and withered herds, they left with plenty.

And from Egypt, Abram went up into the Negev, with his wife and all that he possessed, and with Lot. Now Abram was very rich in cattle, in silver, and in gold. And he proceeded by stages from the Negev as far as Bethel. And there Abram called on the name of the Lord.

Abram thanked the Lord for delivering him out of Egypt with his wife and his nephew and all that they owned.

THE HIGH COST OF SURVIVAL

Abraham and Sarah leave Haran to pursue a spiritual path. But the daily routine of life on earth, with all its travails and tough choices, continues. They are very quickly confronted with life-and-death decisions that fly in the face of our romantic concepts of marriage and a spiritual journey. But this seeming paradox underscores one of the Bible's great gifts: it shows us life and people as they really are, not as we wish them to be. A spiritual journey does not exempt us from the ups and downs of daily life, and even the great matriarchs and patriarchs sometimes behave less than virtuously. But Abraham and Sarah eventually emerge as heroes because they are willing to face tough choices head-on, act decisively, and take responsibility for their choices.

Sarah and Abraham are pursuing two often conflicting goals: survival versus building a new life for their family based on moral choices. No sooner are they promised the land of Canaan for their offspring than that same soil dries up and stops yielding life. They must either migrate to a hostile country or starve to death in the wilderness. And when the chastity of their marriage is jeopardized, they have to weigh their romantic sentiments against the survival of their clan. Abraham asks Sarah to masquerade as his sister so that his *soul may survive*. What he's so desperate to preserve is not so much his own life, but their dream of a future for their people. It is only after the two of them wrestle with their painful decision that God weighs in with His emphatic directive: Sarah is no more expendable to their future than Abraham. She is no incidental vessel for the future of the tribe, but God's choice as its indispensable matriarch. *And the Lord afflicted Pharaoh and his household with great plagues on account of Sarai, Abram's wife.*

What we must do to survive—and what we are morally entitled to do—is a profoundly spiritual issue. The Talmud teaches that there are only three absolute limits to self-preservation: regardless of the threat to our lives, we must not murder, commit incest, or blaspheme God. Other religious doctrines dictate other limits. But every religious creed understands that there must be a bottom line of individual accountability for action we take in the interest of survival. After the famous airplane crash in the Andes that drove the survivors to eat their dead companions, the Pope granted them a special dispensation in light of their extreme circumstances. Individuals placed in extreme circumstances—warfare, imprisonment, natural disasters—often face excruciating choices about how far to go to survive. Until we are tested, none of us knows what acts we are capable of performing or enduring. And no one who has never faced a life-and-death choice can stand in judgment of those who have.

The Hebrew Bible takes a relentlessly pragmatic approach to survival: it refuses to glorify martyrdom and exalts the preservation of life as the highest good. According to the Talmud, "the Torah is given to live by, not to die by." Genesis teaches us that no matter how degrading or difficult the means, survival is a vital end in itself. Without a commitment to survival, there can be no future. And no matter how bleak the present, the future remains a realm of hope and possibility.

Whether it is the survival of an individual, a marriage, or a family that is at stake, we must personally take responsibility for saving ourselves—rather than turning to God and praying for deliverance. When faced with famine, we must first find food, then question its cost. If, like Abraham and Sarah, we are forced to choose between the chastity of our marriage and survival, we must choose survival. If we must fight to save ourselves or our family, so be it.

FAITH IN A MARRIAGE

Many biblical commentators have faulted Abraham for presenting Sarah to Pharaoh as his sister. But from what we know of their marriage, it is clearly a joint decision, painfully arrived at in shared recognition of their responsibilities to the rest of the clan. Agonizing as it must have been, their decision does not become a point of contention or recrimination between them. Their marriage emerges as a partnership working in harmony toward a shared goal. When necessary, they act independently of each other to safeguard the family's future. But Sarah is never merely subordinate to Abraham's wishes.

Measured by any standard, ancient or modern, Abraham and Sarah's marriage is a model of devotion. They are not newlyweds, but a mature couple that has not only survived adversity, but grown closer by facing it together. In a polygamous culture, they sustain a distinctly monogamous commitment to each other. Despite the fact that Sarah is barren, Abraham consciously chooses not to take other wives. Sarah is not a disposable asset. And after their sojourn in Egypt, Abraham understands even more clearly that she is absolutely crucial to the future of their clan.

They have not allowed their infertility, no matter how painful, to tear their marriage apart. In some respects, their prolonged childlessness has contributed to their extraordinary closeness. While children are a blessing to a marriage, they can also put a strain on the relationship. Most couples have a romantic courtship in early marriage, which is often subordinated to the demands of child-rearing. Not until the children leave the house does the original romantic couple get a chance to reunite. As a childless couple, Abraham and Sarah have had no digressions from their intense and intimate relationship.

Better than any other characters in Genesis, Sarah and Abraham demonstrate that we marry well when we marry character. Individual fortunes rise and fall, and none of us can predict or control the future. Character is the only predictor of how someone will react to circumstances. If we know a person's character when we marry, we know what we can expect from our partner in later life.

When they go forth together from Haran, Sarah and Abraham don't know what obstacles they might find along their path. But they know what to expect from each other—which is all the assurance they need.

If a husband and wife share a vision of their family's future—as Abraham and Sarah do—they can endure sacrifices without becoming embittered. In any marriage, clear and shared goals are the best defense against the myriad forces of circumstance that conspire to drive couples apart.

———

LOT DEPARTS THE CLAN: LETTING GO OF CHILDREN

To everything there is a season,
And a time for every purpose under the heaven.
A time to seek and a time to lose,
A time to weep and a time to laugh.

—*Ecclesiastes 3:8*

I grew up as a highly protected, much loved only child. My parents and I lived in a cozy apartment in Haifa, and I was extremely close to both of them—especially my mother, who was also my best friend. I was always aware of how much she enjoyed my company. She laughed at my jokes and listened intently to all the gossip about my friends. We would spend hours together sitting on our balcony, drinking tea and talking incessantly. We were each other's daily captive audience from the time I was a child until I was called to service in the Israeli Navy.

Then, at age eighteen, I got married and abruptly left Israel to live with my young American husband in New York.

At the time I was young and self-absorbed, totally engrossed in the adventure that lay ahead of me. Only in retrospect did I realize how hard my parents worked to make my breaking away easy for me. They never cried in front of me, never loaded me down with emotional confessions of how much they loved me and what a hardship my departure for a distant country would be for them. When they wrote me letters, they always kept the focus on my new life and my achievements rather than on how much they missed me.

Until my own children left home, I didn't grasp how brave and wise my parents had been. Only then did I comprehend the pervasive loss, sadness, and even depression that comes with separating from our children. When I was struggling through this phase of my own parental life, my mother shared her philosophy with me: "Naomi, this is the way of the world, the way it will always be. The young go forward into life, while we parents stay behind. Children carry with them whatever we've managed to give. Whatever is portable." I was grateful for this piece of wisdom and deeply regret that I never thanked her for it.

Letting go of our children is a hard challenge to respond to gracefully. We bring up our children to be independent of us. But when the time comes for them to walk alone in the world, we are filled with anxiety. We are afraid for our children's safety, and we fear for the changes that their departure will bring to our own lives. It's tough enough for parents to see their children as separate people with their own personalities and aspirations. When the process of psychological separation becomes a physical one, it is a sobering reminder to parents of how little control we have over our children's lives. Regardless of how much of our time, love, and hope we have invested in them, we must eventually surrender them to the vicissitudes of the world outside our home, come what may.

Letting go of children is an ongoing, many-staged process. It begins in infancy when they first learn to crawl, and then to walk, away from us. It continues through the gradual separations of childhood and adolescence, each rife with its own anxieties and tensions. Finally, we face the inevitable. If we have done our job as parents and given our children the self-confidence and self-sufficiency to deal with life on their own, they are now ready to leave home.

Learning to let go of children is a universal parental experience. But we must each reenact it ourselves—in our own circumstances, in our own emotional lives. Hopefully, our sense of loss is balanced by the recognition that our children aren't lost to us, but merely departing the nest. This is a desirable and appropriate transition in our continually evolving relationship with our children. If our children are eager and equipped to embark on life on their own, we've succeeded in our most important task as parents.

Abraham has grown to love his nephew Lot as if he were his own son. In light of Sarah's advanced age, Abraham probably looks to Lot as his heir. But when their clan prospers and their paths begin to diverge, Abraham must weigh his family's hopes against his sentimental attachment to his dead brother's son. With characteristic wisdom and tact, Abraham accepts the inevitable separation and bids Lot depart with his blessing.

After their difficult sojourn in Egypt, Abram and Sarai enjoyed a short interval of peace and prosperity.

From Egypt, Abram went up into the Negev, with his wife, and all that he possessed, together with Lot. Now Abram was very rich in cattle, silver and gold.

They settled in Bethel, and their cattle and sheep multiplied, and their people also increased in number. Years passed. But to Abram and Sarai there was yet no child born.

Lot, who went with Abram, also had flocks and herds and tents. And the land could not support them staying together, for their possessions were great, so that they could not live together. And there was quarrelling between the herdsmen of Abram's cattle and those of Lot's cattle.

Abram sought to discover whether Lot's future lay with him or down a different path. So he made a proposal:

Abram said to Lot, "Let there be no strife, I beg you, between me and you, and between my herdsmen and yours, for we are kinsmen. Is not the whole land before you? Let us

separate: if you go the left, then I will go to the right; or if
you depart to the right, then I will go to the left."

And Lot lifted up his eyes, and saw how well watered
was the whole valley of the Jordan all the way to Zoar, like
the garden of the Lord, like the land of Egypt. So Lot chose
for himself the valley of the Jordan, and Lot journeyed eastward.

Thus they parted from each other: Abram lived in the
land of Canaan, and Lot lived in the cities of the plain,
pitching his tent near Sodom. But the men of Sodom were
exceedingly wicked and sinners before the Lord.

It saddened Abram to see Lot go his own way. He worried
for his nephew, living now in the shadow of Sodom. Had Lot
asked to stay, they could have found a way to dwell together in
peace. But as Abram had suspected, Lot saw opportunity in the
cities, where Abram saw only the folly he had left behind in
Haran. Lot saw the profit of commerce in the well-watered
valley, while Abram saw the promise of peace in the rugged
hills around him.

And the Lord said to Abram, after Lot parted from
him, "Lift up now your eyes, and look out from where you
are, to the north and south, to the east and west, for I give
all the land that you see to you and your offspring forever.
And I will make your seed as the dust of the earth, so that if
a man can count the dust of the earth, then your offspring
too can be counted. Arise, walk through the land in its length
and in its breadth; for I will give it to you."

And Abram did as the Lord said. He walked across the
land and through it, and he looked at it with new eyes. Where
there were only stones and earth, he saw trees and grass.
Where there was emptiness, he saw a multitude of life: his
offspring and their herds in a time to come.

But for now, the land would not support his growing clan,

so he told his men to fold their tents and gather their herds. Then Abram moved his tent, and came to dwell by the terebinths of Mamre, which are in Hebron. And he built an altar there to the Lord.

THE ART OF FAMILY PEACE-KEEPING

Once Abraham's family has escaped from Egypt, it faces dissension within its ranks. As a wise family leader, Abraham realizes that he must confront these internal problems head-on. Denial will only bring a harsher reckoning down the road.

As much as Abraham might hope for family unity and a future heir in his nephew Lot, he cannot shut his eyes to the conflict between their values. He understands that the friction between their camps runs deeper than mere competition between their herds for grass and water. Lot has a fundamentally different agenda from Abraham's. He seeks prosperity and is drawn to the stimulus of the city. Abraham and Sarah didn't go forth to build an empire, but to establish a tribe based on spiritual values. This irreconcilable difference points toward either strife or separation.

Abraham is sad to see Lot go, but he doesn't allow sentimentality to cloud his judgment. He cares enough about family harmony to take prompt measures toward an amicable parting of the ways and to execute the separation graciously. By generously giving Lot his choice of which land to inhabit, Abraham allows his nephew to feel like the master of his fate, rather than the subject of his uncle's will.

God is gradually becoming an internal force in Abraham's life. On a day-to-day level He remains in the background, leaving Abraham to make the crucial moral choices for himself. But God reemerges as an inspirational presence when Abraham needs Him most. After Lot departs for Sodom with his clan—when Abraham feels most alone in his role as patriarch—God returns to reassure Abraham that he has acted wisely. He not only deeds the land he inhabits to Abraham for future generations, He instructs him to become intimate with his clan's future homeland—to *walk the width and breadth of the land,* to know the land the way he would know the curves and crevices of his wife's body. By comparing Abraham's seed to the countless dust of the earth, God links Abraham's future to the land, both literally and symbolically.

By linking His promise for the future to a promised land, God reveals much about His plan. The land represents our need to have our feet planted firmly on the ground, even as we pursue a spiritual ideal. As early settlers in Israel were fond of saying: "There is only as much heaven overhead as there is land beneath our feet." Regardless of our spiritual aspirations, we never stop living and navigating in the real world. This emphasis on the land—rather than the kingdom of heaven—is a daily reminder to us that our human destiny is to live on earth among people, not as astral beings detached from earthly concerns.

When I was a child in Israel, hiking the countryside was an integral part of my upbringing and education. As soon as I was old enough to walk, I was taken on hikes—up and down and across the land in every direction. At an early age I was invested with a sense of belonging to the land, and I remember feeling extremely protective of it. At age ten, while hiking along the parched and cracked soil of the Negev, I remember spitting in front of my dusty boots to try to water the thirsty ground.

As we grew older, my classmates and I became increasingly attached to the land. We were constantly being reminded of our historical roots. The land of Israel was more than just a tract of real estate. It was a living organism, wholly dependent on our care and protection for sustenance. Our task was to turn its arid plains into green fields. And when the time came for us to defend the land, we would stand ready to answer the call.

One day a messenger arrived at Abraham's camp with a desperate plea from his nephew Lot. A war had broken out between four kings of Mesopotamia and five kings of Canaan. The kings of the north had overrun Sodom, taking Lot and his people captive and seizing all of their possessions. The messenger had barely escaped with his life.

Abram surveyed his tribe. There were three hundred and eighteen men he had trained in the use of arms. Though no man of war, Abram had not entrusted the survival of his tribe to the mercy of his neighbors. He mustered his men at once and told them to prepare to decamp the next day.

That night he lay with Sarai and tried to soothe away her fears. He explained that Lot was his still his nephew. They had no choice but to rescue him and his people. Sarai feared that her husband was too old to fight, but dared not give voice to her thoughts. Instead she simply asked that, in the heat of battle, he remember why they had come so far—and how far they still had to travel.

They were sleepless that night, gripped by their silent fear of war. Abram remembered how the soldiers of Haran had made tributes to their martial gods before heading off to battle. But he would not beseech God's blessing for the bloody task that lay ahead. He only prayed that his nephew be spared and that his own courage not fail him.

Abram pursued Lot's captors across the length of Canaan, finally catching up to them when they were encamped for the night. Since his force was the smaller, Abram set upon his enemies under cover of darkness and surprised them in their beds. Thus Abram won the release of Lot and his people and all of their possessions.

Then Abram delivered his kinsmen safely back to Sodom, along with the other citizens of that city who had been taken captive with their possessions.

The king of Sodom said to Abram, "Give me the persons, and take the goods for yourself."

But Abram said to the king of Sodom, "I swear to the Lord, God Most High, Creator of heaven and earth, I will not take so much as a thread or a sandal strap of what is yours. You shall not say, 'It is I who made Abram rich.'"

So Lot remained in Sodom, and Abram returned to Mamre where Sarai stood watch for him. When they were alone, she surveyed every part of his body to see that he was whole, then looked into his eyes to make sure he was not hurt.

THE LONELY PATH OF LEADERSHIP

Making tough, lonely decisions is the most demanding part of leadership. Like any strong leader, Abraham doesn't shrink from making hard choices and taking responsibility for them. He may anguish over decisions, but he is not conflicted.

Despite the strains of leadership, Abraham doesn't invoke God's help in solving his problems. He goes forth with the faith that God will guide him and guard him, but he understands that he must act on his own if he is to be a leader of men. When famine strikes, he leads his people down into Egypt. When Lot is captured by enemies, he doesn't hesitate to go into battle to rescue him.

Abraham doesn't abandon Lot once he has departed for Sodom, any more than God abandons Abraham when he goes down into Egypt. He does not shrink from becoming his "brother's keeper," even when it means risking his own life. And even amid the heated emotions of war, Abraham is not swayed by the temptations of revenge or greed. To a person less secure in his faith and his priorities, the booty offered by the king of Sodom would have been a difficult temptation to resist. But Abraham possesses enough maturity and clarity regarding his future not to be diverted from the path to his promised land.

By rising to the role of reluctant warrior, Abraham sends an important message to the alien tribes that surround him. Though he will remain a sojourner in their midst, Abraham will not play the victim. His neighbors learn that if they attack his family, they can expect an immediate response. Abraham emerges as an adversary to be respected and an ally who can be trusted. Because he cannot be bought or sold—*"I will not take so much as a thread or a sandal strap of what is yours. You shall not say, 'It is I who made Abram rich' "*—he establishes his clan as a self-reliant force. He is a leader who solicits no followers and invites no quarrels.

Only in retrospect does God's presence throughout Abraham's trials become evident. God delivers Abraham from Egypt and returns him home from war unscathed. In the end, Abraham learns that wherever he goes—whether to a foreign land, to war, or into the unknown realm of the future—God remains by his side, gradually revealing His intended path.

God's earlier promises of a blessing, offspring, and a homeland will become increasingly tangible in the course of Abraham's journey. God promises to bless Abraham, and indeed Abraham prospers during famine and survives warfare intact. As promised, God "curses" Abraham's enemies, be they Pharaoh or marauding kings. And God gradually reveals His plans for the "great people" Abraham will father: Sarah is in no way expendable as the matriarch, and Lot clearly does not make the grade as future leader of the clan. Though Lot left Haran with his uncle and aunt, their paths are destined to diverge. Abraham and Sarah's route leads ever forward toward a blessed future—while Lot is headed down a road to ruin. Even after he is rescued by Abraham, Lot returns to dwell among the men of Sodom, who are *exceedingly wicked and sinners before the Lord.*

Abraham teaches us the practical advantage of internalizing core values. If we have integrity—values that are integrated into our daily lives—we won't flounder when a crisis arises. If we know where we are headed in life, and why, we can circumvent obstacles we encounter along the way without undue anguish. Moral dilemmas arise daily in virtually every arena of our lives. The more we are at peace with our *weltanschauung,* or world view, the more self-evident the answers to our moral quandaries will become.

GOD SEALS HIS COVENANT WITH ABRAHAM: LEARNING TO "FEAR NOT" IN THE FACE OF DOUBT

And I looked, and behold, a stormy wind came out of the north, a great cloud, with a fire flashing up, so that a brightness was round about it; and out of the midst thereof, as the color of electrum, out of the midst of the fire. . . . And when I saw it, I fell upon my face and I heard a voice of one that spoke.

—*Ezekiel 1:4–5*

The upcoming episode is one of the most enigmatic in Genesis. People have puzzled over its meaning for centuries, and my students have found it a most difficult biblical story to relate to their own lives.

Abraham is the first visionary in the Bible. At the most crucial crossroads in his life, Abraham reaches out to God in a series of visions and dreams. There is a rich tradition of visionary prophets in the Bible. These men and women are not merely empty vessels for God's message. Each prophet's vision is narrated through a passionate personal idiom. The dream described in this episode is no different. It has become known as the "Covenant of the Pieces" because it revolves around an ancient ritual of severing animals in half as a means of sealing a contract. Abraham's dream incorporates a grandiose reenactment of this ritual as a way of sealing his own covenant with God. And the unmistakably sexual imagery that runs through the dream is directly related to Abraham's fervent wish for progeny.

The vision described in this episode follows shortly on his return from war. Abraham is filled with doubts about his mission in the promised land, and he's particularly anxious about the fulfillment of God's promise to give him offspring.

God responds to Abraham's doubts through an explosive dream-vision, complete with fire, smoke, and severed animal parts. Like any mystical encounter with the divine, Abraham's is an overwhelming experience that, by its very nature, defies the power of written description. As we read this story, it's less important to decode the specific imagery of Abraham's dream-vision than to experience it subjectively and impressionistically, as he did.

We all yearn for mystical experiences that transcend the mundane routines of our day-to-day lives. But I fear that our culture may be trivializing mysticism by turning it into a commodity and packaging it in how-to guides—whether in books, audiotapes, or videos. The prophets of the Bible didn't seek visions simply for the sake of having visions. There was always a serious message embedded in their revelations—social justice being the chief concern of the later prophets such as Isaiah, Ezekiel, and Jeremiah. In this episode, God's prophecy forewarns Abraham that his people will have to endure a long period of suffering before reaching the promised land.

In our rushed and crowded lives, transcendent experiences are hard to come by. Unlike our biblical forebears, we don't pitch our tents on vast desert landscapes beneath the star-studded sky with all its power and mystery. Even under the most conducive circumstances, personal epiphanies can't be summoned on demand. Just as in therapy, one can't program the timing of an insight or breakthrough. My work has taught me just how much patience we all need in the slow journey of spiritual growth. It's also shown me what a rich reservoir of personal imagery we each carry within our unconscious mind and in our nightly dreams.

Abram came back from war a changed man. He had never before endured the madness or the cold cruelty of battle. He had never killed, never sensed his own death so close at hand.

He could so easily have died like the many souls who perished at the point of his own sword. And there would have been no one from his own family to inherit his blessing now that his hoped-for heir, Lot, had become a citizen of Sodom. With each passing season he watched over the spring flocks and looked on as other couples conceived and bore new life. Was the Lord testing his faith, or merely mocking him? Had He preserved Abram for his promised future, or simply to endure more torment?

Sarai knew of his turmoil, though he rarely spoke of it to her. Ever since returning from war, he kept more to himself, sharing less of his heart with her. She watched him work the land from dawn to dusk, while the peace of sleep eluded him at night. She had never seen him so exhausted and alone.

Some time later, the word of the Lord came to Abram in a vision, saying, "Fear not, Abram, I am your shield, and your reward will be great."

Abram stirred in his tent. Did he wake or sleep? He had heard the word of the Lord before and knew His voice. Abram had never dared address Him directly, but in the midst of this dark night his soul cried out for comfort.

Abram said, "O Lord God, what can You give me, seeing that I shall die childless, and the one in charge of my house is Eliezer of Damascus? Behold, since You have granted me no offspring, my steward will be my heir."

The word of the Lord came to him in reply, "This one shall not be your heir; none but he who comes forth from your very body shall be your heir."

Abram gazed down at his withered legs, his knees and ankles bony with age. Were there yet the seeds of life in these limbs, as dry and brittle as a tamarisk tree?

God brought him outside, and said, "Look now toward heaven, and count the stars, if you are able to count them. So shall your seed be."

Abram lay on his back on the cool desert floor. Lying there against the earth, he felt the sand begin to flow vivid and bright through his limbs. He opened his eyes to find the black and starry sky spread wide above him. A deep dark field alive with the light of his seed—a shower of stars sprayed across the night sky He was filled with the sight of it—clusters and constellations of his seed They were truly beyond number.

Abram was afraid no more. Peace settled on his soul, and he believed what the Lord had promised him.

And because Abraham put his trust in the Lord, God reckoned it to his merit. Then God said to him, "I am the Lord who brought you out from Ur of the Chaldeans, to give you this land to inherit."

Abram wanted to believe that the land would be his. But his time remaining on earth was brief, and he was yet a sojourner in a land of strangers. So he ventured yet another question.

"Lord God, how shall I know that I shall inherit it?"

And God answered, "Bring Me a three-year-old heifer, a three-year-old she-goat, a three-year-old ram, a turtledove, and a young bird."

And the animals were arrayed before Abram, as if for sacrifice.

And he cut them in two, placing each half opposite the other. But the birds he divided not. Then vultures came down upon the carcasses, but Abram drove them away.

Through the endless day, Abram stood guard over the

severed animals, beating away the vultures till he was weary in every bone.

And as the sun was about to set, a deep sleep fell upon Abram, and a great dark dread descended upon him.

And though he slept, Abram could clearly hear the awesome words of the Lord as He confided to Abram the truth about his future.

And He said to Abram, "Know well that your offspring shall be strangers in a land not theirs, and they shall be enslaved and oppressed four hundred years. But I will execute judgment on the nation they shall serve, and in the end they shall go free with great wealth. And they shall return here in the fourth generation.

"As for you, you shall go to your fathers in peace. You shall be buried at a good old age."

Now Abram tried to rouse himself from his deep sleep, but he was staked like a tent to the spot where he lay between the severed animals. And the dread was yet heavy on his heart.

When the sun set, there appeared in the thick darkness a smoking furnace and a burning torch that passed between those pieces.

The darkness was obliterated by the blazing torch as it passed between the pieces. And Abram's soul was filled with the sound and the smell of the searing flesh. He could feel the heavy heat of the torch firing through his loins, though it burned him not.

And all became still. And Abram came back to himself, lying outside his tent in the cool night air.

And on that day, the Lord made a covenant with Abram, saying, "To your offspring I give this land, from the river of Egypt to the great river, the river Euphrates."

FINDING THE FAITH
TO "FEAR NOT"

During his crisis of faith, Abraham behaves very much in character. He carries his pain alone until it is more than he can bear, then reaches inside for a vision that will sustain him through the midnight of his soul. He has survived his foray into battle, but as every soldier knows, even the victor emerges from war with internal injuries. The peace of mind Abram now seeks cannot be won by bold strokes of daring. Instead, he draws inspiration from his ability to hear and receive the word of God.

We learn from Abraham's experience that none of us is immune to doubts and fears—including leaders who often have no one to turn to for advice or comfort. Genesis teaches us that we don't have to be heroes twenty-four hours a day in order to face life with courage. There are crossroads in each of our life journeys when we lose our way and become frightened for our future. When Abraham most needs reassurance, God calls out to him. "Fear not" becomes the spiritual counterpoint to His initial urging to "Go forth." In succeeding generations, God exhorts each of the patriarchs to "Fear not," and so enables them to prevail over their moments of personal crisis.

The development of faith doesn't happen in an instant. It can only be built over time, by facing and overcoming our fears. We learn to have faith in ourselves by first building trust in our parents through their consistent and reliable love. Whether as children or adults, we all need to be reassured that we are loved, and we need to be shown that love in tangible terms. Like a good parent, God assures Abraham that He will be a continuous and stable presence in his life. He endows Abraham with the confidence to question His promises and to ask for tangible proof when he needs it.

"Fear not" does not mean that there won't be obstacles on the way. "We worship God," writes Rabbi Harold Kushner, "not because He will make our path smooth, but because He gives us the grace and determination to keep walking even when the path is rocky."

THE CUTTING OF A COVENANT

The universal human need for demonstrable "proof" underlies our attachment to rituals. Marriage ceremonies allow us to declare our vows of fidelity before God and family in the hope that these public wishes for the union will help preserve it. Public officials take oaths of office to seal the covenant of trust with their community. We bury our dead in a ritual manner in order to face the finality of death and bid farewell to the departed.

God gives Abraham ritual "proof" in the form of a dream of conception. This dream enacts the ceremony of consummation that Abraham's soul cries out for—a promise of fertility and an ongoing alliance with God. For a visionary soul like Abraham's, this ritualized dream is as binding as any legal contract.

Biblical scholars and psychoanalysts have had a field day trying to decipher the symbols of this mysterious visionary episode, known as the Covenant of the Pieces. What is the meaning of the various animals, and why are they cut in half? Why are the turtledove and young bird not divided also? Medieval rabbis interpreted the uncut birds as Israel and the three cut animals as Egypt, Greece, and Rome, to whom the children of Israel will become enslaved. Freudian analysts such as Dorothy Zeligs have interpreted the entire incident as Abraham's attempt to work through his Oedipus complex and resolve his conflicted desire to possess the mother, represented by the land.

To me, the Covenant of the Pieces is Abraham's wish-fulfillment dream consummating his relationship with God. His vision is clothed in vivid sexual imagery, which speaks to both Abraham's pent-up paternity drive and his passion for spiritual union with God. To Abraham, the imagery of the *burning torch that passed between those pieces* must have conjured strong associations with the sexual act between a husband and wife. It connotes the same transcendent "knowledge," intimacy, and passion. What's fascinating to me is not simply the presence of sexual imagery in this dream, but the way in which Genesis transposes the human sexual drive into a spiritual dimension.

Abraham is clearly obsessed with discovering his true heir. His closest blood relative, Lot, has fallen prey to the seductions of Sodom. Under Canaanite law, the steward of his house, Eliezer of Damascus, could become Abraham's heir, but only as a course of last resort. At the root of all these anxieties may lie the elderly Abraham's doubts about his fertility, despite the fact that in biblical times barrenness was invariably laid at the feet of the female.

By way of reassuring him of his future paternity, God leads Abraham outside the tent of his earthly concerns and compares Abraham's "seed," or sperm, to the multitude of stars overhead. *"Count the stars, if you are able to count them. So shall your seed be."* This celestial image of fertility, paired with the terrestrial *dust of the earth* to which God has previously made comparison, reassures Abraham that his seed will take root both in heaven and on earth.

We are told that Abraham believes God's promise of offspring, and that God *reckons it to his merit* that he makes this leap of faith. But when God reminds Abraham that He has brought him out of Mesopotamia to give him the land of Canaan, Abraham asks for proof that he will inherit it. God responds in terms that Abraham can understand, sealing their covenant by the severing of animals. The Hebrew word for contract or covenant is *brit*, and in biblical times, contracts were sealed with the cutting of an animal's body. This "cutting" custom survives to this day in the form of ribbon-cutting ceremonies. Thirteen years after this sealing of God's covenant with Abraham, the "cutting of a covenant" will be personalized into the rite of circumcision.

At Abraham's moment of greatest receptivity, God entrusts him with a fleeting glimpse into the future. Instead of sugar-coating His prophecy, God reveals that the journey of Abraham's people will be long and tortuous. *"Know well that your offspring shall be strangers in a land not theirs, and they shall be enslaved and oppressed four hundred years."* By trusting Abraham to hear this terrifying prophecy, God elevates him to a more equal level of partnership.

The climax of this scene is ripe with sexual imagery symbolizing the union of God with His people and is rendered with all the Cinemascope pyrotechnics of a Cecil B. De Mille epic. The sun sets and the landscape is plunged into *thick darkness*. Abraham waits on the darkened plain between the opened pieces of animal flesh—a vivid symbol of female anatomy—as God's phallic torch emerges from a smoking furnace and passes between the exposed pieces of flesh. Abraham survives this trial by fire with his faith restored, ready to receive the "great reward" God has promised him. As the smoke clears, God recites His solemn vow to deed all the land from the Euphrates to the Nile to Abraham's offspring. Finally, He assures Abraham of a long and fruitful life: *"You shall go to your fathers in peace. You shall be buried at a good old age."*

SARAH CHOOSES A SURROGATE MOTHER: THE EMOTIONAL PITFALLS OF SELFLESS ACTS

You must fulfill what has crossed your lips and perform what you have voluntarily vowed, having made the promise with your own mouth.

—Deuteronomy 23:24

We all want to make commitments and promises in good faith. We want to believe ourselves capable of good deeds and selfless acts. And sometimes we are.

But how often do our best intentions seem to turn back on us like a bad dream? Why is it that we frequently start out to fix a problem, only to find we've created a worse one?

When our spouse gets a job offer in another city, and we offer to relocate for the sake of his or her career . . . only to realize, after our spouse has accepted the job, that we can't bear to leave friends and family behind and that the very idea of packing boxes plunges us into anxiety and depression.

When we generously invite an elderly and infirm relative to live with us . . . only to feel emotionally overwhelmed by the situation three weeks later.

When we decide to help a friend out by offering him a job at our company . . . only to discover that the same easygoing quality that so endears him to us makes our friend a disastrous employee.

We like to imagine that we are equal to any commitment we take on. But when we try to fix other people's problems it takes humility and maturity to avoid getting in over our heads. When our altruistic impulses collide with our human limitations, it's tempting to simply withdraw and resolve not to get involved anymore. Where's the wise middle ground?

Genesis teaches us how carefully we need to weigh the consequences of our well-intended acts. Since none of us is a saint, we owe it to ourselves and everyone else involved to be realistic about our limitations. In the following episode, Sarah makes the critical error of underestimating her susceptibility to that most agonizing of human emotions: jealousy.

Sarai, Abram's wife, had borne him no children.
The time for waiting had passed. For ten years now they had dwelt in the promised land, but God's pledge of offspring remained unfulfilled. Sarai's hopes for motherhood dwindled as her body slipped further past the time of childbearing with each passing season. Whenever her gaze settled on an infant with its mother, her heart clenched tight in her chest. And for the first time, she had begun to fear for her and Abram's future. On three separate occasions God had promised them a child— but those promises had borne no fruit.

If God meant for Abram to father a great people, Sarai began to doubt it would be through her womb. Either Abram would finally give up waiting and take another wife, or else, through loyalty to her, he would squander the opportunity that God had offered him to father *a great people*. Better that she, Abram's wife, select the biological mother of their clan. If she designated a maidservant of her household, the law permitted her to claim the offspring as her own.

*Sarai had an Egyptian maidservant whose name was
Hagar. And Sarai said to Abram, "Behold, the Lord has
prevented me from bearing. Consort with my maid. Perhaps I
shall have a son through her."*

And Abram heeded Sarai's request.

Sarai didn't know how to take it when Abram accepted
her offer without hesitation. She studied his face when she first
made her proposal, but he betrayed no emotion. Had he been
waiting and hoping for her to take this step? Or was he simply
trying to keep peace in his tents by not questioning her plan?

Abram wasn't one to avoid thorny problems—except
where their relationship was concerned. He would go to war to
protect his kinsmen or set forth from the ease of his father's
house to forge a new life in the wilderness. But when it came to
his wife's wishes, he avoided a confrontation at any cost. He
feared that any argument might unearth old wounds and
quickly lead to recrimination.

Hagar was young and attractive in the way of all youth.
Her Egyptian features gave her a certain exotic allure, Sarai
thought. It was good that their child would be handsome to
look upon. And ever since Sarai acquired her during their time
in Egypt, Hagar had proved both honest and loyal—good
qualities to pass on to their child.

*So Sarai took Hagar the Egyptian—after Abram had
lived ten years in the land of Canaan—and gave her to her
husband Abram as a concubine. And he went in to Hagar,
and she conceived.*

*And when Hagar saw that she had conceived, her mis-
tress became lowered in her esteem.*

The humiliation was more than Sarai could bear. It wasn't
enough that Sarai had acknowledged her barrenness in front of
all their tribe and delivered her maidservant into the arms of
her husband. Was this her reward for her selfless act—to be
sneered at and condescended to by a servant?

First there were Hagar's gestures of thinly veiled contempt

—neglecting her tasks, claiming she was too tired to wash and cook. Then came the demands for special foods and a larger tent. And just that morning Sarai had overhead her talking to another servant, boasting there would be many more children after this one, that Abram would be sharing her tent for a long time to come.

What a fool she'd been to trust Abram not to get attached to the girl. Men were perfectly pragmatic in the management of herds and the conduct of war. But when it came to sex, they were so easily taken in. She'd seen it happen before with other women's men. Particularly when they were feeling their age and their mortality. Once that slave girl got hold of Abram's heart, she would never relinquish it.

Sarai couldn't stand the sight of her. Every feature of her swollen body proclaimed her intimacy with her husband.

Abram returned from fleecing the spring herd to find Sarai in a tearful heap in their tent. When he stooped to comfort her, she struck at him with the back of her hand. He caught the blow on his shoulder, and then another. She delivered a series of blows to his chest that surprised him with their ferocity. All the while his mind was racing to uncover what unintended hurt he might have caused her.

And Sarai said to Abram, "My wrath be upon you! I have given my maid to your bosom, and when she saw that she had conceived, I became despised in her eyes. The Lord judge between me and you!"

Of course, that was it. He'd done everything he could to avoid this scene. Never going to Hagar's tent until after the fires had burned low and all the camp had retired. Always returning to Sarai's tent before the first light of morning. Naturally, in the privacy of Hagar's tent, soft words had been spoken, intimacies exchanged. Perhaps even promises made. He honestly couldn't remember. But during the day he had avoided her altogether. And when Hagar told him she had conceived, Abram had mentioned it to Sarai only in passing, as if reporting the birth of a spring calf. He had been too elated to take careful notice of Sarai's feelings. After so many childless

years, he'd wanted some time to savor the sensation of fatherhood.

Now he was in a bind. If he took Hagar's side, Sarai would
feel abandoned. And if he disciplined Hagar, she would be
disgraced before the tribe. So he took the path of least resis-
tance.

Abram said to Sarai, "Your maid is in your hands.
Deal with her as you think right."

Then Sarai dealt harshly with her, and Hagar fled from
her.

She hadn't meant to chase Hagar away from their camp.
She only wanted to teach her her place, remind her who was
the wife and who the servant. It was only fitting that Hagar
resume her household chores—as well as some extra tasks Sarai
required. Sarai was well within her rights to make Hagar share
her tent with other servant girls and forbid her to speak to
Abram. She went too far by beating her, and deeply regretted
it. But Hagar had provoked her with her insolence, and Sarai
had been careful only to strike her on the hands and feet, so as
not to harm the child.

The morning she realized Hagar was missing, Sarai hadn't
wanted to arouse the camp unnecessarily. Where could she go,
after all, a pregnant woman in the wilderness? By the time
Abram heard of her flight, Hagar had already disappeared beyond the horizon.

An angel of the Lord found Hagar by a spring of water
in the wilderness, by the fountain on the road to Shur. And
he said, "Hagar, Sarai's maid, where have you come from,
and where are you going?"

And she said, "I flee from the face of my mistress,
Sarai."

And the angel of the Lord said to her, "Return to your
mistress, and submit to her harsh treatment. I will greatly
increase your offspring, and they shall be too many to count.

Behold, you are with child and shall bear a son. You shall call him Ishmael, for the Lord has paid heed to your suffering. And he will be a wild ass of a man, his hand against every man, and every man's hand against him. And he shall dwell alongside all of his kinsmen."

When Hagar returned to camp, Abram was careful to conceal his relief. Sarai gave thanks to the Lord that Hagar had been spared and that the death of Abram's child would not be upon her head. She and Abram never spoke of it again, and Sarai avoided Hagar for the rest of her pregnancy.

Hagar bore Abram a son, and Abram gave the son that Hagar bore him the name Ishmael. And Abram was eighty-six years old when Hagar bore Ishmael to him.

SOLVING PROBLEMS AND CREATING CRISES

Sarah takes an altogether different approach from Abraham's to resolving her anxieties about their future. She believes that God intends Abraham to father a great people, but she has lost hope of being its mother. Rather than wait passively for God to show her the way, Sarah boldly takes hold of her family's destiny. She makes a huge personal sacrifice for her husband's sake, and for the sake of the vision they both embrace. Her only failing is in underestimating the emotional price of that gesture.

Ancient history suggests that Sarah didn't invent the concept of surrogate motherhood. Babylonian laws of the day permitted a wife to adopt children by a surrogate mother who was chosen from her own household. But as both this story and contemporary headlines illustrate, legal provisions in no way diminish the emotional conflicts inherent to such arrangements. Society is still grappling with the moral and legal implications of surrogate motherhood, and every advance in fertility research brings with it new ethical questions about what the boundaries of human reproduction should be.

When Sarah decides to take an active role in resolving her fertility problem, Hagar proves to be the unforeseen wild card in her careful calculations. Sarah makes the mistake of taking Hagar for granted, simply because she's a servant. Whether through denial or insensitivity, Sarah and Abraham view Hagar as a mere vessel for their child—an object rather than a person. Though Hagar behaves tactlessly, she remains a human being created in the image of God and deserving of respect.

As the first matriarch, Sarah embodies many strong leadership qualities. But like the other leaders in Genesis, her human frailties are also apparent. She's clearly seduced by the selflessness of offering her maidservant to her husband, and she fails to take into account the emotional cost of her initiative. When her plan comes to fruition and Hagar conceives, Sarai flies into a jealous rage, which she projects onto Abraham. Her initial selflessness deteriorates into angry recriminations against her husband and cruelty toward Hagar. Though the Bible isn't specific about the "harsh treatment" she subjects Hagar to, we know it was extreme enough to cause her to flee into the wilderness.

Considering how intimate we know them to be, it is notable that Abraham and Sarah find it so difficult to talk about their predicament. Every marriage has threatening issues that couples avoid raising at any cost. In Abraham and Sarah's marriage, the issue of sexual jealousy has become too painful for them to discuss openly. Their marriage has been sustained by loyal devotion, despite the strains of infertility and Sarah's stay in Pharaoh's court. But the introduction of Hagar into their relationship proves too explosive to handle. The same woman who didn't flinch from sacrificing her chastity in Pharaoh's palace—and who initiated offering her maidservant to Abraham—can't handle having another woman flaunt her intimacy with her husband. Luckily for Sarah, there is enough trust in her marriage to allow her to vent her rage at Abraham, no matter how irrational its expression.

I have tremendous compassion for her predicament. Anyone who has ever been in love can relate to her feelings of jealousy. And no one should underestimate how hard it must have been in ancient times for an infertile woman to maintain her self-esteem. But Sarah's dilemma demonstrates how important it is for us to weigh the consequences of personal commitments before we take them on. We often get in over our heads in relationships when we act on our wishful fantasies about ourselves rather than the realities of our emotional limitations.

THE ASYMMETRY OF COMMUNICATION BETWEEN MEN AND WOMEN

In the Garden of Eden, we saw how the generic differences between men and women were expressed through their sexual responses. In this episode, we see what author Deborah Tannen describes as the psychological asymmetries of men and women displayed in the miscommunication between Abraham and Sarah. "When sincere attempts to communicate end in stalemate," Tannen writes, "and a beloved partner seems irrational and obstinate, the different languages that men and women speak can shake the foundations of our lives."

Sarah is jealous of Hagar's fertility and angry at her indiscreet behavior. When she lashes out at Abraham—*"My wrath be upon you! The Lord judge between me and you!"*—he's at a loss as to how to respond. As Tannen explains in *You Just Don't Understand*, women often want "the gift of understanding" and men respond with "the gift of advice." Sarah knows she's being irrational, that she's the person who presented Hagar to Abraham in the first place. She merely wants Abraham to acknowledge her feelings, not resolve them. In *Men Are from Mars, Women Are from Venus*, John Gray tells us men need to remember that women talk about their problems in order "to get close and not necessarily to get solutions." According to Gray, the mistake many men, including Abraham, make is "trying to change a woman's feelings when she is upset by becoming Mr. Fix-It and offering solutions to her problems that invalidate her feelings."

Instead of listening to Sarah and trying to comfort her, Abraham avoids the delicate subject altogether and jumps straight to a quick-fix solution. But as we see, his response—*"Your maid is in your hands. Do with her as you see best"*—avoids rather than confronts the problem. They have a serious crisis on their hands, which affects both of them deeply, but Abraham behaves as if it's her problem to deal with independently. And when she feels she has not been understood by Abraham, Sarah takes her anger out on Hagar.

How can we reconcile the asymmetry of men's and women's emotional needs? The first step is to recognize that we don't get a finely tuned relationship ready-made. But we do possess the tools to harmonize our differences. Perhaps the best advice we can follow is also the simplest: "The first duty of love," according to theologian Paul Tillich, "is to listen."

As if to counterpoint Abraham's emotional clumsiness, God signals His attentiveness to Hagar by sending an angel to retrieve her from the wilderness. The Hebrew word for angels, *mal'akim,* means "messengers," and in the biblical narrative angels often appear as God's messengers on earth. Speaking through His angel, God's message of mercy is clear: even a slave girl is worthy of His care and concern. He gives her child the name Ishmael, meaning "the Lord has paid heed to my suffering," to underscore His eternal watchfulness and love.

THE STRUGGLE OF FAITH OVER CIRCUMSTANCES

Abraham and Sarah's story offers a poignant portrayal of a couple coping with the anguish of infertility. Today, raising children is a costly undertaking. But in Abraham and Sarah's time, when children were an important part of a family's assets, barrenness was considered catastrophic. And since their entire vision of the future depends on producing a child to carry forth their covenant with God, they may appear to have more at stake than most modern couples. But Sarah and Abraham's travails in trying to conceive a child are remarkably contemporary.

In spite of four thousand years of technological advances, conception remains a largely mysterious phenomenon. And while modern medicine has achieved some impressive breakthroughs, modern lifestyles have erected new barriers to conception—higher stress levels at work and home, more premarital sex resulting in more sexually transmitted diseases, women working into their mid-to-late thirties before attempting pregnancy. In our material culture where virtually anything can be acquired with sufficient expenditure of effort or money, childbearing remains an often elusive blessing bestowed by chance rather than by merit. As we see from this story, the options available to infertile couples who want children, such as adoption and surrogate motherhood, have changed relatively little. And the emotional toll of infertility has not changed at all.

We can assume that Abraham and Sarah struggle, as any modern couple would, to keep their intimacy intact despite the awesome pressure exerted by circumstances. We watch them move through a familiar cycle of doubt bordering on despair, periodically renewed hope, emotional denial, and finally, pragmatic action. As with most family crises, their struggle brings out both the best and worst in their natures. Their marriage endures—in the midst of a polygamous society—because they refuse to measure it purely in terms of biological productivity. In the end they are sustained by their companionship and their shared faith.

Their continuing struggle to conceive, against tremendous odds, is emblematic of their faith in their future. They have nothing tangible to lend them encouragement, and certainly no guarantees. But they cling tenaciously to their belief in their special destiny. Whether we interpret the role of God in their struggle literally or symbolically, Abraham and Sarah believe that their best efforts as a loving couple—informed by a vision larger than the sum of their two souls—will eventually see them through.

Chapter Twelve
(Genesis 17)

THE COVENANT
OF CIRCUMCISION:
INTEGRATING RITUAL
INTO OUR LIVES

Train a child in the way he should go;
And when he is old, he will not depart from it.

—*Proverbs 22:6*

Observing rituals, both secular and religious, is an invaluable way to restore a measure of order and predictability to the days and seasons of our lives. When we pause to acknowledge the beginning of spring or the onset of autumn, we remind ourselves that there is a patterned cycle to the world that transcends our personal schedules and calendars. Even the simple ritual of eating familiar foods—fish on Friday or turkey and cranberry sauce on Thanksgiving—is a reassuring and comforting act.

The frenzied pace of modern existence exerts a centrifugal force on our lives, pushing us constantly away from our spiritual center. Observing religious rituals allows us to transcend the parameters of our own lives and surrender to a larger timetable. When we congregate in churches and synagogues for prayer and ritual observance, we return to a still point in our ever-changing lives. We acknowledge the timeless in an overscheduled and hectic world.

Our families are more fragmented than ever before. Society's increased mobility creates huge geographic divides. In our highly individualized society, getting together for traditional holidays is a way of fighting isolation and strengthening bonds of belonging. Holidays force us to reconvene as a family at regular intervals. At weddings and funerals, families and friends join together to celebrate and mourn, to heal and to share, to take note of the important milestones in our lives.

As our culture grows increasingly secular, ever more dominated by mass media, we have to work consciously to endow our rituals with transcendent meaning. It's not surprising that our society's ritual observances—watching the Super Bowl or the Academy Awards ceremony—are so frequently dispiriting affairs. When cultural bonding rituals become passive spectator activities devoid of enduring value, they deflate rather than uplift us. When Labor Day or Memorial Day becomes merely another Sale Day, we lose a precious part of our national identity. When Thanksgiving and New Year's Day revolve around televised football games, we mortgage important seasonal observances to the ephemeral rewards of spectator sports.

Abraham and Sarah are building a new family in an alien culture. In this story God offers them a sacred ritual with which to mark their unique family identity and bind one generation to the next. This ritual will be a signpost on their journey toward a promised land, a reminder of their sacred covenant with God and with each other.

The years passed. Ishmael grew up under the loving instruction of his father and the protective gaze of his mother, Hagar. As God had foreseen, he was endowed with a wild nature, but his father saw the promise of great leadership in him. Sarai never developed maternal feelings for the boy, and Abram didn't have the heart to separate his son from his natural mother. So Ishmael remained with Hagar in her tent, and Sarai dwelt with Abram at the other end of the camp.

It had been thirteen years since God last spoke to Abram and sealed their covenant with His flaming torch. He had no way of knowing that God would return to bestow a final gift.

When Abram was ninety-nine years old, the Lord appeared to him and said, "I am the Almighty God. Walk in My ways and be righteous. I will establish My covenant between Me and you, and will make you exceedingly numerous.

"As for Me, this is My covenant with you: You shall be the father of a multitude of nations. And you shall no longer be called Abram, but your name shall be Abraham, for a father of many nations have I made you.

"I will maintain My covenant between Me and you and your offspring to come as an everlasting covenant throughout the ages, to be a God to you and to your offspring to come. I give the land you sojourn in to you and your offspring to come, all the land of Canaan, for an everlasting possession. I will be their God."

And God said to Abraham, "As for you, you and your offspring to come throughout the ages shall keep My covenant. This is My covenant, which you shall keep: every male child among you shall be circumcised. You shall circumcise the flesh of your foreskin, and that shall be the sign of the covenant between Me and you. And throughout the generations, every male among you shall be circumcised at the age of eight days. Thus shall My covenant be marked in your flesh as an everlasting pact. And the uncircumcised male child whose flesh of his foreskin is not circumcised, that soul shall be cut off from his people; he has broken My covenant."

And God said to Abraham, "As for your wife Sarai: you shall not call her Sarai, but her name shall be Sarah. And I will bless her, and give you a son by her. I shall bless her, and she shall be a mother of nations; rulers of people shall issue from her."

Then Abraham fell upon his face, and laughed, and said in his heart, "Can a child be born to a man who is a hundred years old? And shall Sarah bear a child at ninety?" And Abraham said to God, "Oh that Ishmael might live by Your favor."

And God said, "Sarah your wife shall bear you a son indeed. And you shall name him Isaac. And I will establish My covenant with him for an everlasting covenant, and with his seed after him.

"And as for Ishmael, I have heeded you. I hereby bless him. I will make him fruitful and exceedingly numerous. Twelve princes shall he father, and I will make of him a great nation. But My covenant I will establish with Isaac, whom Sarah shall bear to you at this season next year." And He left off talking with him, and God was gone from Abraham.

Then Abraham took his son Ishmael and all the males of his household, and he circumcised the flesh of their foreskins on that very day, as God had said to him. Abraham was ninety-nine years old when he circumcised the flesh of his foreskin, and Ishmael his son was thirteen years old.

THE BLESSING OF AN EVERLASTING COVENANT

Sarah and Abraham have to wait twenty-five years after they depart from Haran and thirteen years after Ishmael's birth before God reveals the details of His plan for their family. God repeats the promises He has made on several previous occasions. But this time He clearly establishes Sarah as the intended matriarch of the clan, and He describes the way in which His covenant must be affirmed in each generation: through the ritual of circumcision.

First, God commands Abraham: *"Walk in My ways and be righteous."* This simple imperative statement is a capsule summary of God's proposed covenant, a synthesis of its spiritual and moral components. God declares Himself to be a righteous God and invites Abraham to walk with Him as a partner. He is not a capricious deity who must be appeased, but a just God whom Abraham can emulate as a righteous role model.

Next, God promises a partnership that will stretch endlessly into the future: *"I will maintain My covenant between Me and you and your offspring to come as <u>an everlasting covenant throughout the ages,</u> to be a God to you and to your offspring to come."*

God forges an ongoing and binding partnership with Abraham that continues through his descendants to the present day. With this everlasting commitment, God's promise made back in Haran to bless Abraham is finally realized. Abraham has earned the blessing of an everlasting covenant by demonstrating the maturity to look beyond immediate gratification toward long-term goals, and by exhibiting the spiritual depth to embrace a vision whose fulfillment lies well beyond his own life span.

WHAT'S IN A NAME?

God signals the profound identity shift that comes with a covenantal relationship by conferring new names on Abraham and Sarah.

This tradition of taking on new names to reflect an elevation in status has been continued through modern times by popes and kings. Sarah's name change is particularly significant. While other men in the Bible are given new names by God in recognition of their spiritual transformations—Abraham's grandson Jacob will become Israel—Sarah is the only woman accorded this honor. Her change of name reflects her elevated status after God declares that she alone will be the matriarch of this clan, and that God's covenant will be with *her* son, not Hagar's. Despite Abraham's incredulity, God insists that *"Sarah your wife shall bear you a son indeed. . . . And I will establish My covenant with him for an everlasting covenant, and with his seed after him."* God also heeds Abraham's request that He bless Ishmael by granting him his own great nation.

In biblical times—and until very recently—a name reflected the values and historical roots of the family or person who carried it. Ishmael is named "God heeds" because God heeded both Hagar's outcast state and Abraham's wish that God bless his first son. Isaac's name, which means "laughter," might seem an inauspicious title for a future patriarch. But it captures the spiritual significance of his parents' reaction to news of his impending birth—the first time that laughter is mentioned in the Bible. Abraham and Sarah are so incredulous and giddy at God's promise to bestow a child on a ninety-year-old woman that they are both moved to laughter. Isaac's name reminds Abraham and Sarah—and teaches us—that while human faith has limits, God's power to perform wondrous deeds is infinite.

THE RITUAL OF CIRCUMCISION

When it comes time to seal the covenant between God and Abraham's progeny, the ancient tradition of cutting of an animal is transposed to the human rite of circumcision. The *brit milah*, the "covenant of the circumcision," becomes the totem of this family's alliance with God, marked indelibly in the flesh of each of its men: *"You shall circumcise the flesh of your foreskin, and that shall be the sign of the covenant between Me and you. . . . Thus shall My covenant be marked in your flesh as an everlasting pact."* Though this covenant is everlasting, it must be renewed in each generation by the father circumcising his sons in memory of the historical link to his forefathers, and to God.

Circumcision was widely practiced by non-Jews in biblical times, often as part of elaborate fertility rites. Some local religious cults took the ritual of phallic mutilation to grotesque extremes in the worship of their earth mother goddess, whom they believed controlled the fertility of their animals and crops. Certain male devotees of these early agricultural societies of Babylonia and Canaan—which were totally dependent on the unreliable cycle of their crops for survival—would dance and sing themselves into ecstatic frenzies, then castrate themselves as a gesture of appeasement to their earth goddess. Having watered the earth with their blood to ensure a rich harvest for their people, these castrated males spent the rest of their lives dressed in women's clothing, wandering the countryside as eunuch priestesses.

Egyptians and Canaanites practiced circumcision for reasons of health and hygiene, and as a rite of passage for males entering puberty. As is so often the case in Genesis, a local pagan ritual was adapted by the patriarchs into a monotheistic framework.

By moving the date of circumcision from the beginning of adolescence to the eighth day of life, the Bible shifts its emphasis from puberty to birth, from the sexual to the spiritual. Circumcision introduces a spiritual element into the earliest stage of a child's life by acknowledging God's role in his conception and celebrating his birth as more than a merely biological event. By forging a direct link between his son and the Creator, the father marks the starting point of his child's spiritual journey while renewing his own covenant of faith with God.

Many women readers may take issue with the central affirmation of the covenant being so literally tied to male anatomy. Some might see circumcision as a phallocentric ritual in a male-oriented religion. There is no doubt that the family of Genesis favored sons over daughters, as was the case throughout the ancient world. But I would argue that the rite of circumcision is less a glorification of maleness than an attempt to address the myriad insecurities men harbor about their gender and genitals.

The male's preoccupation with his sex organ, known affectionately by many men as "the one-eyed god," is well documented. But it's easy to lose sight of the deep-seated anxieties—ranging from castration fears to performance anxiety—that this phallic obsession engenders. To comprehend the level of men's emotional fixation on their penis, women would have to envision all the emotional baggage attached to their face, breasts, buttocks, and legs piled onto one luggage cart.

One plausible interpretation of circumcision is to see it as a safe way for men to sublimate their castration fears. By willfully circumcising their sons' foreskins, men enact a ritual castration in the hope of warding off the real thing. Anyone who doubts the hold that castration fears have over men need only recall the profusion of nervous jokes that surrounded the obsessive media coverage of the Lorena and John Wayne Bobbitt trials.

I believe that circumcision evolved as a compensation for men's exclusion from the birth experience—essentially womb envy. Women are physically linked to the mystery of conception by their uterus, and to the process of child-rearing by their breasts. Childbirth is the woman's ultimate affirmation of her connection to the Creator. Females gestate and bring forth all human life on the planet. They are linked through their bodies to their mothers and their children in an endless chain of conception and birth. Men have a much more tenuous connection to the birth process, beginning with the unresolvable doubts they may harbor about their paternity. By performing the ritual of circumcision on their sons, men have the opportunity to bridge this gender gap and fuse with past and future generations of fathers and sons.

I would also argue that circumcision directly benefits mothers and children. Women, unlike men, have never been far removed from the consequences of their sexual drives—specifically conception and the responsibilities of child-rearing. Fathers have none of the mothers' tangible ties to their offspring and are much more likely than mothers to neglect or abandon them. As an affirmation of their covenant with God, circumcision heightens men's awareness of the responsibility—both biological and emotional—inherent in sexual relations. For Abraham's clan, circumcision is first and foremost a commitment by the father to raise his son in God's path and to play an ongoing role in his child's upbringing. The covenant men reaffirm with God through circumcision is a *direct corollary* to the covenantal relationship of marriage, particularly the commitment to work together to raise children. For this reason, the rite of circumcision is considered as important an obligation in Judaism as the vows of matrimony. I'm always impressed by the wisdom of the Bible in recognizing how indispensable a stable paternal presence is to a family, as well as the need to reenforce that presence through ritual.

ELEVATING THE SEXUAL TO THE SPIRITUAL

Clearly, the ritual of circumcision also has an explicit sexual dimension. By circumcising his most primal body part as an ongoing mark of his covenant with God, Abraham establishes his sexuality as central to his spiritual identity. Ritual transforms the mundane into the sacred; by circumcising his foreskin, Abraham elevates his sexuality to a spiritual realm. By uniting body and soul, by integrating men's physical and spiritual domains, circumcision combats the male tendency to compartmentalize sex. Circumcision becomes a tangible daily reminder that, endowed with free will, man stands apart from animals who are driven solely by blind instincts to copulate and procreate. Human sexuality is no mere biological reflex, but an intimate interpersonal communication between living souls.

Although the medieval theologian Maimonides viewed circumcision as God's way of reining in male sexuality, it would be a mistake to construe circumcision as in any way a denial of sexual enjoyment. On the contrary, it sanctifies an activity between men and women that is inherently pleasurable and endows it with spiritual significance. If God's defining attribute is to create, humans can best walk in His way by creating new life as God does—not casually or accidentally, but as the expression of a conscious design. The first family of Genesis is characterized by positive and loving sexual relationships between husbands and wives. And the Bible clearly recognizes that a strong sexual bond between spouses not only cements a marriage, it creates a stable foundation for the entire family.

FORGING IDENTITY
THROUGH RITUAL TRADITION

Until now, Abraham's path has marked a departure from the traditions of Mesopotamia. With the rite of circumcision, ritual tradition reasserts itself as a vital anchor for spiritual and historical identity. Circumcision in Genesis is a voluntary and irrevocable act of tribal self-identification. On the level of simple survival, Abraham needs to separate his clan from the tribes that surround him—or else face extinction through assimilation. For a people ardent to forge an identity in a land not their own, circumcision becomes a symbol of the sacred covenant binding parents to children, and children to an ancestral body of belief and tradition. It continues to speak to our persistent human need to belong and to express our belonging in tangible terms. And it reminds us that, as parents, we have the power and responsibility to bestow a lasting identity on our children.

Throughout Jewish history, circumcision has played a crucial role in forging identity, both in public and in private life. By graphically connecting man's religious obligations to his most primal body part, circumcision goes to the core of a male identity. And because that body part is private and hidden from view, it reminds Jews of the deeply personal nature of their covenant with God.

To this day, circumcision remains central to Jewish religious identity. Jews continue to circumcise their sons eight days after birth, and following the tradition of Abraham's name change, Jewish boys are named on the day of their circumcision. Moslems throughout the world circumcise their sons after the age of seven, a nonreligious custom dating back to ancient times. The Christian New Year, falling on the eighth day of Jesus' life, commemorates the naming of Jesus, which coincided with his circumcision. Baptism later replaced circumcision as a sanctifying and naming ritual for Christian newborns.

The path has finally been cleared of all obstacles for Abraham and Sarah to bear a child of their own. Their spiritual evolution, signified by their name change, is mirrored by their physical metamorphosis. Literally turning back the biological clock, Sarah will soon reenter her reproductive cycle, while Abraham has sanctified his reproductive organ through circumcision. Having endured the self-doubt of infertility and the marital strife of seeking an heir through a surrogate mother, they will finally be blessed with their own child.

But the story of Genesis repeatedly illustrates that achieving a primary goal only signals the onset of new challenges. No sooner do Abraham and Sarah emerge from the sorrows of childlessness than they are plunged neck-deep into the travails of parenthood. Though they have waited most of their lives to conceive and bear a child, their ultimate test of faith still lies before them.

ABRAHAM HOSTS
THE STRANGERS:
RECLAIMING THE ART
OF HOSPITALITY

Every man shall give as he is able, according to the
blessing of the Lord thy God which
He hath given me.

—*Deuteronomy 16:17*

Time is an indispensable ingredient of all intimate relationships. Columnist Ellen Goodman notes that in our overscheduled and overcommitted modern lives "the currency
in shortest supply and greatest demand is one called time." Sharing
this precious commodity is the most generous gift we can bestow.

For me, one of the saddest casualties of our time-deprived culture is hospitality. With working hours extending into evenings and
weekends, and with both spouses usually working outside the home,
we simply don't find enough time to make visitors feel wanted and

welcome, to share with them all the comforts of our home and our companionship.

Sharing time and extending hospitality to friends and visitors is a highly therapeutic activity for all of us. It answers a fundamental human need for nurture, communion, and relaxation. In his wonderful memoir, *Growing Up*, Russell Baker points out a hidden social dividend of the Great Depression. With so much unemployment and so little expendable income, everyone had plenty of time to sit around the kitchen table drinking tea and talking. Conversation and storytelling were the poor man's entertainment and the young Baker's endless source of enjoyment and education.

We can't turn back the clock to an era when families sat out on front porches with friends and neighbors in the evening instead of watching television or logging on to computer "chat lines." But we *can* recover the joys of hospitality if we choose to draw lines around our working hours and protect our leisure time as the valuable treasure it is. There is always more work to do and more money to make. But in the constant pursuit of a higher standard of living, we are sacrificing what we most crave and need: the comfort of human companionship, of familiar faces and easy laughter. We Americans are no less social or hospitable than any other people. We're simply less protective of our leisure time.

In the biblical era, when people's work schedule was tied to sunlight and the seasons, people had the time—whether in the heat of the midday or around campfires at night—to develop refined customs of hospitality. Despite the simplicity of desert life and its often primitive rigors, Abraham displays a rich tradition of graciousness and hospitality.

It was the hottest hour of a very hot day. The heat rose in waves off the sand, bending the blazing light so the earth and the sky became one. Though his tent was pitched in the shade of a great terebinth tree, Abraham chose not to venture outside. He was still recovering from his circumcision, and he was most comfortable lying inside his tent or sitting quietly at the entrance, as he was now.

It had taken him two days to circumcise all the men in his camp. Ishmael went first, submitting bravely to the flint knife. The others could hardly object once the boy had gone ahead of them. Abraham cut them quickly and cleanly, then gave them each a compress of crushed herbs to guard against infection. A few days later the camp was still quiet, the men keeping to their tents and the women sauntering out to the well to draw water or gossip about how their husbands were healing. The only noise came from the animal pens, where the unmilked goats bleated plaintively at the sheep standing like stone statues in the heat.

It pleased Abraham to contemplate the son that Sarah would bear. He had told her about the covenant of the circumcision, of course, but not about Isaac. He hadn't found the words to explain what he still couldn't understand himself. Better to wait until he was healed and whole again before speaking to her of the child they would create with the help of God.

The Lord appeared to Abraham by the terebinths of Mamre.

Abraham closed his eyes against the glare of the sun and was pleasantly surprised to feel a light breeze caress his face. A bird's cry—was it a raven?—stirred Abraham from his reverie.

He lifted up his eyes and saw three men standing near him. He hadn't seen them approach, and he couldn't tell from what direction or by what means they had journeyed. The sun was at their backs, but they cast no shadows in the blank sand. He didn't recognize these strangers, yet Abraham knew them to be fellow travelers, sojourners like himself in this arid land. Rising to greet them, Abraham was pleased to notice that the pain had altogether vanished from his loins.

As soon as he saw them, he ran from the door of his tent to meet them. Bowing to the ground, he said, "My lords, if it please you, do not go past your servant. Let a little water be brought. Bathe your feet and rest yourselves under the tree. And let me fetch you a morsel of bread, that it may comfort your hearts. After that you shall pass on, seeing that you have come your servant's way."

And they replied, "Do as you have said."

He led them to the base of the tree and bade them sit among its wide roots. While a servant-girl brought them water to bathe their feet, *Abraham hurried into the tent to Sarah, and said, "Quick, three measures of choice flour—knead it, and make cakes!"*

Then Abraham ran to the herd, fetched a calf tender and good, and gave it to a servant-boy who hastened to prepare it. And he took butter, and milk, and the calf which he had prepared, and set it before them. Abraham did not eat with his guests, but remained standing while they ate, hovering over them and attending to their needs.

One of them said to him, "Where is Sarah your wife?"

"There, in the tent," replied Abraham, wondering how they came to know her new name, since he had yet to announce it to his own tribe.

Then one said, "I will return to you at this season next year, and your wife Sarah shall have a son!"

Sarah was listening inside the tent door, which was behind him. Now Abraham and Sarah were old and well advanced in years. And Sarah had ceased having the periods of women. Therefore Sarah laughed to herself, saying, "Now that I am withered, shall I have enjoyment—with my husband so old also?"

And the Lord spoke to Abraham through the mouth of one of the men. *"Why did Sarah laugh, saying, 'Shall I in truth bear a child, now that I am old?' Is anything too wondrous for the Lord? At the time appointed I will return to you, at this season, and Sarah shall have a son."*

When she heard the word of the Lord, Sarah became frightened and called out from inside the tent, *"I laughed not."*

But the Lord who hears every whisper within the hearts of men and women, replied, *"No, you did indeed laugh."*

And the men rose up from there, and looked down toward Sodom. And Abraham went with them to see them on their way.

THE MUTUAL BENEFITS OF HOSPITALITY

We already know Abraham to be a leader of great vision, wisdom, and courage. But in this scene, he exemplifies another virtue: hospitality. The reception he offers his unexpected visitors comprises a virtual etiquette manual for desert hosts. Despite his weakened condition, Abraham falls over himself in his haste to extend every comfort to the three strangers who have wandered out of the desert. He *runs* to greet them and offer them shade and water, *hurries* to have Sarah make cakes, *runs* to fetch a calf and urges the servant boy *hasten* to prepare it. The consummate host, he humbly offers his guests a *morsel of food to comfort your hearts,* then presents them with a feast. Though Abraham has enough food to feed visitors without going hungry himself, he takes pains to provide his guests with the best of everything in his larder—*choice flour* and *a calf tender and good.* And in the custom of his day, Abraham stands over his guests while they eat, rather than joining them in their meal.

Nothing in the text suggests that Abraham recognizes the three strangers as the angels of the Lord they are later revealed to be. He is simply responding in character to the appearance of three strangers in his camp—which is precisely what makes Abraham's behavior so extraordinary. Abraham reaches out to these men because he recognizes the face of God in *everyone* he meets, because he perceives all humans as created in God's image. He embraces all men as his brothers and happily accepts the responsibility of being his "brother's keeper."

As a stranger in a strange land, Abraham is particularly attuned to the precarious position of outsiders, and this sensitivity no doubt informs his behavior. His concern for the welfare of the three strangers foreshadows the myriad laws and precepts that later evolve among the Israelites concerning the protection of strangers.

This scene illustrates an often-expressed rabbinical sentiment about how we draw closest to God: not by sequestering ourselves on mountaintop retreats or communing with our souls in the splendid isolation of meditation, but by tending to the everyday needs of others, face-to-face, in the most ordinary of settings.

Like any enduring virtue, hospitality in the desert culture is grounded in pragmatism. Among desert nomads, offering a stranger food, water, and shelter constitutes a policy of enlightened self-interest. The desert is a fearsome place to find oneself alone without shelter. The stranger you feed and house today may well be your lifeline tomorrow should you become lost in the dunes with no food or water. If you travel today in the Judean desert, you will often find an earthenware jar of water by the entrance of the caves that dot the landscape. The nomadic bedouins who frequent the region still observe the practice of leaving water for the next sojourner who passes by.

The interdependence of desert wanderers is a compelling metaphor for interdependence in the wider world. Whether in our family or in our community, we all rely on the reciprocal advantages of cooperation. Social security, unemployment compensation, and welfare are all ways we help each other in the expectation that someday we, too, may need a helping hand. Just as the desert nomad has learned the value of a communal jar of water, we have learned that cooperative safety nets are our best defense against the vicissitudes of life. Institutionalized altruism, we've found, is the most effective means of protecting our self-interests.

———

ABRAHAM QUESTIONS GOD: TESTING THE LIMITS OF JUSTICE AND COMPASSION

And justice is turned away backward, and
righteousness standeth afar off; for truth has
stumbled in the broad place, and uprightness
cannot enter.

—Isaiah 59:14

A woman in one of my classes arrived at our weekly meeting with a disturbing anecdote. She had been walking with her eight-year-old daughter when they passed a homeless man camped out on the sidewalk with his mangy dog. A block later her daughter turned to her with great consternation: "Mommy, what will happen to that dog if it has nothing to eat?"

The woman was stricken with doubt and guilt. How had her child become so numb to the plight of homeless people that she saw only the suffering of the dog? Had she communicated her own lack of sensitivity to the suffering of the homeless to her child? What should she be teaching her children about their personal responsibility to help others?

Our class wrestled with these questions for over an hour. Not surprisingly, we came up with very few answers and plenty of new questions. What are our obligations to a person living on the sidewalk? With so much suffering around us, how do we fight our own sense of helplessness and eventual numbness? How can we convert our compassion into effective action?

Asking questions doesn't always produce satisfying answers. But any serious exploration—either intellectual, moral, or spiritual—begins with a question. This process of asking hard questions and pressing for meaningful answers is epitomized by the following dialogue between Abraham and God. For the first time in Genesis, a human being challenges God to explain the moral underpinnings of His acts. Once that process begins, the spiritual horizons of human conscience are never the same. Once we give ourselves permission to question the most basic assumptions about our faith and about the way the world works, the boundaries to our intellectual and spiritual growth are ever-expanding. Abraham's relentless interrogation of God shows us that complacency is not the desired expression of faith—that questioning, doubt, and sometimes anger are our only tools for exploring the limits of justice and compassion.

The best advice that the group could come up with for the troubled mother was this: Give your daughter the security and encouragement to ask tough questions. Of her parents, of her teachers, of her friends, and of herself. The child's eternal "Why?" is the starting point of all learning, all morality, and all justice. The story of Genesis narrates the human evolution from the questioning child —Eve asking, "Why shouldn't I eat of the fruit of the tree of knowledge?"—to the questioning adult: Abraham asking, *Will You sweep away the righteous along with the wicked? Shall not the Judge of all the earth do justly?*

Having announced to Abraham and Sarah the imminent birth of their heir, God finally reveals why He has chosen to elevate Abraham to the level of partner and confidant. The scene that follows is one of the most remarkable dialogues between man and God in the entire Bible. It marks a watershed in their relationship, and Abraham's finest hour. He sets a standard of moral conscience that all subsequent biblical leaders will be measured by.

Now the Lord said, "Shall I hide from Abraham what I am about to do, seeing that Abraham shall surely become a great and populous nation, and all the nations of the earth shall be blessed by him? For I know him to be one who will instruct his children and his household after him to keep the way of the Lord by doing what is just and compassionate, in order that the Lord may bring about for Abraham what He has promised him."

And the Lord said to Abraham, "The outrage of Sodom and Gomorrah is great! Because their sin is so grave, I will go down and see whether they have acted altogether according to the outcry that has come to Me. If not, I want to know."

The men went on from there to Sodom, while Abraham remained standing before the Lord. Abraham was moved that God had confided in him. But he was troubled to think that his God would destroy a whole city for the sins of the majority, that He would not spare a whole city to save a few righteous citizens.

Abraham drew near to God and said, "Will You sweep away the righteous along with the wicked? What if there should be fifty innocent inside the city; will You then destroy the place and not spare it for the sake of the fifty innocent? Far be it from You to do such a thing, to slay the righteous with the wicked, so that the innocent and the guilty fare alike. Far be it from You! Shall not the Judge of all the earth do justly?"

Silence. Had the Lord even heard Abraham's plea?

Then the Lord said, "If I find within the city of Sodom fifty innocent ones, then I will spare the whole place for their sake."

Abraham heard the Lord's response and wondered if he dared argue further. *And he said, "Here I venture to speak to the Lord, I who am but dust and ashes: What if the fifty innocent should lack five? Will You destroy the whole city for want of the five?"*

This time, there was a much shorter pause before *the Lord answered, "If I find there forty-five, I will not destroy it."*

Abraham couldn't resist pressing his case, *and he spoke to Him yet again, saying, "What if forty shall be found there?"*

And He answered, "I will not do it for the sake of the forty."

And he said to Him, "Let not the Lord be angry if I go on: What if thirty be found there?"

And the Lord answered, "I will not do it if I find thirty there."

And he said, "I venture again to speak to my Lord: What if twenty should be found there?"

And He answered, "I will not destroy it for twenty's sake."

And he said, "Let not the Lord be angry if I speak but this last time: Possibly ten shall be found there."

And He answered, "I will not destroy it, for the sake of ten."

When the Lord had finished speaking with Abraham, He departed. Abraham returned to his tent and spoke to Sarah of his wondrous dialogue with the Lord. He worried for his nephew Lot, who dwelt with his family in Sodom, and he hoped that God would heed his plea and spare the innocent souls of that city.

THE ADVENT OF ALTRUISM

Sodom and Gomorrah have become synonymous in the modern mind with evil and corruption. But the focus of this episode in Genesis is less on the nature of evil than on the mitigating influence of compassion and justice on a violent world. By pleading with God to spare the citizens of Sodom, Abraham extends the biblical dictum of "loving the stranger" from his own tent to the world around him. The citizens of Sodom are total strangers to Abraham's way of life. Not only do they belong to a different tribe and worship other gods, but the selfish values of that city embody everything Abraham spurned when he left Haran. Despite their differences, Abraham regards the citizens of Sodom, like *all* people, as created in the image of God, and therefore his kinsmen deserving of justice and compassion. The ultimate brother's keeper, Abraham regards each of their lives as precious and worth defending to the last.

Abraham's defense of the citizens of Sodom is the first pure act of altruism described in the Bible. This is no small addition to Abraham's complement of virtues, and it highlights a uniquely human attribute. Virtually unknown in the animal kingdom, altruism is rare even among humans. But only human beings have the potential to act out of true selflessness, and perhaps nothing more purely epitomizes altruism than the defense of the rights of strangers.

The last time God faced a critical decision about how to cope with human evil, He turned to Noah and commanded him to build an ark. Though Noah was described as *a righteous man in his generation,* he followed God's instructions without question. Noah saved his own family, but he never spoke out on behalf of the rest of humanity swept away in the Flood. Abraham has immediate family living in Sodom, but he never pleads with God on their behalf. Abraham shows himself to be not only righteous, but brave enough and compassionate enough to stick his neck out for his fellow man.

When I was a girl in Haifa, I once witnessed a scene that illustrated to me, on a small scale, why Abraham was more righteous than Noah. My mother and I were shopping at the grocer's when we ran into a neighbor, Mrs. Kempner. The two women got to talking about how difficult it had become to get food for their families. It was 1950, and Israel was still in the grip of strict rationing. Mrs. Kempner boasted to my mother, "To get food for my children, I'd deny myself anything. For months I won't even buy stockings, so I can buy my children eggs at black market prices. The sky's the limit for my children." As we trudged up Mount Carmel with our groceries, my mother told me, "If she were paying black market prices to buy food for the orphan down the street, then I'd be impressed. But taking care of your own children is like taking care of yourself. Where's the virtue in that?"

THE FREEDOM TO QUESTION AUTHORITY

Even more important than Abraham's goodwill toward an alien culture is the way this dialogue illuminates the evolving relationship between God and His new covenantal partner. The first rule of this new, groundbreaking relationship is that man's right to question God is without limits. Not only is Abraham permitted to challenge God's actions, God invites him to do so. For the first time, the reader is privy to God's internal monologue as He decides to elevate Abraham from the status of loyal servant to confidant: *"Shall I hide from Abraham what I am about to do, seeing that Abraham shall surely become a great and populous nation, and all the nations of the earth shall be blessed by him?"* God injects a new level of trust in their relationship, even as He tests Abraham to discover if he will indeed prove a blessing to all the nations of the earth.

Next, God reveals for the first time explicitly why He has chosen Abraham, above all other people, to be His partner now and in the future: *"For I know him to be one who will instruct his children and his household after him to keep the way of the Lord by doing what is just and compassionate."*

God's simple statement *I know him* is infused with meaning. He has an intimate understanding of Abraham, having watched him deal with difficult moral dilemmas over the course of several decades. Abraham and Sarah have earned God's confidence in both their righteousness and their commitment to pass that code on to their children. God bestows a child on them so that the covenant can be carried forward into the future. Justice and compassion are clearly the pedestals on which the covenant rests, and these values define the *way of the Lord,* which the children of this covenant must walk. We can demonstrate fidelity to God's path only by our just and compassionate deeds, not by our words.

In Hebrew, the words "justice" and "compassion" are expressed by a single word, *tsadakah,* which implies that true justice must always be mingled with compassion. Justice without compassion is heartless; compassion without justice has no moral authority.

Abraham's faith may be strong, but it is not blind. He presses God relentlessly to establish whether He will deliver on His expressed code of justice and compassion. Abraham musters all his courage and tact to deliver a challenge to God that reverberates to this day: *"Shall not the Judge of all the earth do justly?"* When God proves responsive to each of Abraham's questions, He validates the power of one man of integrity to be the conscience of the world. We learn from their exchange that one of the most solemn privileges and responsibilities of free choice is to question authority and demand justice, no matter what the personal cost. Adam and Eve could challenge God only by disobeying, the way children resort to disobedience in the face of overpowering parents. But as a morally centered adult who cares about the plight of the world around him, Abraham learns that he can challenge God on His own terms and hold Him accountable to His own high standard of justice.

This dialogue marks a watershed in the evolution of the human spirit. Never again will man be a fearful supplicant before God—or subordinate to a god who hides behind a veil of inaccessibility. Abraham's spiritual leap delivers all humanity from the pagan culture of capricious gods demanding appeasement. Once God is questioned and responds in kind, no earthly authority will ever again wield absolute power over the souls of men.

EXPLORING THE LIMITS OF JUSTICE

In the course of his negotiation with God, Abraham shows off his finely honed rhetorical skills. His line of questioning shifts deftly from courteous to defiant, from humble to demanding. His goal is not so much to win his argument with God as it is to discover for himself the limits of God's moral law. When he asks, *"Will You sweep away the righteous along with the wicked?"* Abraham poses a timeless moral question of how to mete out justice to the guilty without punishing the innocent.

In a world of perfect justice, the urge to punish the wicked is outweighed by the need to protect the innocent. The best argument against the death penalty is the contention that if only one innocent man is accidentally executed out of a hundred guilty murderers, justice has been subverted. Better to spare the hundred than to unjustly destroy the one innocent soul. Likewise, civil libertarians argue that it is better to defend the absolute right of free speech— even of those whose ideas we find repugnant—than to risk limiting the rights of individual citizens to speak out in a free society. And in the conduct of war, always a slippery moral slope, we are constantly forced to consider the cost to the innocent of attacking the guilty. Firebombing Dresden may have broken the morale of the Third Reich and hastened its demise, but only at the cost of a hundred thousand civilians. Should the citizens of Hiroshima and Nagasaki have been swept away with their militarist leaders in order to speed the end of the war? When we impose economic sanctions on countries run by ruthless dictators, can we justify the suffering it inevitably causes the poorest members of the society?

Many of Abraham's questions about the limits of justice and compassion remain unanswerable. But that does not relieve us of the obligation to persist in asking them. We cannot immunize the world against violence, but we must always cry out against it. Prejudice and injustice will always plague society, but that in no way relieves us of our obligation to oppose them.

Abraham is not a passive bystander who simply watches as Sodom burns. He acts to prevent its destruction. His passionate plea for mercy fails to rescue the citizens of Sodom, since, as we will see, God cannot find even ten righteous men in the doomed city. But Abraham has not acted in vain. His display of moral courage reminds all of us that being informed spectators of world events will not suffice. All the sophisticated news gathering in our electronic age is pointless unless it inspires us to respond to scenes of injustice and suffering. When we turn away from these images we forfeit our capacity for active compassion.

SODOM AND GOMORRAH: OVERCOMING SUSPICION OF STRANGERS

When a stranger sojourns with you in your land,
you shall do him no wrong. The stranger who
sojourns with you shall be to you as the native
among you, and you shall love him as yourself, for
you were strangers in the land of Egypt.

—*Leviticus 19:33*

Human history is a never-ending chronicle of people drawing personal and national boundaries separating "them" from "us." Our primal fear of the unknown speaks to our subconscious fear of the "other." The most American genres of film and fiction—Westerns, science fiction, and "slasher" movies—are all built around our collective fear of the stranger. Whether it's a nameless gunslinger arriving in town, an "alien" from outer space, or a crazed chain-saw killer, we are psychologically and culturally obsessed with the perceived threat of the stranger in our midst.

Our deeply ingrained distrust of strangers has actually been traced back to our genetic programming. Primatologists have long observed this same xenophobic tendency in apes. When a strange ape enters the perimeter of some primate clans, the males will almost always band together to chase him away. If he resists, the clan will physically assault him, or even kill him. Humans were once thought to be the only species capable of murder. But a few decades ago, primatologist Jane Goodall was shocked to observe chimpanzees in the wild ambush and kill another ape whose only crime was belonging to a different clan.

We naturally fear strangers because we don't know their history and we perceive them as having no stake in the future of our community. The Book of Leviticus directs us to transcend our instinctual suspiciousness and to protect the helpless in our midst—specifically, to *love the stranger as thyself*. To put the concept of *loving the stranger* to work in our own lives, we have to extend ourselves as human beings. It is precisely because this distrust of strangers is so deeply embedded in our natures—and magnified by our human imagination—that the Bible instructs us to protect them.

The Bible cautions us to remain vigilant against our innate suspicion toward human beings who look or sound different from us. Though we are a nation built on successive waves of immigration, each new group to reach our shores has to deal with our suspicion and ridicule, simply because they have not yet assimilated themselves into the mainstream culture. How quickly we forget that our ancestors were once strangers in a strange land who had to accommodate themselves to a new set of customs and traditions. Society needs laws to protect strangers expressly because they have proven vulnerable to discrimination from biblical times to the present.

Part of the terrible price of urban violence is our growing reluctance to extend even common courtesy to strangers. When strangers knock at our door, our first impulse is to check the lock. Prudent parents are conflicted. They feel obliged to teach their children to be wary of strangers without becoming consumed by fear and distrust. Eventually, everyone on the other side of our locked gate becomes the "other," and we become our own jailors.

The angels whom Abraham had welcomed into his camp now descend into Sodom on a reconnaissance mission for God. They are sent to investigate the nature and degree of wickedness in Sodom and to discover if there are ten righteous souls remaining in the city.

The two angels arrived in Sodom in the evening, as Lot was sitting in the gate of Sodom. When Lot saw them, he rose to greet them and, bowing low with his face to the ground, he said, "Please, my lords, turn aside to your servant's house to spend the night, and bathe your feet. Then you may be on your way early."

But they said, "No, we will spend the night in the square."

Lot knew the evil that stalked the streets of Sodom by night, and he urged the strangers to accept his invitation to lodge. *So they turned his way and entered his house. He prepared a feast for them and baked unleavened bread, and they ate.*

They had not yet lain down, when the townspeople, the men of Sodom, young and old—all the people to the last man— encircled the house. And they called to Lot, "Where are the men who came to you this night? Bring them out to us, that we may 'know' them!"

And Lot went out to them, shutting the door behind him. He saw that his house was encircled with angry faces and hungry eyes. And he sought to appease them, saying, *"I beg you, my brothers, do not be so wicked. Behold, I have two daughters who have not known a man. Let me bring them out to you, and you may do to them as you please. Only to these men do nothing, for they have come under the shadow of my roof."*

But his offer only fanned the flames of their hatred. They cried out as one, *"Step aside!" And they said to one another,*

"This fellow came here as an alien, and already he acts the judge! Now will we deal worse with you than with them."

And they pressed hard upon the person of Lot and moved forward to break down the door.

But the angels stretched out their hands, and pulled Lot back into the house with them, and shut the door. And they struck the men who were at the entrance to the house with dazzling light, so they were unable to find the door.

And the angels said to Lot, "Whom else have you here? Sons-in-law, your sons and daughters, or anyone else you have in the city—bring them out of this place. For we are about to destroy this place, because the outcry against them before the Lord has become so great."

So Lot went out and spoke to his sons-in-law who had married his daughters, and said, "Arise, get out from this place, for the Lord is about to destroy this city." But to his sons-in-law he seemed as one who jests. All through the night, Lot argued with his wife and his sons-in-law about whether they should flee and what they should carry with them.

At dawn the angels urged Lot on, saying, "Arise, take your wife and your two remaining daughters, lest you will be swept away because of the iniquity of the city." But still he delayed, so the angels seized his hand, and the hands of his wife and two daughters—the Lord being merciful to him—and they brought him out and set him outside the city. And one of them said, "Flee for your life! Look not behind you, nor stop anywhere in the plain. Flee to the hills, lest you be swept away."

But Lot said, "I cannot escape to the hills, lest evil over-take me and I die."

As the sun rose upon the earth, the Lord rained down

brimstone and fire upon Sodom and upon Gomorrah from out of heaven. He annihilated those cities and the entire plain, and all the inhabitants of the cities and the vegetation of the soil.

But Lot's wife looked back, and she thereupon turned into a pillar of salt.

Next morning, Abraham hurried to the place where he had stood before the Lord. And he looked down toward Sodom and Gomorrah and toward all the land of the plain, and he saw the smoke of the land rise up like the smoke of a furnace. Thus it was that when God destroyed the cities of the plain and annihilated the cities where Lot dwelt, God was mindful of Abraham and removed Lot from the midst of the upheaval.

THE SINS OF SODOM

Archaeologists have yet to confirm the location of Sodom and Gomorrah, but scriptural references place their probable coordinates to the south of the Dead Sea, where today's city of Sodom now stands. What *is* known, from the study of local geology, is that a major earthquake occurred in this region about four thousand years ago. And the bitumen and natural underground gases in the area could certainly have ignited during a geological upheaval to create the rain of "fire and brimstone" described in the Bible. Greek and Latin historians also corroborate reports of an earthquake or other cataclysm that corresponds roughly to the details of the biblical narrative. But the purpose of the story of Sodom and Gomorrah is not to explain a natural catastrophe, but a human one.

There are many legends surrounding the sins of Sodom, ranging from extreme greed to cruel injustice. By all accounts it was a prosperous city, *watered like the garden of the Lord* (Genesis 13:10). According to the prophet Ezekiel, Sodom had *pride, surfeit of food, and prosperous ease, but did not aid the poor and the needy.* Affluence devoid of social responsibility is clearly condemned as a moral crime, particularly in a culture that exalted hospitality as the highest virtue. The story in Genesis depicts Sodom's extreme hostility toward strangers—expressed graphically in the attempted homosexual gang rape of the two visitors by the mob outside Lot's house. While Sodom has come to be connected linguistically with sodomy, this story is not an indictment of homosexuality, but of rape. And as is the case with most rape, this assault is motivated less by sex than by violence.

TURNING A VIRTUE INTO A VICE

Lot exhibits an instinctual protectiveness toward the strangers, which he probably learned from his uncle, Abraham. But a comparison of how these two men display their hospitality highlights their essential character differences. Like Abraham, who sits in the entrance to his tent, Lot is posted at the gate of the city and immediately intercepts the two angels. He understands only too well how these strangers will fare if they spend the night in the town square, and insists that they lodge the night with him in his house. And, like Abraham, he treats his guests to a feast.

When the citizens of Sodom surround his house and clamor for the strangers so that they *"may 'know' them"* (remember that the Hebrew word for "knowledge" also means "sexual intercourse"), Lot implores the mob to spare his guests who are under his protection, since they have *"come under the shadow of my roof."* He then turns the virtue of hospitality into a vice by offering his two virgin daughters to the mob to *"do to them as you please,"* so long as they don't molest his guests. Like any doctrine taken to an extreme, Lot's blind devotion to the ideal of hospitality becomes an idolatrous evil. At the moment he offers up his daughters to the mob, Lot abdicates his moral authority as a parent and as a human being. Measured against Abraham's acute sense of right and wrong, Lot emerges as a mediocre man, intending good but lacking the moral fiber to convert his good intentions into righteous actions.

This story cautions us that whatever our best intentions may be, our behavior under fire is the final measure of our character. Abraham is a great leader because he behaves consistently whether in the heat of battle, in a debate with God, or in the privacy of his tent.

THE SEDUCTION OF THE MOB MENTALITY

The confrontation outside Lot's house, which we are told includes every man in Sodom, draws a chilling portrait of mob violence. Individual morality and accountability are subsumed by the collective lawlessness and anonymity of a crowd. History has shown repeatedly the dangers of relinquishing our individual code of ethics to the ever-present reservoir of violence that dwells within the untamed mob. In every generation, hatemongers and demagogues have exploited the human propensity for violence when excused from individual accountability. Genesis recognizes just how dark our primal urges can be—and how easily seduced we are by opportunities to vent them with impunity. In Sodom, the lure of mob violence is so great that it sweeps up *the men of Sodom, young and old—all the people to the last man.*

The story of Sodom demonstrates that a society's fate is ultimately determined by its moral and social behavior. Violence begets violence, ultimately consuming itself, as it did during the time of the Flood. The violence of fascism in Europe, appeased for years by its fearful neighbors, eventually engulfed the entire globe in war. In light of the burgeoning violence in our own urban areas, we cannot ignore this somber story. While we often despair of solving the roots of violence in our culture, Abraham's example teaches us that one person's concern and active intervention *can* have an impact, even if it only rescues one man or one family.

While most of us will never become part of an angry mob, we are all subject to peer pressure and the temptation to take advantage of the anonymity of a group. At some point in our lives we are bound to find ourselves in situations where our personal accountability is submerged in a group activity, and we will feel pressure—either internal or external—to act on our worst instincts.

We've all read about how otherwise well-behaved young college men, under the influence of alcohol and group pressure, can lose their moral bearings to the point of participating in a gang rape. The Tailhook scandal showed how the lowered constraints of a group celebration emboldened servicemen to harass and attack women sexually. And the My Lai massacre stands as an extreme example of how the anonymity of a uniform and the suspended morality of warfare allow normally decent individuals to commit a group atrocity.

White-collar crime also flourishes when people feel they are operating behind the protective anonymity of a corporate superstructure. Whether in the recent S&L banking scandals or insider trading violations within major financial firms, many seemingly "upstanding" executives with much more to lose than to gain stepped across established legal boundaries in the belief that "everyone was doing it" and that no one was watching.

LOT'S WIFE:
A MONUMENT TO INERTIA

Lot's wife, who looks back at the destruction of Sodom and is turned into a pillar of salt, is one of the most intriguingly ill-fated characters in the Bible. There is an underlying geological corollary to her "pillar of salt" destiny: the many tower-shaped salt formations still plainly visible near the shores of the Dead Sea. But to discover the underlying meaning of this story, we should compare Lot and his wife to Abraham and Sarah.

When God commands Abraham to "Go forth" from Haran, he and Sarah don't hesitate to depart. They understand that their destiny lies in the future God has promised, not in the past. Lot's family, on the other hand, is a study in denial and inertia. When Lot tells his sons-in-law to flee for their lives, they laugh at him. And when it comes time for Lot himself to depart with his wife and daughters, he finds one reason after another to delay, until the angels literally have to drag him out of the city. Despite all the evidence, he shuts his eyes to the difficult truth. When Lot's wife looks back, instead of "going forth," she becomes a haunting metaphor for the perils of inertia. Her preoccupation with the past literally paralyzes her in the face of danger, freezes her in time, and turns her into the most inert and lifeless of substances—salt.

Denial and delay can be deadly faults, as the fate of so many victims of genocide attests. Jews in Germany had ample warning of Nazism's peril, yet in many cases people couldn't bring themselves to abandon their houses, furniture, and friends. Despite clear evidence to the contrary, many of them couldn't believe that calamity lay just around the corner. The truth was too painful to accept and the cost of rapid departure too steep. Attachment to material possessions, coupled with denial of evil, can create a fatal blind spot.

Fleeing from danger is one of our innate, God-given survival mechanisms. Lot's wife, and the legions of procrastinators who have followed her through history, teach us that we suppress our instinctual flight-response at our peril.

Lot's personal saga does not end on a high note of escape from the rain of fire and brimstone. Genesis offers us a sordid epilogue to his family's fate following his wife's transformation into a pillar of salt.

And Lot went up and settled in the hill country with his two daughters; and he lived in a cave, he and his two daughters. And the older one said to the younger, "Our father is old, and there is not a man on earth to consort with us in the way of the world. Come, let us make our father drink wine, and we will lie with him, that we may maintain life through our father."

And they made their father drink wine that night, and the older went in and lay with her father. And he did not know when she lay down, nor when she arose.

The next day, the older said to the younger, "Behold, I lay last night with my father. Let us make him drink wine

*tonight also, and you go in and lie with him, that we may
maintain life through our father." And they made their father
drink wine that night also, and the younger went and lay
with him; and he did not know when she lay down, nor when
she arose.*

*Thus the two daughters of Lot came to be with child by
their father. The older one bore a son and named him Moab,
meaning "from my father." He is the father of the Moabites
today. And the younger also bore a son, and she called him
Benammi, meaning "son of my people." He is the father of
the Ammonites today.*

LOT AND HIS DAUGHTERS:
THE DARK CAVE WITHIN

The Book of Genesis reveals human character through its narrative, and Lot's true character is scathingly exposed in the final chapter of this story. God rescues Lot from the inferno of Sodom, but in the end, Lot cannot rescue himself from his own demons. Uprooted from his familiar surroundings, bereft of his wife, and fearful of annihilation, he retreats into a dark cave. But no matter how far he flees, he cannot escape his flawed character or the dark desires of his unconscious.

The cave that Lot and his daughters retreat to offers some biblical interpreters an irresistible Freudian symbol of the characters' unconscious desires. In her book, *Psychoanalysis and the Bible*, psychoanalyst Dorothy Zeligs suggests that this story dramatizes Lot and his daughters' unsuccessful struggle to repress their powerful incestuous drives—which Freud labeled as the Electra complex. A strict Freudian would probably interpret Lot's invitation to the mob to *"do to them as you please"* as a sublimation of his own incestuous urge.

I see this story as an illustration of woman's unstoppable drive to procreate, since the daughters express the belief that the rest of the men on earth have been destroyed: *"There is not a man on earth to consort with us in the way of the world. Come, let us make our father drink wine, and we will lie with him, that we may maintain life through our father."* But the Bible makes it clear that satisfying their maternal instincts through an incestuous relationship is unacceptable. Though incest is not explicitly outlawed until the Book of Leviticus, the Moabite and Ammonite tribes who are spawned by the incestuous unions between Lot and his daughters—notorious enemies who will prove a constant thorn in the Israelites' side—serve as an indirect indictment of incest.

Another explanation for the daughters' behavior is as vengeance for their father's betrayal in Sodom. At the moment he offered them up to the mob, Lot abdicated all moral authority as their father and became their tormentor. Once in the cave, the daughters were in control of their powerless father, humiliating and disabling him with wine.

The story of Lot and his daughters is a telling counterpoint to the mob scene in Sodom. It shows us that extreme isolation from society can lower our inhibitions just as readily as an anonymous mob. And when we wish to further release ourselves from personal accountability, we often enlist the inhibition-reducing effects of alcohol or other drugs. When Lot confides to the angels, *"I cannot escape to the hills, lest evil overtake me and I die,"* he may well be alluding to his distrust of the darker urges within him and his inability to rein them in. The bleak ending of this story confirms Lot's worst fears about himself.

Chapter Sixteen

(Genesis 21)

———

HAGAR'S BANISHMENT: HARNESSING MATERNAL INSTINCTS

And her rival vexed her sore, to make her fret,
because the Lord had shut up her womb.

—*First Samuel 1:6*

*D*reaming about the future is a vital part of setting and pursuing life goals. Dreams energize and motivate us. They help us overcome the anxieties and inertia that keep us from setting forth toward distant horizons.

It's in the nature of dreams that they be bound up with fantasy and imagination. Whether we dream of becoming a professional athlete, a corporate CEO, or an award-winning playwright, we rely on the fantasy aspects of our dreams to counteract our fear of failure.

When we do achieve a long-held dream, we are often puzzled

and upset by how deeply our feelings conflict with our expectations of happiness. Why do we feel so different about our dream's fulfillment from the way we imagined we would?

I witness this collision of fantasy and reality in my therapy practice all the time—in people's professional, romantic, and family lives:

- A woman convinces her longtime lover to marry her, only to find the level of romance and passion has not kept pace with her expectations.
- An unhappily married man imagines exhilarating freedom after his divorce, but discovers loneliness and depression instead.
- A young professional gets a fantasy job working in the White House, only to find herself consumed by endless hours of work, tremendous stress, and none of the glamour she had imagined.
- A woman goes through arduous in vitro fertilization to bear a child, only to become racked by guilt because she begins missing her law career after three months of motherhood.

We all seem to anticipate a dream's fulfillment as an end point, when it usually turns out to be a new beginning with a new set of difficult challenges. And yet, if we stop dreaming, we stop moving forward in life. We still need to dream in order go forth into the unknown and often daunting future.

The promised land for Abraham and Sarah is a far-off destination that they know lies beyond their own lifetimes. For them, the dream of a child of their own is the tangible fulfillment of their vision. But when that dream is finally realized, they are caught unprepared for the onslaught of emotions that awaits them.

With Lot's tale concluded, the narrative now returns to Abraham and Sarah, whose promised son is about to make his long-awaited appearance. Though initially a cause for joy, his birth soon precipitates a new crisis in Abraham's camp. The patriarch is compelled to weigh the commands of his conscience against his conflicting loyalties to his two sons and their mothers. God intercedes in this family quarrel, but the resolution He imposes allows Abraham only a short respite before the final face-off with his faith.

The Lord visited Sarah as He had promised, and the Lord did for Sarah as He had spoken. Sarah conceived and bore Abraham a son in his old age, at the set time of which God had spoken. Abraham gave his new-born, whom Sarah had borne him, the name of Isaac. Abraham thanked the Lord for granting him a son with his beloved wife, Sarah, and he vowed to raise him in the ways of the Lord. *And when his son Isaac was eight days old, Abraham circumcised him, as God had commanded him. Now Abraham was a hundred years old when his son Isaac was born to him.*

And Sarah said, "God has brought me laughter, everyone who hears will laugh with me." And she added, "Who would have said to Abraham that Sarah would suckle children! Yet I have borne him a son in his old age."

And the child grew up and was weaned, and Abraham made a great feast on the day that Isaac was weaned. And Sarah saw Ishmael, the son of Hagar the Egyptian, mocking Isaac. It pierced an old wound in Sarah's heart, the pain still fresh from the time when Hagar, heavy with child, mocked her in her barrenness.

Now Sarah beheld Ishmael, a hearty youth of sixteen, standing astride her infant boy. Isaac was barely weaned from her breast, a mere child still tottering on rounded legs. She and Abraham were well advanced in years, and she feared for the future of her son. *So she said to Abraham, "Cast out this slavewoman and her son; for the son of this slave shall not share in the inheritance with my son, Isaac."*

The matter distressed Abraham greatly, for it concerned a son of his. Ishmael was his firstborn, whom he had raised with the care of his own hand to take his father's place at the head of the tribe. How could he now banish Ishmael and his mother to the wilderness, where they would surely perish?

But God said to Abraham, "Do not be distressed over the boy or your slavewoman. In all that Sarah says to you, harken to her voice. For it is through Isaac that your offspring shall be continued. As for the son of the slavewoman, I will make a nation of him too, because he is your seed."

Abraham rose up early the next morning and took some bread and a skin of water, and he gave them to Hagar, placing them upon her shoulder. He neither looked her in the eye nor hugged the boy to his breast, for he was afraid to weep before them. *And he sent her away, along with her child, and she departed and wandered about in the wilderness of Beersheba.*

When the water was spent from the skin, she left the child under one of the bushes and went and sat down at a distance, a bowshot away. For she thought, "Let me not look on as the child dies." And sitting thus afar, she lifted up her voice and wept.

But God heard the cry of the boy, and the angel of God called to Hagar from heaven, and said to her, "What troubles you, Hagar? Fear not, for God has heard the voice of the boy where he is. Arise, lift up the boy, and hold him by the hand, for I will make of him a great people."

Then God opened her eyes, and she saw a well of water. She went and filled the skin with water, and gave the boy a drink.

And God was with the boy, and he grew up and lived in the wilderness of Paran and became a bowman. And his mother got a wife for him from the land of Egypt.

THE TYRANNY OF A MOTHER'S HEART

God's promise is finally fulfilled. Beyond all human hope, Sarah and Abraham have been blessed with a child in their old age. Sarah's initial laughter of incredulity is now transformed into the giddy laughter of joy at her long-postponed motherhood. But the mood of rejoicing with which this episode begins is soon overshadowed by the fiercely protective aspect of Sarah's maternal nature.

In the midst of celebrating Isaac's weaning—an important rite of passage marking his first step toward manhood—Sarah becomes consumed once again by her resentment of Hagar. Ishmael is a living reminder to Sarah of her humiliation at the hands of another woman. Now that she has a son of her own, Sarah is emboldened to pursue a dual goal: to secure Isaac's future ascendancy in the tribe while settling an old score with her rival.

Sarah's motives are understandable from an emotional point of view. She has borne the stigma of barrenness for her entire adult life, while Hagar has shared her husband's bed and carried his child. And considering how old Sarah and Abraham are, she may well fear for her young son's welfare after their death. Obviously we'd prefer to view this matriarch as a saintly figure endowed with selfless compassion. But that would rob Sarah of her human dimension—and deprive us of the lessons we can learn from this very human predicament. Our heart goes out to all of the players caught in this web of competing maternal interests: the father, the mothers, and their sons.

Even if we sympathize with Sarah's motives, we feel compassion for Hagar and Ishmael. Though Ishmael is certainly blameless of any sins, his very existence arouses Sarah's most primitive maternal instincts. Like a mother bear protecting her cub—and like countless queens and empresses throughout time who will stop at nothing to ensure the ascendancy of their children—Sarah lashes out at her rivals.

Abraham is once again caught in the middle between Sarah and Hagar, but this time the stakes have escalated. Like many a contemporary husband, he must navigate between two sets of wives and their children's competing interests. The Bible emphasizes that Abraham's first loyalty is to his wife and lifelong companion, Sarah —as well as to their son, Isaac, whom God has designated as the new heir. But Sarah's demand that he "cast out" Hagar and Ishmael is totally at odds with Abraham's sense of justice. If the sinners of Sodom deserved compassion, how can he deal so heartlessly with his own flesh and blood? He's deeply attached to Ishmael, who for thirteen years had been his only son and intended heir. How can he sentence him and his mother to banishment and near-certain death?

This chapter of Genesis highlights the gender gap between the way mothers and fathers deal with their children. While Abraham clearly loves his sons, his actions are constantly balanced between moral and domestic considerations. Sarah and Hagar, on the other hand, have more basic, less conflicted drives. Their fierce maternal instincts transcend situational ethics or social boundaries. They both love their sons intensely and will do whatever necessary to ensure their survival. Hagar's despairing cry: *"Let me not look on as the child dies,"* has endured as an icon of maternal love, inspiring painters and poets alike.

I think this gender discrepancy owes more to the male's comparative remove from his offspring than to an innate moral sense. Sarah's visceral connection to the son she has carried in her womb overrides the ethical conflicts that plague Abraham's conscience. And while Sarah is hardly held up as a paragon of virtue, Isaac clearly benefits—as any child does—from his mother's single-minded devotion. In the following episode, when Isaac's fate rests solely in his father's hands, we will see just how perilous a father's conflicted feelings for his son can be.

Narratively, God has once again emphasized the centrality of Sarah to the future of the clan. He deliberately selected her as matriarch back in Haran, and He preserves her throughout her trials in Egypt and Canaan. This tribe is in a crucial and formative stage of self-definition, continually dividing and separating to clarify its intended lineage. At each narrative juncture, the family path forks off in two directions—Abraham and Sarah take one road while the rest of the clan detours in the opposite direction. When Abraham departs from his father's house, his brother Nahor remains behind in Haran. Lot abandons the rigors of the nomadic life in the promised land for the allure of Sodom. Now, with God's blessing, Ishmael and

Hagar head off toward a separate destiny. Ishmael will go on to lead a great people, and Islam will someday embrace him as one of its patriarchs. He will return to help Isaac bury their father, and Isaac's firstborn son, Esau, will take one of Ishmael's daughters as a wife. But with the resolution of this episode, the narrative spotlight shifts focus to Sarah's son, Isaac, now the sole hope for the future of the tribe.

BALANCING THE COMPETING INTERESTS OF STEPFAMILIES

Most of us set out to build a tightly knit and self-contained nuclear family fashioned on an Ozzie and Harriet motif of domestic harmony. But as often as not, we find ourselves with an amalgam of children, stepchildren, spouses, ex-spouses, and somebody else's furniture and pets. Much as we may sometimes wish to, we don't have Sarah's recourse of simply casting out the characters who are complicating the family mix. We have to work with what we have, which often requires a sensitive balancing act.

Stepmothers have been maligned in folktales throughout history. As this biblical story about Sarah and her stepson teaches us, and as anthropological studies attest, there is an innate conflict of interests between a stepmother and her stepchildren. The stepmother may see the stepchild as encroaching on her relationship with her husband. And if she has her own child, as Sarah does, she may see a stepchild as competition for the father's resources and attention. The absence of a biological bond only exacerbates this perceived threat.

How can we reconcile the conflicting interests of a modern compound family? Here are some suggestions for women who are trying to fill the demanding role of stepmother:

- Have realistic expectations. Expect conflict with your stepchildren—it's a complex and difficult relationship. Don't expect to build love and trust overnight. If you start with respect and cooperation, love may well follow.

- Don't try to "cast out" the biological mother. Don't try to replace her. Whether you like it or not, she's part of the extended family. Try to be tolerant and flexible.
- Assume that the father will have divided loyalties. He will always be linked to his children and, to a lesser degree, their mother.
- Remember that you can grow to love your stepchild without betraying your own children.

If our hopes for a happy family are inclusive and realistic enough to embrace the complicated configuration we find ourselves in, then we will not have dreamed in vain.

THE BINDING OF ISAAC:
THE ANATOMY OF FAITH

You shall love the Lord your God with all your heart

and with all your soul and with all your might. Take

to heart these instructions with which I charge you

this day and impress them upon your children.

—Deuteronomy 6:5–6

Here in America, our convictions are rarely tested. Thanks to the rights written into our constitution, we are free to worship as we please and to speak our beliefs without fear of persecution. Our geographic isolation has spared us invasion by enemies, and our volunteer army allows us to choose whether or not to put our lives at risk.

Do we ever ask ourselves how much we'd be willing to sacrifice for our beliefs? For love? For country? For our children? For our ideals of justice?

How would we respond if our faith was truly tested? How

would we act if called upon to sacrifice our comfort, our livelihood, or our personal safety for what we believed in?

It's not surprising that we avoid tests, that we devote much of our energy and prayers to protecting ourselves from being tested. What this next story tells us is that we depend on life's tests to teach us about ourselves. Only when we are tested do we discover the limits of our character, the depth of our commitments. Only when tested do we find out how much suffering we will tolerate for the sake of our beliefs.

Most of us will never be tested in as dramatic a fashion as Abraham. But every day, in ways large and small, life offers us tests to gauge ourselves by. As Genesis never fails to remind us, the only meaningful measure of our humanity is our ability to convert our values into action. And as this story so starkly illustrates, our commitment to the values we profess is finally measured by what we are prepared to sacrifice for them.

In the previous chapter we explored the challenges we face when our long-held dreams are finally fulfilled. Now Abraham confronts a more daunting dilemma. What would happen if our worst fears came true? What if we were called upon to pay the ultimate price for what we believe?

We have now arrived at the climactic episode in Abraham's century-long life—arguably the most dramatic scene in Genesis. The story of the binding of Isaac—known in Hebrew as the *Akedah*: "The Binding"—remains one of the most difficult in all the Bible. Volumes have been written about the heartbreaking test to which God subjects Abraham. Poets and philosophers, rabbis and priests have debated the meaning of God's test and Abraham's response: Did Abraham pass the test? Was he perhaps testing God—or exploring the depth of his own commitment? How would we respond to such an extreme challenge to our own faith, our own ideals? The resolution of this drama is at once chilling and inspiring, shocking and uplifting.

The literary style of this episode exemplifies the Bible's genius for simplicity and emotional power. Despite the pathos of the plot line, it is written with remarkable restraint and terseness, the austerity of the language heightening the tension of the scene almost to the breaking point. The very sparseness of the narrative, devoid of

all psychological reflection or physical detail, invites every generation of readers to reinterpret it against the backdrop of its life and
times. In order to comprehend the hidden meanings of this passage,
we need to burrow beneath the spare prose and uncover the primal
confrontation of doubt and belief, of betrayal and fidelity, of sacrifice and surrender.

No matter how many times I read this story, I always approach
it with awe and trepidation.

*Some time afterward, God put Abraham to the test. He
called to him, "Abraham."*

Though his ears were dimmed with age, Abraham heard
God's call once more resounding in his soul. *And he answered,
"Here am I."*

*And God said, "Pray, take your son, your only son,
Isaac, whom you love. And go forth to the land of Moriah, and
offer him there as a burnt sacrifice on one of the mountains
which I will point out to you."*

Abraham's mind stopped. His heart froze. Why? Why
Isaac? Why now? Why must the promise be revoked?

In the hour before Sarah awoke, he took hold of his sleeping son and bore him from their tent. *Early that morning,
Abraham saddled his ass and took with him two of his servants
and his son Isaac. He split wood for the burnt offering, and he
set out for the place of which God had told him.*

For three days they walked. Grimly and in silence, save
for the sound of their sandals and the donkey's hooves. Could
he yet turn back and retrace his steps?

*On the third day Abraham looked up and saw the place
from afar. Then Abraham said to his servants, "You stay here
with the ass. The boy and I will go up there; we will worship,
and we will return to you."* It was a wish from the depths of his
soul, but had he the power to make it come true?

*Abraham took the wood for the burnt offering and laid it
upon his son Isaac. He himself took the firestone and the knife.*

And the two walked off together.

Isaac sensed the gravity of their mission and the tension in the air. Anxious and excited, he clasped his father's hand. *Isaac called to his father Abraham, "Father!"*

And he answered "Here am I, my son."

And Isaac said, "Here are the firestone and the wood, but where is the sheep for the burnt offering?" Isaac looked up, searching his father's face for explanation.

The dread rose in Abraham as the question resounded in his head. *And Abraham said, "God will see to the sheep for His burnt offering."*

And the two of them walked on together.

They arrived at the place of which God had told him. Abraham built an altar there. He laid out the wood. He bound his son Isaac and laid him on the altar, on top of the wood. And Abraham stretched forth his hand and took the knife to slay his son. The same knife he had used to circumcise him on his eighth day of life. He had marked the covenant in his son's flesh so that God would remember His promise.

Then an angel of the Lord called to him from heaven: "Abraham! Abraham!"

And he answered, "Here am I."

And He said, "Do not raise your hand against the boy, or do anything to him. For now I know that you are in awe of God, since you have not withheld your son, your only son, from Me."

And Abraham looked up, and his eye fell upon a ram, caught in the thicket by its horns. So Abraham went and took the ram and offered it up as a burnt offering in place of his son.

And Abraham named that site Adonai-yireh, "God will provide"—as it is said to this day, "On the mountain of the Lord, it will be seen."

THE BINDING OF ISAAC: NIGHTMARE OR WISH FULFILLMENT?

Despite its seeming happy ending, we stagger away from this story, as if having narrowly averted a fatal car wreck. Our minds reel with unanswered questions: How could God, who rules by justice and compassion, sanction such a crime? And how could Abraham, who has pleaded so eloquently for the lives of the sinners of Sodom, say nothing to defend his innocent son against this calamitous decree?

Many interpretations have been offered to explain Abraham's baffling and uncharacteristic behavior. But only one approach to this story helps me comprehend God's command to Abraham that he sacrifice his beloved son Isaac: that this entire drama takes place in Abraham's dreams. After hundreds of readings of this enigmatic tale, I am struck by its many dreamlike elements:

First, there are the eerie time references in the story—*Some time afterwards . . . early the next morning . . . on the third day* —which echo the passage of time in dreams. Place is also only vaguely described—*". . . one of the heights which I will show you . . ."* *. . . the place of which God had told him . . .* the mysterious "Mount Moriah," about whose actual location many have speculated.

Second, there is the surrealistic nature of Abraham and Isaac's journey to the mountain: Sarah's mysterious absence at their departure, the three days of silent walking with no sense of destination. And then the abrupt arrival—*Abraham looked up and saw the place from afar.* And after the sacrifice is averted, Abraham is said to descend the mountain alone. Isaac is nowhere to be seen.

If we view this episode through the window of Abraham's unconscious fears and hopes, many of the unexplained elements take on meaning. Sarah's unnatural absence speaks to the loneliness of Abraham's situation. The young Isaac becomes a mouthpiece for Abraham's unspoken anxieties. And the larger framework of the story comes into focus as a portrait of Abraham's anguished psyche.

Every episode of Abraham's life story is telescoped into the terrible moment when he binds Isaac and raises the sacrificial knife aloft. It has been twenty-five years since God first bid him "Go forth" from Haran in search of a promised land and the promise of fathering a new line of people. Finally, after decades of waiting and hoping, after prayers and visions, after tests of patience and endurance, Abraham and Sarah are blessed with the miraculous gift of a child in their old age. All of Abraham's hopes for the future hang by this slender human thread. His young son, Isaac, whom Abraham has circumcised as a sign of his compact with God, is now the sole link to the future generations of the covenant.

Armed only with his faith in the future and his trust in God, Abraham confronts his worst nightmare—the death of his clan at his own hand.

In his dream, Abraham is wrestling with his doubts and anxieties—about the vulnerability of his young son, about the demands of his covenant with God, and about the possible risks to Isaac of inheriting this weighty commitment. By conjuring his worst fear—that his covenant with God would compel him to sacrifice his son, that the promise of the covenant could be arbitrarily reversed by the God of justice and compassion—Abraham is able to work through his anxieties and discover the comforting power of faith.

Abraham has never been anxious about his own physical safety —whether in famine or in war. Now that he has been blessed with a child, Abraham is overcome with anxiety. Only now does Abraham realize how fragile and precious this link to the promised future of the covenant is. He's frightened that he will not be able to protect his son from harm—or worse yet, might actually prove to be the instrument of that harm. Perhaps Abraham's covenant with God holds unseen risks for this child. Abraham and Sarah are nearing the end of their lives. Who will take care of their boy when they're gone?

Abraham's faith in God "solves" Abraham's problem in the dream, which begins in anxiety and ends in a wish fulfillment. Though he trusts that *"God will see to the sheep for His burnt offering,"* Abraham is unsure of who that sheep will prove to be until the very last moment. At the point of greatest danger, when he holds the knife over his helpless son, an angel of God stays his hand. God reassures Abraham that the covenant will prove a blessing, not a hazard, to his child.

Only a heartbeat stands between Abraham and the extinction of his seed. But he goes on trusting in God, as the Book of Deuteronomy directs us, *with all your heart and with all your soul and with all your might.*

THE BURDEN OF FREE WILL

The most agonizing aspect of Abraham's dream dilemma is that he has a choice. God can command him to sacrifice his son, but only Abraham can execute the order. Like any true test—any authentic sacrifice—this one is voluntary. Abraham understands that he can obey or refuse God's request. Free will lies at the heart of his terrible decision.

The burden of choice falls squarely on Abraham's shoulders. Like all of life's toughest decisions, Abraham must make this one alone. Not only must he make this choice without Sarah, he must take pains to calm the boy's fears—which represent, as we've noted, Abraham's own doubts.

Abraham has three long days during his trek to Mount Moriah in which to contemplate his choices:

His first option is simply to reject God and His command. Who could fault a loving parent for putting his child's life above obedience to God? But to do so—to conclude that God is complicit in the senseless slaughter of the innocent and that any previous claim to justice was a lie—would repudiate everything Abraham had lived for over the past twenty-five years. At every turn he has made a leap of faith, trusting God to deliver on His promise of a land and a people of great destiny. To reject God now in the face of His seemingly capricious request would mark the end of the covenant, the end of all promises. Abraham would save his son, but only by forfeiting his future and denying his past.

The other option, to sacrifice his only remaining son to a God whose will he can no longer comprehend, would also negate the dream Abraham has journeyed toward for so long. Without Isaac, there would be no seed, no "countless offspring"—no great people of destiny.

ARE LEAPS OF FAITH
ALWAYS BLIND?

The most perplexing question remains: Why doesn't Abraham confront God directly with his agonizing dilemma? Abraham established through his petition for Sodom that he holds God accountable for His actions. Why doesn't Abraham now plead for his son's life as aggressively as he pleaded for the lives of the wicked citizens of Sodom?

If we look back at how he has managed the crises in his life, we see that Abraham has proved tenaciously self-sufficient—perhaps to a fault. Abraham has always been loath to ask God for help on his own behalf. Whether his tribe was beset by famine or faced with war, Abraham always took the initiative for resolving his predicaments. Like a man who, no matter how lost, refuses to ask directions, Abraham cannot bring himself to plead for a path out of his nightmare.

It is not until his son finally gives voice to the very question which weighs so heavily on Abraham's heart that he begins to find his way. Once he hears the awful question, as if spoken from his own heart—*"Here are the firestone and the wood, but where is the sheep for the burnt offering?"*—Abraham knows the answer: *"God will see to the sheep for His burnt offering."*

His reply is not the statement of blind faith it might first appear. Abraham doesn't know what is going to happen when he reaches the mountaintop. But he realizes that his relationship with God has been built exclusively on trust, earned gradually over time by promises made and kept on both sides. Abraham trusts that despite every rational impulse crying out within him to defy God's request, his only choice is to "go forth" once again and "fear not." At this point Abraham realizes that he and God are bound together in their covenant. Only by moving forward in his life path can Abraham prove his faith and reaffirm his destiny.

Throughout their relationship Abraham has been tested, the binding of Isaac being the final test of Abraham's commitment to his covenant with God. By enduring this nightmare test, Abraham learns several important lessons. By staying his hand at the last moment, God demonstrates once and for all that their covenant is bound by justice, love, and compassion. This dream also gives Abraham the chance to explore the limits of his own commitment to the covenant—not for God's sake, but for his own. When he is asked to give up what he loves most, and then has his hand stayed at the last moment, Abraham learns that God values human life above all else and does not require its sacrifice.

CHILD SACRIFICE VERSUS SACRIFICE FOR THE CHILD

It's important for us to keep in mind that child sacrifice was common among Canaanite tribes in Abraham's day. On an historical level, this episode further defines the covenant by rejecting human sacrifice, once and for all, in favor of sacrifices of the heart. Marking the sign of the covenant in Isaac's flesh through circumcision is the only bloodletting required of Abraham. And circumcision represents not a token sacrifice of the child but a sanctification of his life and the commitment of the father to raise his child in a spiritual path.

Psychologically, the binding of Isaac symbolizes the complex web of emotions that tie children to their parents, and parents to their impossible roles as protectors of their children. This story shines a spotlight on the parent-child dynamic in all its complexity. It teaches us that, while we will be called upon to make endless sacrifices *for* our children, we must always resist the temptation to sacrifice our children on the altar of our own ambitions. A father may feel he is providing for his children by working weekends and evenings, when in fact he is merely depriving them of what they need most—an available, accessible father. In order to give our children the love and guidance they need, parents may have to sacrifice a portion of their professional glory.

We are all to some degree susceptible to the temptation of

making our children over in our own images. In the purported best interests of the child, fathers pressure children to join a family business or profession. Mothers raise their daughters to be the popular teenager or successful professional they never became. When we exhort our children to gain admission to prestigious colleges, how much are we driven by pride, and how much by our children's best interest? Perhaps God is warning Abraham against overweening religious zeal, reminding him that even devotion to God, when taken to an extreme, is idolatrous and self-serving. It is often easier to pray to God than to make sacrifices for our children. This story—a precursor of the later teachings of the prophets—tells us that whatever we do in service to God is an empty ritual unless it benefits human beings.

The binding of Isaac is a warning about the destructive potential that lies beneath the loving surface of the parent-child relationship. Even acts that begin in love can veer into narcissism or selfishness—which is why we must heed the angel's plea to *"not raise your hand against the boy."*

The vulnerability of children to their parents' influence endows our parental role with much more than mere biological significance. For better or for worse, we bestow on our children an identity that goes well beyond their genetic inheritance. As a cautionary tale, this story reminds us that the ideals we pass on to our children may someday exact a high cost. When we teach a child to love country or justice or freedom, we do so with the solemn knowledge that they may someday be called upon to put their lives on the line for their beliefs. The Hebrew Bible in no way glorifies martyrdom. But it is realistic enough to recognize that ideological commitments find their fullest expression in action—often at a heavy price.

When God says to Abraham, *"Take your son, your only son, Isaac, whom you love . . ."* it marks the first mention of the word "love" in the Bible. This is no accident. Love relationships, as the rest of Genesis will demonstrate, are always laced with the possibility of heartbreak. In the end we are bound up with those we love in an inescapable *akedah* of interdependence.

"*HINENI.* HERE AM I": THE COVENANT'S REFRAIN

Abraham's response to the challenges of his life is encapsulated in a single Hebrew word, which is repeated three times in this short episode: *Hineni.* "Here am I." When God calls out to Abraham, he responds simply, "Here am I." With this simple phrase Abraham signals his total spiritual and emotional receptivity.

As the ubiquitous byword of this story, *Hineni* suggests the universality of the covenantal relationship. When Isaac turns to his father for reassurance, Abraham responds, *"Hineni.* Here am I." The spirit of this transcendent statement of accessibility resounds throughout all human relationships. When an infant stirs in her bedside cradle, the mother calls out, "I'm here." When a lover calls out in passion or in need, the partner responds, "Here I am." When a friend turns to us for a favor, large or small, the true friend responds: "I am here for you."

As a therapist, it is my role to be totally receptive and available to my patients. The covenant defining the therapeutic relationship is built on trust: the patient reveals himself without reservation, and the therapist listens with compassion and without prejudgment. The more I can convey the spirit of *Hineni,* the more trust I can engender, and the more freedom the patient will feel to face change.

THE COVENANT AS A MODEL FOR HUMAN RELATIONSHIPS

God has been building Abraham's faith and trust over the course of his adult lifetime by giving him tangible tokens of their covenant: the land, sons, a vision of his future. In his final encounter with God, Abraham comes away with an intangible but invaluable lesson: the understanding that his covenant with God is also a blueprint for his relationship with other human beings. The covenant between God and Abraham's clan in Genesis is symbolic of the trust that we all have to share with each other in order to survive. This covenant stands as an idealized model for all the deeply committed, covenantal relationships in our lives.

The measure of these relationships is our readiness to make unforeseen sacrifices for them. I always cry at weddings, but not for purely sentimental reasons. What moves me is how innocently the bride and groom make absolute pledges of fidelity and devotion. Little do they imagine the sacrifices they may someday be called upon to make in the course of their marriage.

Consensual covenants govern virtually all our relationships—in love, in friendship, in political life, and in business. Even contracts and treaties between nations are modeled after the covenants forged in Genesis. However, the binding power of each of these covenants is measured by the level of sacrifice the participants are willing to make on its behalf. Unlike a morally accountable covenant, a contract carries little expectation of sacrifice—which is why we consult lawyers before signing business contracts and clergy before we wed.

However we personally conceive of God, the covenant between God and the human race in Genesis celebrates our extraordinary drive to elevate ourselves to our highest potential. The covenant embodies our yearning to transcend the narrow confines of our individual lives, to offer ourselves in service to something larger—to say, "Here am I."

THE DEATH OF SARAH: TAKING CARE OF FINAL TASKS

To everything there is a season, and a time to every
purpose under the heaven:
A time to be born, and a time to die.

—Ecclesiastes 3:1–2

I'm amazed at how Sarah and Abraham, this aged couple who lived four thousand years ago, can serve as contemporary role models for our rapidly growing population of older people. To me, they embody the proverb: "Old age, to the unlearned, is winter; to the learned, it is harvest time."

Their fearless approach to the later stages of life is both inspirational and instructive. And while they would certainly be remarkable in any age, I like to think that Abraham and Sarah would be gratified to see that older people are beginning to reclaim their traditional respect and authority through political activism.

I've found growing older to be a mixed blessing: a constant challenge to my vanity and an ongoing revelation of unexpected personal gains I feel building in my life. Ten years ago I would not have had the confidence to write this book. Only recently have I achieved the sense of security and purpose required for such a daunting undertaking. I applaud the sentiment Betty Friedan expresses in her book *The Fountain of Age*, when she writes about the newfound power and freedom that comes with age: "Saying what we think and feel at last—knowing who we are, realizing that we know more than we ever knew that we knew, not afraid of what anyone thinks of us anymore . . . I have never felt so free."

Abraham is now a very old man with the great tests of his life behind him. But while he has sealed his covenant with God, Abraham must still set his worldly affairs in order. When his lifelong companion, Sarah, dies, Abraham is faced with one of his final tasks: in the midst of his grief he must purchase a burial ground for his wife and himself.

Despite God's promise to someday give all of Canaan to Abraham's offspring, Abraham has no legal claim to any of the land as he approaches death. After decades of a seminomadic existence, he understands the urgency of procuring a permanent family burial ground. As an alien in Canaan, Abraham doesn't even have the legal right to own land. In order to secure a tomb for Sarah and their progeny, he has to win a special dispensation from the local Hittites.

The ensuing scene provides a fascinating glimpse into the art of Near Eastern negotiation. And it shows us how astutely Abraham orders his priorities when conducting important family business. Even though he is still deep in grief for Sarah, Abraham grasps all the subtleties of this important and delicate transaction.

The span of Sarah's life came to a hundred and twenty-seven years. Sarah died in Kiriath-Arba—now Hebron—in the land of Canaan. And Abraham came to mourn for Sarah, and to weep for her.

Then Abraham arose from beside his dead wife and spoke

to the Hittites, saying: "I am a stranger and a sojourner among you. Sell me a burial site among you that I may remove my dead for burial."

And the Hittites answered Abraham, saying: "Hear us, my lord; you are a mighty prince among us. Bury your dead in the choicest of our tombs. None of us will withhold his burial place from you."

Abraham knew exactly which piece of property he wanted to buy. It included a cave for burial and a row of trees that formed a natural fence denoting the boundaries of the plot. To ensure that his descendants' claim to the property would not be contested in the future, Abraham took pains to conduct the negotiation in full view of the townspeople. And he didn't hesitate to humble himself by making the required obeisance to the local Hittites to enlist their goodwill.

Thereupon Abraham bowed low to the people of the land, to the Hittites, and he said to them, "If it is your wish that I remove my dead for burial, then you must intercede for me with Ephron, the son of Zohar. Let him sell me the cave of Machpelah, which he owns, which is at the end of his field. Let him sell it to me, at the full price, for a burial site in your midst."

Ephron answered Abraham in the hearing of the Hittites and of all who entered the gate of his city, saying, "No, my lord, hear me: I give you the field, and I give you the cave that is in it. I give it to you in the presence of my people. Bury your dead."

The owner of the property had opened the negotiations by facetiously offering to give the land to Abraham outright. Abraham understood this to be a mere formality and insisted that he wanted to pay full price for the land so that no one could ever challenge his ownership.

And Abraham bowed low before the people of the land, and he spoke to Ephron in the hearing of the people, saying, "If only you will hear me out. Let me pay the price of the land. Accept it from me that I may bury my dead there."

Ephron then quoted a highly inflated price with dismissive bravado:

And Ephron answered Abraham, saying: "My lord, listen to me: A piece of land worth four hundred shekels of silver— What is that between you and me? Go and bury your dead."

Abraham accepted Ephron's terms. Abraham paid out to Ephron the money he had named in the hearing of the Hittites —four hundred shekels of silver at the going merchant's rate.

Abraham surprised his counterpart by immediately accepting this opening offer. Though we know Abraham to have been a skillful negotiator—and we know historically that four hundred shekels was a large sum of money for a simple plot of land—he chose not to haggle over price. Abraham understood that in some matters a binding covenant is more important than a good price.

So Ephron's land in Machpelah, near Mamre—the field with its cave and all the trees that were within the borders of the field—passed to Abraham as a possession in the presence of the Hittites, before all who went in the gate of his city.

And after this, Abraham buried Sarah his wife in the cave of the field of Machpelah, facing Mamre—now Hebron—in the land of Canaan. Thus the field with its cave passed from the Hittites to Abraham as a burial site.

THE IMPORTANCE OF
A FAMILY BURIAL SITE

Living in Washington, DC, I'm always struck by how people are drawn from all over the country to the various memorials we've built to our dead. Whether it's the Vietnam Memorial, Arlington National Cemetery, memorials to our founding fathers, or the haunting testament of the Holocaust Museum, we all seem comforted by coming together to commemorate those who have gone before us. These gatherings offer us a sense of belonging, an awareness of our historical roots, and shared memories of pride and loss.

The importance of a burial ground to the fledgling identity of Abraham's clan applies equally to our own families. By establishing continuity amd connection between the generations, grave sites allow us to share a collective memory of our forebears. Congregating at cemeteries offers us quiet moments of reflection, remembrance, and storytelling.

Every culture and religion has developed its own burial ritual as a hallmark of its spiritual identity. Whether we cremate our dead on the banks of the Ganges, embalm them and entomb them beneath great pyramids, or bury them in simple pine boxes in the ground, our burial rites speak directly to our understanding of life, death, and its aftermath.

Abraham's acquisition of the cave of Machpelah represents his family's first legal foothold in the promised land. Though it is merely a single field with trees and a cave, this tiny piece of real estate will be the ancestral tomb of the patriarchs and matriarchs, the family's only fixed point of return for many generations. Abraham and Sarah will be buried there, as will their son, Isaac, his wife, Rebekah, their son, Jacob, and his first wife, Leah.

Even at the last stage of his life Abraham fully embodies his role as patriarch, doing whatever is necessary to provide for his family's welfare and continuity. By securing a family burial ground, he is reminding his children of the importance of this land to the future of their family. By choosing to be buried in Canaan, rather than back in the land of their birth, he and Sarah are symbolically putting down roots in its soil.

Though we remember him largely as the spiritual leader of his clan, Abraham shows us that worldly affairs are not separate from or less important than spiritual concerns. Both are parts of an integrated life requiring equal measures of attention. Abraham understands that the promised land lies not in the heavens, but in the ground beneath his feet.

THE COVENANT AS A MODEL FOR MONOGAMY

In the polygamous society of their day, Abraham and Sarah's relationship stands as a model of monogamous devotion. Their marriage outlasts the strains of midlife crisis and infertility, the upheavals of war, famine, sexual jealousy, and intrafamily rivalry. Abraham and Sarah's marriage, like their covenant with God, is built on trust and fidelity.

Genesis suggests a direct connection between the developments of monotheism and monogamy. It is no accident that these two concepts emerge simultaneously from a polytheistic and polygamous culture. The advent of a covenant between an individual and a single God is mirrored by the covenant between two individuals in a marriage.

It is particularly noteworthy that a couple rather than an individual is chosen to lead the way down a new spiritual path. God doesn't choose only Abraham to embark for Canaan; Abraham wouldn't have made it alone. Neither does He select only Sarah. He chooses a couple—a middle-aged man and woman who have already demonstrated their maturity, wisdom, and loyalty to each other. God emphasizes their equal importance to the covenant by conferring new names on both of them as a sign of their spiritual transformation. And when God seals His covenant with this couple by blessing them with fertility, they undergo concurrent physical metamorphoses of circumcision and menstruation.

At every turn in this story, God intervenes to assure the survival of Abraham and Sarah's exclusive relationship. He commands them to go forth from Haran together. He rescues Sarah from Pharaoh's harem. He derails their experiment with surrogate mother-hood and prophesies that the covenant will continue exclusively through their child, Isaac.

Abraham and Sarah endure as a couple not merely because of God's intervention, but because they are prepared to make sacrifices for each other and for a shared set of ideals. This devoted couple will be a model for later generations of this family. Isaac and Rebekah will continue this tradition of monogamy, while the source of many of their son Jacob's woes can be traced to his multiple wives and the ensuing rivalries between them and their offspring.

Although sibling relationships will remain thorny, and conflicts between parents and children will emerge and persist, strong emotional bonds between spouses will be the bedrock of this family. In an age of arranged marriages and institutionalized polygamy, the pattern of romantic love between spouses is remarkable. Genesis describes a family that endures tremendous strife because it remains anchored by strong couples bound together by a commitment to a shared faith, to their family, and to each other.

Part Three

Jacob Becomes Israel: Wrestling with the Challenges of Family Relationships

Jacob Wrestling with the Angel

With Sarah's death and burial, the saga of the first generation of this family draws to a close. Abraham and Sarah have forged an identity for their family that revolves around an ongoing, transcendent covenant with God. But their foothold in the land of Canaan is still tenuous. The question remains: Will this clan survive with all its vitality and sense of destiny? And for how long? Will their covenant with God and the land be transmitted to the next generation?

Genesis depicts how the men and women of the next three generations of this family incorporate the covenant into their personal lives. Each generation marks a new beginning, a new test case for the values that underlie its interactive covenant with God. Each character's different needs, strengths, and weakness shape his or her relationship to the blessings and obligations of the covenant. Each character must wrestle with his or her personal demons and angels in the universal human quest to feel blessed and whole.

Throughout the next three generations, Abraham and Sarah remain the towering beacons of faith to the men and women who follow them. No one else will have Abraham's sustained dialogue with God, though He will continue to visit the patriarchs and matriarchs, reassuring them that He remains by their side and that His covenant with them endures intact. The process by which each character reaffirms the covenant in his or her own life and transmits it to the next generation is the narrative through line of the rest of Genesis. Abraham and Sarah, the pioneering visionaries, are gone. But the covenant remains as a lifeline for their family. As long as they are spiritually and psychologically grounded in this legacy, the family will always have a defined sense of purpose and a vision of the future that helps them hurdle obstacles and cope with the vicissitudes of life.

Spiritually, the men and women of Genesis stand on the shoulders of those who came before them. But each generation must work through the same thorny issues of family relations: marital strife, child-rearing, sibling rivalry. We each have to rework the same issues that confronted our parents, grandparents, and great-grandparents. None of us is spared the anguish and joy of growing up through the graduated phases of family life.

With the second and third generations, the family tree begins to take shape. Abraham and Sarah's son, Isaac, is a transitional figure, the stabilizer who sinks roots into the land. In his generation it is the matriarch, his wife Rebekah, who surfaces as the active, dynamic force and passes the torch of leadership to their son Jacob. Jacob emerges as the pivotal character in Genesis —the most contemporary and accessible personality in the book. Nowhere is the dictum "Character is fate" better illustrated than in the life of Jacob. As in a finely wrought tragedy, the traits exposed in his youth provide a telling blueprint for the anguish of his later life.

Though totally enmeshed in the fabric of family life, Jacob struggles mightily in his roles as son, brother, son-in-law, husband, and father. All of these relationships are conflicted, troubled, and painful. But he strives and he endures. What redeems him, despite his personal failings, is his tenacity. He falls and he gets up and continues on his way. Despite all his missteps, he aspires to do good. In the face of monumental emotional blind spots that persist until his dying days, Jacob succeeds in his most important task as patriarch: he transmits a strong sense of family identity and destiny to his twelve sons, the founders of the future twelve tribes of Israel.

Like no other character in the Bible, Jacob embodies the human potential for both inner conflicts, and transcendent spiritual epiphanies of astounding clarity. His life story is heartbreaking, inspirational, and totally believable.

ISAAC WEDS REBEKAH: CHOOSING A MATE FOR LIFE

*Whosoever findeth a wife, findeth a good thing and
obtaineth favor from the Lord.*

—*Proverbs 18:22*

Winston Churchill once remarked in a speech to the House of Commons that "democracy is the worst form of government—except for all those other forms that have been tried from time to time." I feel the same way about marriage. It's not a perfect institution, because it involves human beings who are innately imperfect. We bring all of our unresolved conflicts and unrealistic expectations to our marriages, which inevitably reflect those problems. But I fully believe that, in the long run, a good marriage is the best platform for achieving personal growth and fulfillment.

Embracing the concept of marriage is relatively easy. Making a wise choice about whom to join with in this long-distance journey is much more complicated. Selecting a partner for life, and then making the ongoing commitment to that choice, is an awesome challenge. In biblical times, the burden of that choice was left to parents to arrange. The concept of older, presumably wiser, adults evaluating the strengths and weaknesses of a proposed match had a lot going for it. Arranged marriages built on similarity of background, traditions, and expectations offer newlyweds a large measure of stability and continuity—two ingredients that are sorely missed in today's marriages.

Today, we are encouraged to believe that unless and until lightning strikes and we "fall" in love, we cannot hope to find happiness. While falling in love is certainly an exhilarating and bonding experience, it's not always a reliable guide to long-term compatibility and commitment. The hazards of youthful romantic choices are reflected in the high failure rate of first marriages. These "starter marriages," as unions between people in their early twenties have recently been dubbed by sociologists, have only a one in three chance of survival. But when these same people remarry in their late twenties or early thirties, more than 50 percent of them remain married for life. The degree to which we can bring wisdom and maturity to our decisions about marriage—whether we marry at sixteen or sixty—is our best defense against the upheaval of divorce.

Isaac and Rebekah are the only absolutely monogamous life-long couple in this first family of Genesis. The story of how Abraham goes about choosing a wife for his son teaches us that when it comes to making this most important of life decisions, it is best to proceed with caution and deliberation.

Abraham was old, and well advanced in age, and the Lord had blessed Abraham in all things.

Before he died, Abraham performed one last task to ensure the continuity of his clan. He wanted to arrange a proper marriage for his son, Isaac, who was forty years old and not yet wed. As a man who had relied heavily on the support of a strong mate throughout his life, Abraham understood the importance of choosing the right partner for his son. And he realized that as the future matriarch of the family, Isaac's wife would play a key role in raising the next generation of children and transmitting the traditions that he and Sarah had established. He needed to find a woman who would embrace not only Isaac but also his family's commitment to physical and spiritual continuity. That, above all else, had to be preserved.

Abraham resolved to find for Isaac a wife who came from his old home in Mesopotamia, and from his own family. He didn't want Isaac to make the journey himself, for fear that his son would be so seduced by the blandishments of city life that he might never return to Canaan. Since Abraham was too old to make the trip himself, he delegated the task to his most loyal servant.

Abraham said to the oldest servant of his house, who ruled over all that he had, "Place your hand beneath my thigh. I will make you swear by the Lord, the God of heaven, and the God of the earth, that you will not take a wife for my son from the daughters of the Canaanites, among whom I dwell, but you will go to the land of my birth and get a wife for my son Isaac. The Lord God of heaven will send His angel before you, and you will take a wife for my son from there. And if the woman be not willing to follow you, then you will be clear from this oath. Only do not take my son back there."

So the servant put his hand under the thigh of his master Abraham and swore to him as bidden.

Abraham is preoccupied with preserving continuity in his family. As he sees it, once continuity is interrupted, the covenant is betrayed. Wary of the dangers of mixed marriages and assimilation, Abraham feels more secure going back to "the old country" to select a bride for his son. By bringing a bride from so far away, he hopes that she will be absorbed psychologically, spiritually, and socially into her new family in Canaan.

Today we live in a multicultural society where mixed marriages are common. While many cross-cultural marriages work well, the cultural divide between spouses often gapes wider when conflicts arise, especially around child-rearing issues. Suddenly, the initial cross-cultural attraction between two people can itself become a source of contention and alienation. Both partners end up wondering why these issues weren't discussed before they exchanged marriage vows.

Abraham takes special pains to ensure that Isaac's wife will not be coerced into the marriage. This detail stands out, because in biblical times women didn't have much choice as to where they went and with whom. Such matters were usually decided by a woman's family. But Abraham wants to make sure that when Isaac's wife leaves her home and enters marriage, she does so freely and enthusiastically.

It is worth noting that Abraham secures his servant's oath by commanding him to *"place your hand beneath my thigh."* The thigh in the Bible is often used as a euphemism for sexual organs, which represent the source of Abraham's reproductive powers and the fate of his progeny. The image of having someone swear an oath by placing his hand on another man's genitals might jar us. But this practice, common in the ancient Near East, speaks to the lack of prudishness of those times. The privacy and primacy of a man's genitals were universally appreciated, so placing another man's hand there was a gesture of ultimate trust and solemnity. The word "testament," based on the Latin *testes* or testicles, derives its meaning from this ancient custom. A sanitized version of this oath-taking ritual survives today when a witness testifying under oath in court swears to tell the truth while placing his hand on the Bible.

Our story now turns from the end of an old man's life to the marriage of two young people. And in a refreshing shift from the intensity of the preceding episodes, we get a wonderfully pastoral and romantic tale, full of the joy and hope of a new beginning. Stylistically, it's a radical departure from the laconic style of the earlier chapters. The binding of Isaac runs fewer than twenty lines. The story of Rebekah at the well, the most richly detailed in Genesis, is told at a leisurely pace with mellifluous language.

Abraham's servant took ten of his master's camels, and set out, taking with him all the bounty of his master. And he arose, and went to Mesopotamia, to the city of Nahor, Abraham's brother.

Outside the city, there was a spring where all the women came at sunset to draw water for the evening meal. The servant made the ten camels kneel down in a row near the spring, and he prayed: *"O Lord God, let the maiden to whom I say, 'Let down your water jar, I beg you, that I may drink,' and who replies, 'Drink, and I will also water your camels'—let her be the one whom You have appointed for Your servant Isaac."*

He had scarcely finished speaking, when Rebekah—who was born to Bethuel, the son of Milcah, who was the wife of Nahor, Abraham's brother—came out with her water jar upon her shoulder. The maiden was very beautiful to look upon, a virgin whom no man had known. She went down to the spring, filled her jar, and came up.

The servant ran to meet her, and said, "Please, let me drink a little water from your jar."

And she said, "Drink, my lord," and she lowered her jar upon her hand and let him drink. When she had let him drink his fill, she said, "I will also draw water for your camels, until they have finished drinking." Quickly emptying her water jar into the trough, she ran back to the well to draw water, and drew for all his camels.

The man meanwhile stood gazing at her, silently wondering whether the Lord had made his journey successful or not.

When the camels finished drinking, the man took a golden nose ring weighing half a shekel, and two gold bracelets for her wrists, ten shekels in weight. And said, "Whose daughter are you? Pray tell me, is there room in your father's house for us to spend the night?"

And she said to him, "I am the daughter of Bethuel the son of Milcah, whom she bore to Nahor." And she said to him, "We have both straw and fodder enough, and room to lodge in."

ASSESSING CHARACTER BY OBSERVING ACTION

The biblical authors are clearly fond of wells as backdrops for meeting scenes, since they appear several times in Genesis. At different junctures, the well will symbolize fertility, female sexuality, and the subconscious wellspring of imagination. In this episode, the simple act of drawing water at a well becomes a barometer of a prospective bride's character. In biblical times a town's well was a social grazing ground—like the soda fountain of the 1950s or coffee bar of the 1990s—where a young woman's attributes were put on display. Every response and movement by Rebekah in this scene reveals an important facet of her personality. With no other matriarch, among the four depicted in Genesis, are we given so many details concerning her nature and character.

Though we are told that Rebekah is *very beautiful to look upon,* the major criterion for choosing Isaac's bride is her character rather than her beauty or wealth. Genesis teaches us that, when all is said and done, character is the one sure component we can trust in choosing a mate. The psychosocial test that the servant puts Rebekah through is critical to the future of the story. Circumstances will change. Her marriage will have its ups and downs, its shifting dynamics. But Rebekah's assertiveness and self-confidence will remain constant. The character traits illuminated by this episode in Rebekah's youth will stand her in good stead throughout her life and throughout her marriage to Isaac.

The test is simple: the woman who offers the servant water *and* volunteers to water his ten camels will be Isaac's bride. We can picture the long row of camels kneeling by the spring in the cool of the evening as the women of the city come out to draw water. I see Rebekah in my mind's eye as graceful and slender, with the wonderful posture of women accustomed to balancing jugs of water on their shoulders. She exudes vitality and strength. Hers is the attractiveness of youthful exuberance and physical vigor.

The focus of this story is on Rebekah's warm and spontaneous response to the tired stranger by the well. Not only does she give him water from her jug, but she offers to water his camels *"until they have finished drinking."* Remember that there are *ten* camels, and that these creatures are renowned for their capacity to store enormous amounts of water in their humps at a single session. Watering these animals is no casual task—especially since Rebekah must descend repeatedly to the spring and climb the slope back up to the trough bearing a heavy water jug.

Already the servant has observed several important traits in this bridal candidate. She is strong, healthy, and industrious, and she doesn't shy away from physical labor. We know from earlier chapters the high value her great-uncle Abraham puts on hospitality, and Rebekah certainly scores high marks on this account. We discover that her nurturing and compassionate nature also extends to animals. Ever since the Garden of Eden, humans have been responsible for animal welfare. Later on, in the Book of Exodus, the principle of humane treatment of animals will be codified into law.

When the servant inquires after her identity, Rebekah displays new virtues. She is forthright and articulate in her response, right away giving her name and parentage. She doesn't hem and haw or giggle into her hands. She knows exactly who she is and where she has come from. This strong sense of self will surely be welcomed by Abraham's clan. And when the servant inquires into lodgings, Rebekah again responds with poise and hospitality.

What follows sheds even more light on Rebekah and her family.

And the maiden ran and told her mother's household of these things. Now Rebekah had a brother whose name was Laban. Laban ran out to the man at the spring. And as soon as he saw the nose ring and bracelets upon his sister's wrists, he went up to the man, who was still standing by the camels at the spring. "Come in, O blessed of the Lord," he said. "Why do you remain outside, when I have made ready the house and a place for the camels?"

So the man entered the house, and the camels were unloaded. The camels were given straw and fodder, and water was brought to bathe his feet, and the feet of the men who were with him. But when the food was set before him to eat, he said, "I will not eat until I have told my tale."

And Laban said, "Speak, then."

The servant told them about their relatives Abraham and Sarah, who had departed for Canaan more than half a century before. He told of how they had prospered and borne a son in their old age who would be their sole heir. Then he related how he met Rebekah by the well and the kindness she showed him. *"And now, if you mean to treat my master with true kindness, tell me. And if not, tell me also, that I may consider what course to pursue."*

Then Laban and Bethuel answered, "The matter was decreed by the Lord. We cannot speak to you bad or good. Here is Rebekah before you. Take her and go, and let her be a wife to your master's son, as the Lord has spoken."

When Abraham's servant heard this, he brought forth gifts of jewelry and garments for Rebekah. And he also gave gifts to her brother and her mother. Then they all ate and drank late into the night. *When they rose up in the morning, the servant said, "Give me leave to go to my master."*

And Rebekah's brother and mother said, "Let the girl stay with us a few days, at least ten. After that she shall go."

And he said to them, "Do not delay me, now that the Lord has made my errand successful."

*And they said, "We will call the girl and ask her to reply
from her own mouth." And they called Rebekah, and said to
her, "Will you go with this man?"*

And she said, "I will go."

*Then Rebekah and her maids arose, mounted the camels,
and followed the man. So the servant took Rebekah and went
his way.*

It's interesting to note the way Rebekah's character contrasts
with her brother Laban's. Laban is introduced here as the greedy
schemer in the family. He makes gestures of hospitality that echo
Rebekah's. But while she is moved by genuine openheartedness, his
motives are transparently mercenary and his speeches hypocritical.
On meeting the servant, Laban's eyes immediately latch on to the
jewelry he's brought as a gift for the bride. *As soon as he saw the
nose ring and bracelets upon his sister's wrists, he went up to the
man.* Only then does he invite his guest into his house. And later,
over dinner, after the servant has revealed that Rebekah's husband
would be a man of great wealth and substance, Laban pretends to be
moved by divine Providence—*"The matter was decreed by the
Lord. We cannot speak to you bad or good"*—even though we have
no reason to believe he acknowledges the God of Abraham.

I love the scene in which Rebekah decides to head off and
marry Isaac. When they call her forth and put it to her directly:
"Will you go with this man?" Rebekah doesn't miss a beat. She is
probably no more than fifteen or sixteen years old; Canaan is a
faraway wilderness, and Isaac is an unknown quantity. But the same
decisiveness she exhibited at the well comes through loud and clear:
"I will go."

Why is this woman-child so eager to go forth into the unknown? Apparently she's cut from the same risk-taking, pioneering
cloth as her relatives Abraham and Sarah. Like them, she is prepared
to trade in her comfortable city life for the rigors of a desert existence. Because she knows and trusts herself, she can go forth into an
unknown future without fear. Perhaps she has heard stories about
Abraham and Sarah, about how they tired of the materialistic life—
which her brother Laban exemplifies—and set off in search of a

more meaningful existence. Rebekah's spontaneous decision to marry a man she's never met in a faraway land may stem from her desire to get clear of her rapacious brother. Or maybe she's simply a young girl happy for the chance to leave home and spread her wings.

The meeting of Isaac and Rebekah has always struck me as an understated masterpiece of romantic literature:

> *Isaac, who had settled in the Negev, went out to meditate in the field at eveningtide.*

This was his favorite time of day, when the heat had lifted and the bright sun dimmed. He liked to get away from the noise and commotion of the camp to walk alone at day's end. Ever since his mother died there had been a gap in his life, one that would soon be filled by the arrival of his young bride. Isaac wondered what manner of woman she would be. Strong and hearty like his mother? Or like Hagar, dark and sultry? Would she be kind or shrewish?

As he paced the field, waiting for his bride to be brought to him, he felt as if his life was finally about to begin. Though he was forty years old, he had always dwelt in his father's shadow and still felt more like a boy than a man. Soon it would be his turn to lead, and today he would meet his partner for the future.

> *And he lifted up his eyes and saw camels approaching.*
>
> *Raising her eyes, Rebekah saw Isaac. She alighted from her camel and said to the servant, "Who is that man walking in the field to meet us?"*
>
> *And the servant said, "That is my master."*
>
> *So she took a veil and covered herself.*
>
> *Now the servant recounted to Isaac all things that he had done. And Isaac brought her to his mother Sarah's tent, and he took Rebekah, and she became his wife. Isaac loved her, and thus was comforted after his mother's death.*

When Isaac brings Rebekah into Sarah's tent, the bridge between the departed mother and the new bride is complete. The story highlights a telling psychological detail of their relationship: *Isaac loved her, and thus was comforted after his mother's death.* Though Sarah has been dead for several years, for Isaac, her tent has remained a symbol of maternal love. Rebekah is a comforting mother figure who makes Isaac whole again and enables him to face the future after his parents die.

I've always had a special feeling for Rebekah. I, too, was an only daughter. I met my future husband at the age of fifteen when he was visiting Israel from New York. He proposed almost immediately, and three years later I left Israel to be married and live with him in his country, among his family. Even though I was heartbroken to leave my family and country, I was thrilled at the thought of the unknown path that lay before me. Rather than worrying about what I was leaving behind or my parents' sadness, I put my complete trust in my new partner and the life we would share. Like Rebekah, I was young and fearless. Like Isaac, my young husband was mourning the recent death of his mother. And I was still grieving the loss of a beloved cousin who had fallen in battle. We "entered the tent" of our marriage and found comfort in each other's company.

COMMITTING TO THE FUTURE

Friends often share with me their ambivalence about committing to a marital relationship. "Is he 'Mr. Right'?" "Is she the woman I've been waiting for?" "Am I ready for this commitment?"

I usually respond with a few well-worn questions of my own: At the end of a long day when you are about to close your bedroom door, is this the person you most want to be with?

Next I ask them: When you picture this person in your mind's eye, is this the man or woman you want to be with in your thirties, your forties, your fifties? Is this someone with whom you can envision facing hardship, be it financial, emotional, or physical? Is this someone with whom you can imagine growing old, with all that aging entails?

Have you spent enough time together in varied and difficult circumstances to feel you know each other's character and have seen it tested?

Have you shared each other's life story in detail?

Have you met each other's family?

Is this someone you can laugh and giggle with? Do you bring out the child in each other? Are you comfortable being silly with each other?

And finally: Do you and this person share a common vision of how to raise children?

When conflicts surrounding child-rearing arise in the marriages of my friends and patients, I always ask if these issues were discussed or thought about beforehand. And almost universally, they were not. "We talked about children and both said we wanted them very much," is a typical response. This is a necessary starting point, but should only be the beginning of a more in-depth exploration of topics such as education, religion, parenting roles, and the role of extended family in the children's lives.

A good marriage should serve our psychological, sexual, social, and economic needs. A good marriage is something both partners want to "build up" rather than make sacrifices for. A good marriage should enrich, not diminish, us. A good marriage deserves to be nurtured and protected.

I feel that we need to look upon marriage as an institution that doesn't just serve the bride and groom, but benefits three generations: the grandparents, the parents, and the children. These three generations provide stability, structure, and nurture for each other. And in the end, they provide the only lasting continuity and personal history we can integrate into our lives.

The first family of Genesis continually looks backward to its parents and grandparents for role models and the roots of its identity. And it looks forward to its children's future for hope and continuity. When we choose a mate for life, we share everything that endows our family with strength: our identity, our sense of belonging, and our destiny.

Abraham was old, and well advanced in age; and the Lord had blessed Abraham in all things. And Abraham breathed his last, dying at a good ripe age, old and contented. And he was gathered to his people. And his sons Isaac and Ishmael buried him in the cave of Machpelah, in the field of Ephron the Hittite, which Abraham purchased from the Hittites. There was Abraham buried, and his wife Sarah.

After the death of Abraham, God blessed his son Isaac.

The essence of Abraham's character can be summed up in the single line describing his death: *Abraham breathed his last, dying at a good ripe age, old and contented.* It doesn't suggest that his life was easy. He acted in harmony with his personal values and, to the best of his ability, pursued his goals without moral compromise. His identity was firmly rooted in his fidelity to the covenants he forged—with God, with Sarah, with the land, and with the future generations of his family. Having taken all possible measures to provide for his descendants, Abraham bequeathed them the invaluable legacy of continuity. His two sons, Isaac and Ishmael, are reunited at his funeral. And God's blessing passes, as promised, to Isaac after Abraham's death.

In the end Abraham's faith triumphs over circumstances. At every stage of his life's journey he counts himself as blessed, regardless of the obstacles in his path. The quality that marks Abraham as a great leader and patriarch is his integrity. His faith is integrated into the fabric of his day-to-day life, and his priorities are ordered and clear. As Abraham breathes his last, we know he does not fear death—because he has never feared to go forth into life.

ISAAC RECLAIMS THE LAND: PRESERVING FAMILY TRADITIONS

The wilderness and the parched land shall be glad,
and the desert shall rejoice and blossom as the rose.
. . . For in the wilderness shall waters break out
and streams in the desert.

—Isaiah 35:1–6

In our immigrant society, we admire self-made men and women. Our country was built by aggressive self-starters who weren't afraid to take risks in untried areas—characteristics that our culture exalts and glorifies. But the children who grow up in the shadow of these groundbreaking pioneers often pay a heavy price for their parents' success. They face an uphill struggle to make their own mark in a landscape shaped by those who came before. As Adin Steinsaltz notes in his book *Biblical Images*:

History is full of big fathers who leave no space for their sons to prove themselves. The task of successor has always been one of the most unrewarding of all the tasks in history. It has often been said that "all beginnings are difficult," but continuation can be even more difficult. The capacity to persist is no less important than the power to begin.

The challenge for Isaac is to demonstrate his capacity to persist in his father's daunting footsteps. The stakes are high—the survival of his clan and its special destiny hang in the balance. Once his father is gone, Isaac will have to discover for himself how to adapt his unique talents to his new leadership role. Like Isaac, each of us must draw on our unique talents to create a life in our own image.

From childhood, Isaac had been groomed to be the heir to his father's covenant with God. When Abraham died, Ishmael returned for the funeral at the cave of the Machpelah. Reconciled at their father's graveside, the half brothers went their separate ways once again. Ishmael returned to Paran, and Isaac journeyed south, alone now with Rebekah.

It isn't long before Isaac is faced with his first test as the leader of the clan. Like his father, he is confronted with a drought-ridden landscape and hostile neighbors. Like each of the patriarchs, he has to begin anew to blaze his own path through the wilderness. As we will see, Isaac meets the challenge in his own style and forges a personal bond with his God and the land in harmony with his own personality and temperament.

> *There was a famine in the land and Isaac went to the land of the Philistines in Gerar.*
>
> *And the Lord appeared to Isaac and said, "Do not go down to Egypt. Stay in the land which I point out to you. Reside in this land and I will be with you and bless you. I will give all these lands to you and to your offspring, fulfilling the oath that I swore to your father Abraham. I will make your descendants as numerous as the stars of the heaven, and give to*

them all these lands, so that all the nations of the earth shall bless themselves by your offspring."

Isaac sowed in that land and reaped a hundredfold the same year. The Lord blessed him, and the man grew richer and richer until he was very wealthy. He acquired flocks and herds, and a large household, so that the Philistines envied him. And the Philistines stopped up all the wells which his father's servants had dug in the days of his father Abraham, filling them with earth. And Abimelech, the king of the Philistines, said to Isaac, "Go away from us, for you have become too numerous for us."

So Isaac moved on from that place. He began to redig the wells that his father had dug before him and that the Philistines had filled up after Abraham's death. And he gave these wells the same names that his father had given them. But every time that Isaac's men struck water, the local herdsmen quarreled with Isaac's men, claiming the water as their own. Each time Isaac dug another well, another dispute broke out. And each time Isaac decided not to fight, but to move on to another place. He saw no advantage in a confrontation, and he had the faith that God would guide him to water wherever he dug.

Finally he dug a well that no one else tried to claim, so he called it *Rehoboth*, meaning "broad space," saying, *"Now at last the Lord has granted us ample space to increase in the land."*

From there he went up to Beer-sheba. That night the Lord appeared to him and said, "I am the God of your father Abraham. Fear not, for I am with you, and I will bless you and increase your offspring for the sake of my servant Abraham." So he built an altar there and invoked the Lord by name. Isaac pitched his tent there and his servants started digging a well.

Abimelech came to visit Isaac there, accompanied by his counselor and the chief of his troops. *And Isaac said to them,*

"Why have you come to me, seeing that you have been hostile to me and have driven me away from you?"

And Abimelech said, "We now see plainly that the Lord has been with you, and we thought: 'Let there be a sworn treaty between our two parties, between you and us. Let us make a pact with you that you will not do us harm, just as we have not molested you but have always dealt kindly with you and sent you away in peace. From now on, be you blessed of the Lord!'"
Then Isaac made them a feast, and they ate and drank.

Early in the morning, they exchanged oaths. Isaac then bade them farewell, and they departed from him in peace. That same day Isaac's servants came and told him about the well they had dug and said to him, "We have found water!"

SUSTAINING
THE WELLSPRINGS
OF FAMILY STRENGTH

Like many sons of famous fathers, Isaac has to work hard at establishing his own identity. Born to his parents late in their lives, he has an overprotective mother, a brawny, much older half brother, and a father whose accomplishments he can never hope to equal. But Isaac's reserved personality proves essential to the spiritual continuity and physical survival of his generation.

Again, Steinsaltz emphasizes the importance of the second generation:

In all significant revolutions in history, the "founding fathers" have to struggle against formidable objective forces and circumstances. But the verdict of history concerning their success, whether it was a glorious victory or merely a passing episode, lies with their successors—the generation who has to fix and stabilize the revolution. They have to dig again the wells that the fathers dug before them and that have become blocked up—to release the living waters and let them flow as they will.

Despite the long shadow cast by his father, Isaac plays a crucial role in his family's destiny. Most important, he survives amid hostile neighbors by accommodation and tenacity. While a more bellicose posture toward the Philistines may have been more heroic, it could also have resulted in the extinction of his clan. Isaac's personality—to avoid confrontation and seek stability—suits his position as the patriarch of the second generation, still a sojourner among strangers. When the Philistines fill up the wells his father dug, Isaac digs new wells. And when others claim his well water for their own, he grins and bears it. And then he begins to dig anew.

Isaac has inherited his father's capacity for faith. No matter where he digs, he hits water—not because of any magical powers, but because he believes in God's promise to protect and preserve him. His deeply held belief in their covenant endows his trials with a sense of purpose. So when he is forced away from the wells he has dug, Isaac has confidence that he will find water elsewhere. And when famine comes and God tells him to *reside in the land* and plant, Isaac *reaps a hundredfold in the same year*. Not because of some innate "green thumb," but because he trusts in the internal voice that guides him—and continues to follow that voice until *"at last the Lord has granted us ample space to increase in the land."*

Finally, the Philistines recognize what Isaac has known since childhood: God has blessed him and is watching over him. Though he will never be the pioneering patriarch that his father was, Isaac has inherited his parents' most precious legacy: fidelity to their covenant with God. When Isaac faces his first crisis after his father's death, God appears to him and reassures him that the covenant He made with his father is still in force. God's reminder: *"Fear not! I am with you."* becomes this family's perennial inoculation against despair and defeatism.

Isaac's main task is to put down roots in the land of Canaan, which he achieves literally by planting crops and digging wells to water them. Isaac makes his mark as his family's first farmer. Even though Isaac achieves nothing spectacular in his lifetime, he makes a lasting contribution to his clan by staying on the land, cultivating it, and securing it for future generations. He redigs his father's wells, which are his family's lifeline to the soil. He preserves his family's traditions, ensuring the continuity and stability necessary for the survival of his wandering tribe.

Here in Washington, DC, where so many people have moved from other regions of the country, I am always mindful of the importance of home and place. One of my psychotherapy patients was a foreign-service officer who had been on the move all his adult life, relocating every few years. His father had also worked in the foreign service, moving his family from country to country with every changing assignment. Some time ago my patient inherited his family's farm on the eastern shore of Maryland. It was the place where the family alighted every summer for vacation, a still point in their lives of constant movement.

Over the ensuing years, the farm became a financial burden to his family, as well as a sore point between him and his wife, who resented having to shoulder responsibility for this family "heirloom." But this farm, despite its rocky soil and poor drainage, held the happiest memories of his childhood and of his parents. The more strength he drew from these memories, the more he realized how much of his personal identity was tied up in preserving the farm that his parents had bequeathed to him. He knew that if he sold the farm, his children would be cut off from this wellspring of family continuity that had by now become an indelible part of *their* youth.

What we learn as we grow older is that within our most private selves, we are what we remember. And we remain in touch with who we are *because* we remember.

A wife of another foreign-service officer once confided to me her perennial coping mechanism for maintaining a sense of home amid a life of constant movement. Wherever she and her family relocated, for however short a period of time, she pretended to herself that it was their home for the rest of their lives. As soon as the movers had unpacked, she put the curtains up, hung the family photos on the wall, and adorned the apartment with all the accumulated knickknacks that created a sense of familiarity and continuity.

In this era of constant mobility, it's easy to feel homeless and rootless. We are more and more cut off from our pasts, and in our increasingly peripatetic society, our souls become starved for a place to call our own—a place that was, is, and will always be, home.

JACOB AND ESAU, THE PRIMAL RIVALS: YEARNING FOR A FATHER'S LOVE

The fathers have eaten sour grapes, and the children's teeth are set on edge.

—*Jeremiah 31:29*

Men who grow up with absent or emotionally distant fathers often spend the rest of their lives compensating for the lack of a loving male role model in their youths. If they are fortunate enough to have a strong and supportive mother, they can become high achievers, though they often continue to strive for the approval of surrogate father figures in the worlds of business, the arts, the professions, or politics. Other men face a long uphill struggle against feelings of failure and inadequacy. In Jacob, the Bible presents us with a test case of a neglected son who strives throughout his life to win a father's blessing. His story details the ongoing battle to overcome the insistent doubts and insecurities that haunt him.

Jacob is one of the most compelling characters in Genesis, perhaps because he seems the most modern. Since we are privy to every biographical detail, from his prenatal life to his deathbed, Jacob emerges as Genesis's most psychologically developed personality. In Jacob we meet the Bible's first antihero: emotionally overwrought, easily manipulated, and prone to spontaneous outbursts of weeping. Hardly the cloth that great patriarchs are cut from. And yet we soon recognize Jacob as the hero of his generation, an inspired but flawed figure destined to be both humbled and exalted, disgraced and delivered.

A wayward character propelled by unconscious drives, Jacob's dreams serve as his channel markers through the rocky shoals of life. While his story reads like a melodrama of family discord and marital woe, it is highlighted by Jacob's transcendent visions of his true spiritual identity and destiny. He clings tenaciously to these fleeting epiphanies, endures the endless travails of his life, and eventually emerges as an integrated adult prepared to lead his tribe.

We identify with Jacob's journey because his feelings of inadequacy are so familiar. Like many of us, he feels overwhelmed by the demands and expectations of the people in his life, and trapped by his position in his family. He is the second son in a patriarchal clan, whose mother is overbearing and whose father is emotionally remote. His older brother is overpowering, his father-in-law manipulative, and his wives impossible to please. As a father, Jacob will find only more heartache, visiting the sins of his parents on his own children.

And yet Jacob prevails.

By dint of tenacity and vision, he triumphs over the unfair and uncontrollable circumstances of his life—as well as his self-created obstacles. His struggle becomes heroic when he stops running from adversity and finally musters the courage to face his problems. Jacob's story is a hopeful one for us because it celebrates the power of human endurance and offers the possibility of authentic personal transformation.

Jacob and his twin brother, Esau, act out the most primal of sibling rivalries. Their competition reflects the opposing forces at war within their family, and specifically, within their parents' marriage. But at the end of the story it will fall to the grown brothers to bind their family together and take charge of their own lives. To do so, they must close the cycle of rivalry and betrayal their parents left them, bury decades-old resentments, and find reconciliation in each other's arms.

Isaac and Rebekah were a loving and passionate couple who were once observed through a window by the Philistine king Abimelech *sporting with one another.* But like Abraham and Sarah before them, Isaac and Rebekah were unable to conceive for many years. *Isaac pleaded with the Lord on behalf of his wife, because she was barren. And the Lord responded to his plea, and his wife Rebekah conceived.*

But when Rebekah finally became pregnant, it felt more like a curse than a blessing as her twins battled in her womb. *They struggled within her,* making their mother so miserable that she cried out to God, *"Why do I exist?"* She went to inquire of the Lord, and the Lord answered her:

"Two nations are in thy womb,

Two separate peoples shall issue from thy body;

One people shall be mightier than the other,

And the older shall serve the younger."

Rebekah was racked by pain, as if her womb had become a battleground—which in fact it had. For Jacob and Esau had already begun their decades-long struggle for primacy. They kicked and wrestled in the watery darkness, two bodies feeding off one placenta, fighting for nourishment and—most of all— for a space apart from the other self.

As the labor contractions began, the two infants jockeyed for position, pressing their way down through the birth canal. Esau, the stronger, fought his way out of the womb, winning the status of firstborn son. *Then his brother emerged, holding on to the heel of Esau,* as if to pull him back inside. Jacob had lost the first round of their sibling rivalry, and from that moment forward he would always be playing catch-up, forever chasing the shadow self of his twin brother whom he could never quite catch, and never overcome.

Even at birth Esau emerged ruddy and hairy, flush with male hormones. Jacob, by contrast, was the pale runt of the litter. Their father, Isaac, was watchful for innate signs of strength and leadership. Already sixty years old when his twin sons were born, he naturally saw his firstborn, the stronger of the two, as the spiritual heir promised him that long-ago night in Beersheba when the Lord had appeared to him, saying, *"I am the God of your father Abraham. Fear not, for I am with you, and I will bless you and increase your offspring."*

As he grew into manhood, Esau became *a cunning hunter and a man of the field. Isaac loved Esau, because he did eat of his venison.* Isaac, grown old and infirm, drew comfort from this robust young man who hunted game for his father's pleasure—a welcome contrast to Isaac's own youthful self. Esau reminded Isaac of his older brother, Ishmael, *a wild ass of a man,* who was master of the bow and the sword, if not his own temper. It was best, he thought, that the next generation be led by a virile man of action.

Jacob was a quiet man, dwelling in tents. And Rebekah loved Jacob. Rebekah's marriage to Isaac began as a great romance. But now that she was increasingly deprived of her aged husband's love and attention, Rebekah turned to her younger son for companionship. He became the focus of all her hopes and plans for the future. True, he was introverted, a bit over-sensitive, and quick to tears. But he had her intuition, her intelligence, and, most important, her patience. She taught him the lesson of the disenfranchised: observe your adversary closely, watch for his point of weakness, and wait for the moment to take advantage.

Though secure in his mother's love, the adolescent Jacob yearned to break free of her and replace Esau at the center of his father's affections. Now that he'd grown into manhood, Jacob craved a male role model and a relationship with his emotionally distant father. He resented Esau's ancestral birthright and plotted patiently to win it from him. . . .

Once when Jacob was cooking a stew, Esau came in from the field, famished. Jacob had been inside his tent all day, cooking the lentils and spices over a low heat as his mother had taught him. Esau stuck his red-maned head into the pot and inhaled deeply. He reached a hand inside, his muscular arm drenched and glistening with sweat from his labors. But the stew was boiling to the touch and Jacob clutched his ladle out of sight behind his back.

And Esau said to Jacob, "Give me some of that red pottage to gulp down, for I am faint."

Jacob, sensing for the first time leverage over his older twin brother, held out for a lopsided exchange: *"Sell me first your birthright."*

Esau, who had always taken his father's love for granted and couldn't see beyond the moment, replied, *"I am at the point of death, so what use to me is my birthright?* Give me some stew!"

But Jacob insisted, "Swear to me first."

So he swore to him and sold Jacob his birthright. And Jacob gave Esau bread and lentil stew. And he ate and he drank and he rose and he went off. Thus did Esau spurn his birthright.

THE TYRANNY OF SELF-GRATIFICATION

Jacob doesn't win anything tangible in this scrimmage, which amounts to little more than brotherly horseplay. Esau's agreeing to trade his birthright for a bowl of stew doesn't change their position in the family or the laws of primogeniture, which dictate that the first son will be his father's direct heir. But as a prologue to the future contest for the leadership of their family, this scene offers us important insights into both brothers' character.

Esau takes his privileged position so much for granted that he lightly makes sport of it. When he *spurns his birthright,* Esau rejects his identity and belittles his destiny. He effectively cancels himself out of the future leadership of his clan, in much the same way that Lot secedes from the family when he moves his camp to Sodom. For a moment's pleasure, Esau forfeits his claim to a glorious future. Esau's need for instant gratification is a serious weakness in a leader, and it tips us off to his shortcomings as a potential patriarch. His thoughtless haste is underlined by the string of short verbs used to describe his actions—*And he ate and he drank and he rose and he went off*. His preoccupation with the present moment also blinds him to his brother's jealous scheming.

Jacob's behavior is equally telling. He understands that his brother is the slave, not the master, of his appetites—and he doesn't hesitate to exploit this weakness. As the physically weaker younger brother, Jacob has to press whatever strategic advantage he has, be it through guile or opportunism. Unlike his brother, Jacob is clearly a man who thinks about and plans for the future. Jacob knows that if he patiently bides his time, he will find a way to supplant his older sibling. What he doesn't yet grasp is the high emotional cost of such a gambit.

THE PERENNIAL CURSE OF SIBLING RIVALRY

Sibling rivalry is without doubt *the* defining conflict in this first family of Genesis—and it remains as omnipresent today as it was in biblical times. Why is competition between siblings so universal? Anyone born into a family of more than one child is subject to this innate clash of self-interests. The womb where Jacob and Esau contest for supremacy becomes a symbol of the constricting confines of any sibling relationship. Anyone who's ever seen a sonogram of prenatal twins can appreciate just how physically Jacob and Esau competed for nurture in their mother's womb. There never seems to be enough space, enough food, enough attention.

The family is a microcosm for the larger world, the first place where we learn to compete for the things we need. Ideally, the family offers us an opportunity to learn cooperation and tolerance. But all too often, the first lesson we learn from family life is that there is never quite enough love to go around. No matter how attentive our parents are, we never get all the approval we crave. Esau's anguished cry in the next scene, *"Have you but one blessing, my father?"* resounds in the heart of every child who has ever felt displaced in his parents' heart by a brother or sister.

This points to an important truth about rival siblings: they do not so much compete *with* each other as *for* their parents' attention and love. There is nothing in this story to suggest that Jacob dislikes Esau personally. He's simply jealous of his older brother's access to his father. And like Cain before him, Jacob's compulsion to act out his competitive urges will earn him the exact opposite of the blessing he seeks. Jacob himself will become a fugitive and a wanderer on the earth, on the run from his vengeful brother, cut off from both his father and his mother.

WHEN THE SINS OF THE PARENTS ARE VISITED ON THEIR CHILDREN

When the Book of Exodus speaks of *visiting the guilt of the fathers upon the children, unto the third and fourth generations,* it refers to the destructive patterns of behavior that are passed from parents to children to grandchildren. Whether it is alcoholism, child abuse, or—in the case of this story—parental favoritism, we are likely to transmit our internal conflicts to future generations unless we confront and resolve them.

Jacob and Esau's struggle in their mother's womb symbolizes the degree to which our sibling rivalry is shaped by our family's history. Like any family, this one demonstrates how far back patterns of behavior reach. By examining the building blocks of the family dynamic that these twin brothers inherit, we can trace the cycles of deception and favoritism back several generations to their roots.

Isaac is the textbook son of a famous man, overshadowed by the accomplishments of those who came before him. His father,

Abraham, was a pioneering man of faith who forged a covenant with God and followed a vision to a promised land. Isaac was also preceded by Ishmael—*a wild ass of a man*—his elder half brother by thirteen years who was endowed with both physical strength and a virile personality.

When his twin sons are finally born, Isaac naturally gravitates toward the stronger, more virile of the two—the robust boy Isaac always wanted to be. *Esau was a cunning hunter and a man of the field* who reminds Isaac of his half brother Ishmael who had been so skilled with the bow. Esau courts his father's love by bringing him choice meats and *Isaac loved Esau, because he did eat of his venison.* As with many families, food has become a vehicle for acting out issues of control and love. Isaac returns Esau's love by demonstrating partiality toward the son who hunts for him and through whom he experiences vicarious virility.

Isaac is a patriarch in the twilight of his life who symbolically and literally can't see his sons for who they really are. He mistakes Esau's superficial dominant traits as leadership qualities, and he is blind to Jacob's fierce need for his father's love and blessing. Jacob, deprived of an attentive father figure, will be doomed to repeat his father's favoritism toward his own sons, with disastrous results. Another generation of fraternal harmony will be sacrificed to a father's insensitively apportioned love.

Jacob is fortunate to have a positive role model of male leadership in his grandfather, Abraham. We can assume that Rebekah, who is grooming Jacob to become the next patriarch, has taken care to inculcate her son with stories about his pioneering grandparents. This intergenerational link to the first patriarch, his vision and his covenant with God, will continue to bail this family out of its worst crises. This is the hidden strength of any extended family in any age: children can find role models in several generations, be they parents or grandparents, aunts or uncles.

Having an aggressive older brother precede him into the world makes Jacob feel he can never compete head-to-head with Esau for his father's affections. He has to learn to get around his physically stronger brother by playing on his weaknesses. Thus begins a lifelong pattern of meeting physical strength with cunning. But this survival strategy is ultimately self-defeating. The more successful

Jacob becomes at outwitting his brother, the more precarious his position in the family.

Jacob's bond with his mother is indispensable to his early development. It is from his mother that he learns his leadership skills of perseverance, self-discipline, and strategic planning. And though he doesn't yet grasp his destiny as a patriarch, his mother's focused love clearly builds his sense of identity and purpose. But as he grows older, Jacob needs an adult male role model. Mothers represent the world "inside tents," where Jacob dwells with Rebekah. The knowledge of this domain is intuitive and observational. The father's archetypal domain is the outside world, "in the fields," where Esau hunts for his father's game and learns to survive by the sword. Every child needs both a mother's and a father's love to mature as an integrated adult.

I'm intrigued by how consistently the Book of Genesis stresses the indispensable role of an involved father in a child's upbringing. The enduring value of a strong male presence in a child's life has never been more evident than it is today. In his book *Iron John*, Robert Bly explores the costs to boys of having absent, remote, or alcoholic fathers. He could be describing Jacob when he notes that sons who are deprived of access to their fathers develop a "father-hunger" that will afflict them all their lives. As Bly explains: "Women cannot, no matter how much they sympathize with their starving sons, replace that particular substance." Likewise, "a mother's protection, no matter how well intentioned, will not do as a substitute for a father's protection."

Although Jacob is much more successful than Esau at mastering his appetites, he will never fully recover from his "father-hunger."

THE GREAT DECEPTION:
SEEKING A BLESSING,
FINDING A CURSE

*The bread of deceit is sweet to a man. But
afterwards his mouth shall be filled with gravel.*

—*Proverbs 20:17*

any families that harbor underlying tensions between
the mother and father have a tendency to split into
two camps. More often than not, the family members
remain unconscious or in denial of this truth—until circumstances
bring the two opposing sides into open conflict. But by that time it
is often impossible to prevent a catastrophic head-on collision.

The day of reckoning between Jacob and Esau arrives when the
brothers are approaching manhood and their father, Isaac, is drawing near to death. The fateful showdown between the sibling rivals
is one of the most masterfully conceived dramas in the Bible. While

you read, imagine watching it unfold on a stage divided into two areas: inside of the old patriarch's tent, and just outside it—beyond his sight, but not necessarily beyond his hearing. It's a set piece worthy of Shakespeare—part tragedy, part farce, and altogether human.

> *When Isaac was old and his eyes were too dim to see, he called his older son Esau and said to him, "I am old now, and do not know how soon I may die. Take your gear, your quiver and your bow, and go out into the field and hunt me a deer. Then prepare me a savory stew, such as I like, that I may give you my innermost blessing before I die."*

Standing just outside the tent, Rebekah overheard Isaac's request. Even on his deathbed, her husband's thoughts turned to Esau—not to her, and certainly not to her favorite son. She knew she must act quickly if she was to act at all.

Rebekah had a broader agenda than merely giving Jacob a leg up in the world. And her motives were more complicated than a parent playing favorites with her children. She was haunted by the prophecy revealed to her by God during her painful pregnancy.

> *"Two nations are in thy womb,*
> *two separate peoples shall issue from thy body;*
> *One people shall be mightier than the other,*
> *And the older shall serve the younger."*

For two decades Rebekah had carried this secret inside her heart, watching and waiting for this promise from God to be fulfilled. Now Isaac lay dying. In an hour he would formally bless Esau and anoint him as the leader of the next generation. What should she do? Remain faithful to her husband, or to God's vision for her family? Who knew her sons' character better than the mother who carried them in her womb, and who could better choose between them? If God had elected Jacob to lead, who was Isaac to deny her younger son what God had promised?

She decided. The time had come to intervene in her family's destiny and help bring God's prophecy to fruition. Calling Jacob to her tent, she whispered: *"Now my son, listen carefully as I instruct you. Go to the flock and fetch me two choice goats, and I will make of them a dish for your father, such as he likes. Then take it to your father to eat, in order that he may bless you before he dies."*

Jacob trembled at these words, remembering how his brother hunted wild animals with his bare hands. He answered his mother fearfully in a vain attempt to extricate himself, *"But my brother Esau is a hairy man and I am smooth-skinned. If my father touches me I shall appear to him a trickster and bring upon myself a curse, not a blessing."*

Rebekah considered telling Jacob about the prophecy and explaining all that God had in store for him. But if Jacob understood what was truly at stake he might lose his nerve. She'd seen him go to pieces before, crying like a child at the slightest provocation—his brother's teasing or her own rebuke. Even now she could see the telltale signs of stress quivering around his eyes and lips. But now was the time for action, not handholding. *"Your curse, my son, be upon me! Just do as I say and go fetch the goats for me."*

Jacob hesitated another moment. But she stared him down, and, as usual, he bent to her will.

So he brought Rebekah the goats, averting his eyes as she slit their throats and dressed them for the stew. Skillfully she skinned the animals and wrapped their fur around Jacob's arms, hands, and neck to simulate his brother's hairy body. Jacob recoiled under the touch of the bloody skins, gagging back his disgust. He would not let himself be sick. He would compel his legs to cease their shaking, though his heart raced and cried out for flight.

Next Rebekah dressed him in Esau's clothing, drawing the garment tight around Jacob's slender frame. Then she shut her eyes and ran her hands across his chest and arms. Could this possibly work? Isaac might have been blind, but he still had his wits about him. Could her goat stew pass as venison? The younger son as the elder? She said a silent prayer to God, then gazed into Jacob's eyes, smiling her encouragement. She passed him the piping hot stew and pressed him toward the entrance to Isaac's tent.

Jacob crept inside the tent and stood silently before his father's bed. Isaac stirred at the smell of the stew and turned his head in Jacob's direction.

"Which of my sons are you?"

Jacob was finally facing his father, poised to ask for the blessing and the love he had always craved. But this moment of truth, for which he had waited a lifetime, was doomed to deception. *"I am Esau, your firstborn. I have done as you bid me. Arise, I pray thee, sit and eat my venison, that you may give me your innermost blessing."*

"How did you perform this so quickly, my son?"

A dread pause. Then, on impulse: *"Because the Lord your God granted me good fortune."*

"Come near that I may feel you, whether you be my son Esau or not." Jacob moved closer, and Isaac caressed his goat-skinned arms and hands. *"The voice is the voice of Jacob, yet the hands are the hands of Esau."* But the old man was not altogether convinced. *"Are you really my son Esau?"*

In a deeper voice, *"I am."*

Reassured, Isaac ate the stew and drank the wine Jacob offered him. Jacob watched as his father licked the bowl clean, smiling contentedly.

"Come close and kiss me, my son."

Jacob stiffened. Did he dare kiss his father and risk detection? He moved closer to the old man, and they embraced. Jacob buried his head in his father's neck and kissed him, searching his mind in vain for memories of this fatherly embrace. Perhaps they dwelt only in his dreams. He choked back a sob, clenching his teeth against the tears exploding in his eyes.

Isaac pressed his face into Jacob's shoulder and breathed in deeply. *"Ah, the smell of my son is as the smell of the field which the Lord hath blessed."* Then, holding him at arm's length and gazing at him with sightless eyes, Isaac blessed his son:

"May God give you the dew of heaven,
And the fat of the earth,
And plenty of corn and wine.
Let peoples serve you,
And nations bow down to you.
Be lord over your brothers,
And let thy mother's sons bow down to you.
Cursed be they that curse you,
And blessed be they that bless you."

The blessing conferred, the old man reclined back onto his bed to digest his meal. Without another word, Jacob slipped out of the tent.

No sooner had Jacob left the presence of his father than his brother Esau came back from his hunt. He, too, had prepared a dish and brought it to his father. "Let my father sit up and eat of his son's game, so that you may give me your innermost blessing."

His father said to him, "Who are you?"

"I am your son, Esau, your firstborn!"

Isaac was seized with a violent trembling. "Your brother came with guile and took away your blessing. I blessed him; now he must remain blessed."

When Esau heard his father's words he broke into wild and bitter sobbing. "Have you but one blessing, my father? Bless me too, Father!" And Esau lifted up his voice and wept aloud.

But it was too late. Isaac had bestowed his blessing on Jacob, and Esau was doomed to serve his younger brother. *And Esau hated Jacob because of the blessing that his father had given him. And Esau said in his heart: "Let the days of mourn-*

ing for my father be at hand. Then will I slay my brother Jacob."

When the words of Esau were reported to Rebekah, she sent for her younger son Jacob and said to him, "Your brother Esau is consoling himself by planning to kill you. Now my son, listen to me. Flee at once to Haran, to my brother Laban. Stay with him awhile, until your brother's anger subsides and he forgets what you have done to him. Then I will fetch you from there. Let me not lose you and my husband both in one day."

Then Rebekah, in order to cover her younger son's tracks, told Isaac that she was sending Jacob to her brother's village to find a wife. Like Abraham before her, she argued for the merits of finding her son a bride from the "old country." *"If Jacob marries a Hittite woman from among the native women, what good will life be to me?"*

Strangely, Isaac never raised the issue of the stolen blessing with either Jacob or Rebekah. Could it be that he was somehow complicit in their deception? Perhaps he knew in his soul that Esau, his favorite, lacked the qualities to lead. He would never have had the heart to disinherit Esau himself. But when Rebekah provided him the opportunity to disbelieve his senses . . .

Isaac blessed Jacob, invoking Abraham's name to guide him through his exile:

"May the Lord bless you, make you fertile and numerous so that you become an assembly of peoples. May He grant the blessing of Abraham to you and your offspring, that you may possess the land where you are sojourning, which God gave to Abraham."

Rebekah held her son long and close in her arms—for the last time, she feared. But she had no regrets, and she wept not. With a final kiss and caress, she ushered her son out of her tent, and Jacob departed for Haran.

WHEN CHILDREN
BECOME HOSTAGE TO THEIR
PARENTS' MARRIAGE

It is human and, to some degree, inevitable that every parent develops a closer rapport with one child than with another. Genesis makes no attempt to disguise Isaac and Rebekah's partiality from the very beginning: *Isaac loved Esau, because he did eat of his venison. . . . Jacob was a quiet man, dwelling in tents. . . . And Rebekah loved Jacob.* Because of this innate proclivity, we are cautioned to be especially vigilant in our efforts to make each child feel unique and special to us.

Unfortunately, there is also a natural temptation to use our relationship with a favorite child to compensate for emotional disappointments in our marriage. The story of Jacob and Esau is a strong warning to us of the danger to children when parents draw them into the shifting power balance of their marriage. Children need to grow and develop without feeling responsible for the emotional well-being of the adults in their lives. When we rob children of their childhood, we deprive them of their chance for graduated development and for personal autonomy.

Isaac and Rebekah's marriage begins as intensely romantic and, we are given to believe, passionate. But unlike Sarah and Abraham, who remain equal partners throughout their lives, Rebekah and Isaac drift apart, perhaps because of the age difference or because of his mental and physical decline. By the time they are finally blessed with twin sons, they seem to have lost touch with the intimacy that characterized the earlier years of their marriage. They pair off with their respective favorites and immediately create a schism in the family. To a degree, the parents compensate for the disappointments in their marriage and re-create a primary emotional bond with their favored child. Each child may benefit in the short run from the intense devotion of a single parent. But this new surrogate "marriage" between parent and child is fundamentally unequal and frustrating for the child, who needs the balance of both male and female role models.

As old age descends upon him, Isaac retreats from the demands of his marriage and his leadership position into a simpler relationship with Esau that revolves around traditional male bonding and food. As an old man both physically and emotionally detached from his wife, Isaac now finds his sensual gratification in eating, and this fixation on food becomes his "blind spot." When Rebekah plots to deceive him, she concocts a faux venison stew from goat. Isaac is presumably so focused on his hungry anticipation of his meal that he is distracted from his important paternal task of conferring his blessing on his firstborn son. Esau suffers a similar humiliation at the hands of his brother when he allows his hunger for a bowl of lentil stew to override his judgment.

Starved for her husband's companionship, Rebekah latches on to the younger son, who the father has ignored, who evokes both her love and protectiveness. She recognizes a kindred spirit in Jacob, a boy she can cultivate in her own image. Her maternal side is probably drawn to the physically weaker infant at birth. And as he grows, she keeps him close by her, *dwelling in tents,* where she can teach him to survive by his wits and to cultivate his innate leadership qualities. Though Rebekah is driven by the lofty goal of implementing God's prophecy that her *older shall serve the younger,* her tactics of pitting one son against the other ensure that her family will be driven apart.

Since his father is emotionally unavailable to him, Jacob can't extricate himself from his mother's influence, which only increases his feeling of powerlessness. Jacob's untenable position, pinioned between a strong-willed mother and an emotionally inaccessible father, comes to a head in the blessing scene when he must either defy his mother or deceive his father. By choosing the latter course, he destroys his last chance for what he most craves—his father's love. But Jacob is too tied to his mother to refuse. In the few moments he spends in his father's tent, Jacob tastes the sweet love from his father that Esau has enjoyed for years: the physical affection, the warmth of male bonding over food and drink. Jacob's tragedy is that by glimpsing the wonderful father-love he never received, he feels more deprived than ever. The guilt of deceiving his father and brother will haunt him for the next twenty years.

THE ART OF MAKING HARD CHOICES AND PAINFUL DECISIONS

Rebekah is often condemned for instigating the plot to deceive her husband and bestow Esau's blessing on Jacob. But it is important to keep in mind that Rebekah carries a burden of responsibility that goes beyond the immediate concerns of domestic harmony. As Isaac recedes into the passivity of old age, he leaves a leadership vacuum in the family, which Rebekah must fill. As with many couples where a husband becomes incapacitated by illness, the wife, Rebekah, evolves into the dominant member of the marriage, forced to make independent decisions on behalf of her family's future. But she has to work covertly from "within the tent." She does not have the option of replacing her infirm husband and conferring the blessing on Jacob herself.

Whether we interpret God's prophecy of Jacob's ascendancy literally or as a mother's intuition, it is clear that Rebekah is a keener judge of her sons' character than Isaac. Neither son is perfect, but she understands that Jacob has the tenacity and spiritual depth to become the next patriarch. And she takes her family's destiny seriously enough to intervene on behalf of future generations. The birthright may be Isaac's to bestow, but it is Rebekah who ultimately dictates who will receive it. And while it is easy for us to fault Rebekah for using deception to achieve her goal, she emerges as a proactive pragmatist who is willing and able to make tough decisions when circumstances demand. She, more than the men in her family, understands the gravity of the choices she must make. God speaks to Rebekah, not Isaac, about the future leadership of the family, and she does not shrink from the responsibility that receiving His prophecy confers on her.

Even though everything is foreseen by God—in this case, that her younger son shall rule over her older—Rebekah still has the obligation to exercise her free will. How does she weigh the damage to her family harmony against the larger goal of ensuring its future leadership? The hardest choices in life are the ones that reside in the gray areas. The right and wrong decisions are not always clearly distinguishable. Circumstances often require that we choose between two unsatisfactory options. But choose we must.

A close friend of mine faced one of these gray choices when, as an elderly man, he had to rewrite his will. One of his most valuable assets was a large library of rare books that had been passed down through three generations of the family. Traditionally, the eldest child had inherited the library, along with the responsibility for preserving and expanding it. My friend surmised that his oldest child appreciated the library more for its financial worth than its literary value. He feared that if this child encountered any future financial difficulty, he might begin selling off the library, one volume at a time.

His middle child, on the other hand, had always cherished the library, both as an intellectual property and as a bridge connecting multiple generations of the family. My friend trusted the middle child to preserve the library against the incursions of unforeseen circumstance. So he changed his will and left the library to her. It was an imperfect solution, and one that he agonized over at great length. He knew that by skipping over the eldest child, whom he dearly loved, he might well cause strife in the family after his death. But he felt a personal responsibility to make the wisest long-term decision—not on behalf of the books in the library, but for the sake of future generations of the family who were the heirs to this legacy. He had the maturity to make a tough choice when it would have been easier to simply yield to tradition.

SHIFTING ROLES AS COUPLES AGE

Often I have observed a couple starting out in marriage with carefully delineated gender roles, only to have those roles reverse as a couple matures. The change may occur when a spouse becomes ill and the healthy partner takes over. The role reversal can also result from a shift in family finances or in the changing professional fortunes of one spouse or the other. The most difficult, and not uncommon, shift of power happens when one of the partners becomes mentally infirm—a much tougher adjustment than a mere physical ailment. A trusting marriage will lay the groundwork for an orderly transfer of responsibility. But for most of us, the idea of fundamental change in a marriage due to illness or mental infirmity is too frightening to contemplate, much less plan for.

Rebekah, in contrast to Isaac, is decisive and proactive. When it comes time to wed, Rebekah is the one who leaves her homeland for a new life. When she is pregnant and suffering pain, it is Rebekah, not Isaac, *who inquires of the Lord*—and then keeps the information to herself. When Isaac is ready to pass on his blessing to the next generation, it is she who intervenes in the best way she knows how, and substitutes Jacob for Esau. Meanwhile, we find Isaac in his accustomed passive posture, on his back in his tent, blind to the machinations at work around him.

Rebekah assesses the situation, decides what to do, and takes responsibility for her actions independently, not burdening her aged and blind husband with weighty deliberations. But when reading the scene during which Isaac blesses Jacob, I get the eerie feeling that Isaac is aware that Jacob is dressed up as Esau. While his eyesight is failing, his other senses—smell, taste, and touch—are still acute. So it seems unlikely that he would mistake goat stew for his beloved venison, or Jacob for his favored son, Esau. If only subconsciously, he seems to play along with Rebekah's scheme, relieved that he doesn't have to choose the younger over the older. Rebekah has shielded Isaac from the painful duty of demoting his firstborn son to a subordinate status.

Rebekah goes on to protect Isaac from the painful facts of the violent falling-out between the two brothers. She fibs and says that Jacob is running off to find a suitable wife in Haran—by now a traditional mating ground in their family. The fact that Esau has vowed to murder Jacob is kept from the ailing Isaac, who simply rubber-stamps his wife's suggestion and sends Jacob on his way without reprimand and with yet another blessing.

THE BLESSING OF OUR PARENTS' LOVE

The message that comes through most strongly in the story of Jacob is that we all need to feel loved by our parents, that by internalizing the blessing of our parents' love we acquire self-esteem and self-confidence. God's continual emergence in Genesis as a loving parent figure underlines the direct connection between parental love and an integrated adult identity. The blessing God bestows on each generation of the first family of Genesis can best be understood as the prototype for the unconditional love we all desire from our parents, the approval we need to become self-sufficient adults.

It is impossible to overrate the value of this feeling of blessedness. It is the most fundamental building block of faith in ourselves. We all need to feel chosen and special. We all need to feel that we have a spiritual identity that cannot be undermined even by the most wretched misfortunes. And most of all, we need a sense of purpose, a belief that what we do matters—not just to ourselves but to those who will come after us.

Jacob and Esau show us how desperately children need their parents' love and how explicitly that love needs to be conveyed. The message of this story is that it is not enough for parents to *feel* love for their children. They need to articulate it verbally and express it physically. Parents need to find time to share with children, to listen to them, to teach them. Nothing can replace a parent's loving attention, and no child can get too much of it.

Jacob finds Isaac's blessing powerful because it is so explicit—even if it is intended for his brother. Isaac lays his hands on his son's head and wishes for him all the best that life has to offer. Judaism acknowledges the importance of ritualizing this explicit parent-child bond by instructing parents to bless their children every Friday night at the beginning of the Sabbath.

Being loving toward our children sounds easy. But it takes strength, patience, time, and even courage to give children the emotional affirmation they need—especially when what they need is for us to acknowledge that we may have caused them pain. The famous movie tag line: "Love means never having to say you're sorry" may have looked good on posters, but it stated the inverse of the truth. Had Isaac acknowledged Jacob's need for his attention, and perhaps apologized for his favoritism to Esau, the entire family might have been saved a lot of grief. Admitting to our adult children that we're less than perfect parents is a tough but necessary part of good parenting.

In my work, I have also been privy to the anguish of parents when confronted by accusatory children. It's taught me how important it is for adult children to temper the way they express their anger over past hurts. If the goal of candor in a family is to heal rather than destroy a relationship, we all need to think through the way we confront the people we love. The Fifth Commandment's instruction to *Honor your father and your mother* acknowledges that parents are tremendously vulnerable to the judgments of their children. When children first become aware of their parents' shortcomings, whether at age six or thirty-six, it is traumatic for both generations. Since most of us are someday destined to become parents, it behooves us to deal with our own parents' frailties with a degree of delicacy and respect.

HOW UNDERSTANDING YIELDS COMPASSION

It is often easier to idealize our parents than to acknowledge the real hurts they visited on us. We may feel that we are being unfaithful to our parents by reexamining how their shortcomings affected us. The point is not to assign blame for the problems in our lives. We do not mature or grow by blaming others. We look into our past to understand, not to blame. With understanding comes new insight, compassion, and forgiveness. The goal is to achieve enough understanding and compassion to take responsibility for our lives. The French have a saying that describes this process perfectly: *Tout comprendre c'est tout pardonner.* "When all is understood, all is forgiven."

My father was a strong moral and intellectual presence in my life, but painfully remote emotionally. As a little child I would beg him to let me climb on his knees, and I promised to sit still and not disturb his reading. With a pained expression he would acquiesce, only to put me down a short time later, claiming I was moving around too much. His coldness was deeply hurtful to me, despite all the love my mother lavished on me. As an adult, I came to understand that my father was reared in a Victorian family where displays of affection were frowned upon as overly sentimental. I saw that he simply never learned to express love, and that understanding helped me. But I still carried a lot of residual anger inside.

Not surprisingly, this anger resurfaced in my marriage. It used to depress me when my husband, Peter, chose to read on weekend afternoons instead of focusing on me. Reading was his way of unwinding from the week's work, but it made me feel neglected and ignored. When I criticized him for reading, he became irritated with me. I felt like a nag, which is something I'd sworn I'd never become. I felt unattractive and pathetic begging for his attention. And of course, his behavior never altered, because no one responds to hectoring. Worst of all, my anger kept ruining otherwise beautiful weekend afternoons.

One day, when I'd worked myself into a fury over Peter's reading a book instead of paying more attention to me, I had a strong emotional memory from my childhood. In retrospect the connection was obvious, but I had never made the association before. My father was a very scholarly man who would spend hours at home reading. When "Daddy" was reading, he always got the best armchair and was never to be disturbed. Of course, he seemed much more interested in his books than in me. But because reading was valued so highly in my family, I didn't allow myself to be angry. There was always a halo around him in that armchair, and he was always reading something esoteric—like twelfth-century Chinese history—which only made his preoccupation more sacrosanct and unassailable.

Once I realized that my anger at my husband had more to do with my father than with him, I could explain my feelings to Peter instead of just being upset with him. He wasn't magically transformed into the all-attentive male figure I probably yearned for on those weekend afternoons, but he was much more sensitive to my feelings on the subject. And more important, I felt less controlled by the situation. I've actually learned to enjoy the simple pleasure of sharing a quiet Sunday afternoon reading together on the back patio.

This is hardly an earthshaking insight, but it's the small victories over our personal demons that allow us to keep growing and enjoying life more fully. If there's one truth that Jacob's struggle illustrates, it's that there are no permanent solutions to life's problems, and there is certainly no state of ultimate perfection. Life is an unfolding mystery that demands our total ongoing involvement.

JACOB'S LADDER:
BEGINNING THE SLOW
CLIMB OUT OF DESPAIR

For He will give His angels charge over thee,

to keep thee in all thy ways.

—Psalms 91:11

Leaving home as a young person is one of the most stressful transitions in life. Whether we are going off to war or simply to college, cutting the ties to our parents and facing adult challenges for the first time is anxiety-provoking. Particularly when one sets out, as Jacob does, plagued by guilt, pursued by doubts, and propelled by adolescent yearnings. Jacob's exile is a long, lonely journey that will lead him from adolescence to mature middle age before finally carrying him home.

Like many mythic heroes, Jacob must seek out his destiny and forge his adult identity away from his clan. Abraham had to "Go forth" from Haran to find the promised land, and Jacob's son Joseph will also have to travel to a distant land before he rises to power and influence. Only Isaac remains in the land of Canaan throughout his life. And because he stays "at home," as God commands him, Isaac never experiences the cathartic personal transformation that the other patriarchs undergo.

In this episode Jacob's life "bottoms out." But he demonstrates the resilience to push off the floor of his despair and begin the long climb upward. He reaches out to his God at his moment of greatest need—and is answered. As Joseph Campbell has observed:

> From the bottom of the abyss comes the voice of salvation. The black moment is the moment when the real message of transformation is going to come. At the darkest moment comes the light.

Jacob left Beer-sheba and set out for Haran.

Jacob had not yet grasped the magnitude of his exile, nor realized that he would never see his mother or his father again. All he knew was that he was terribly alone—banished from his homeland, despised by his brother, and shamed before his dying father. The stolen blessing and birthright hung on him like a millstone. Grasping for love and acceptance, he had earned only hatred and self-contempt. How did he become an outcast from his own life, an orphan in the wilderness?

The road stretched before him, lonely and desolate as his heart. As the sun set, he crawled along the roadside, groping in the near-darkness for a place to rest. His hands found a round stone, still warm from the sun, and he drew it toward him. He rested his temple on the stone, a silent, soothing pillow, and prayed for refuge in sleep. . . .

He had a dream.

A ladder was set on the ground and its top reached the sky, and angels of God were going up and down on it.

And the Lord was standing beside him and He said, "I am the Lord, the God of your father Abraham and the God of Isaac. The ground on which you are lying I will give to you and your offspring. Your descendants shall be as the dust of the earth; you shall spread out to the west and the east, to the north and to the south. All the families of the earth shall bless themselves by you and your descendants. Remember, I am with you: I will protect you wherever you go and will bring you back to this land. I will not leave you until I have done what I have promised you."

Jacob awoke from his sleep and said, "Surely the Lord is present in this place, and I did not know it! This is the gateway to heaven."

Early in the morning, Jacob took the stone that he had put under his head and set it up as a pillar and poured oil on the top of it. He named that site Bethel, meaning "house of God."

Jacob then made a vow, saying, "If God remains with me, if He protects me on this journey that I am making, and gives me bread to eat and clothing to wear, and if I return safe to my father's house—the Lord shall be my God."

JACOB, THE FUGITIVE DREAMER

Jacob's ladder is the first explicitly recorded dream in the Bible. Writers and poets, philosophers and theologians have been busy deciphering and interpreting its symbols to this very day. This first biblical dream paints a compelling portrait of the psychological crossroads where Jacob now finds himself. And it shows us just how sophisticated the biblical authors were in portraying the unconscious mind several millennia before the advent of modern psychology.

The hidden meaning of dreams can often be traced to events and anxieties of the preceding day—what Freud described as "the day's residue." Freud also viewed dreams as "a disguised fulfillment of a repressed wish." If we examine the juxtaposition of Jacob's miserable day and the symbols at work in his dream, we can see how his unconscious mind is working overtime to resolve the conflicts that threaten to tear him apart.

Jacob is a fugitive, on the run from his brother's wrath and from his own shame. Even though he was manipulated by his mother into stealing his brother's blessing, Jacob is racked by guilt. Now that he has usurped the mantle of the covenant, he doubts whether he can fulfill its obligations. Having acquired his father's blessing under false pretenses, Jacob feels none of the validation he had hoped for. In fact, he feels the opposite: like a fraud and a thief. Though he was chosen by God to lead the next generation, Jacob doesn't feel deserving or blessed. He is starting out on a lonely journey of indeterminate length and uncertain destination. He feels lost and vulnerable, unsure of his ability to persevere.

Jacob manages to prevail over his moment of crisis. By tapping in to the same source of faith and inspiration as his father and grandfather before him. The ladder expresses his desire for upward transcendence, for deliverance from his earthly conflicts. Significantly, the angels are first going up, and then returning down the ladder. They are Jacob's messengers to God, expressing hope for inheriting the covenant, imploring comfort from the pain of his current crisis.

In his moment of most abject dejection and loneliness, Jacob cries out for help. God visits him for the first time in what we could call a wish-fulfillment dream. God promises him all that he has lost and has almost despaired of ever recovering: a family, a homeland, and most important, a feeling of being blessed. He offers Jacob a ladder out of his despair, a bridge connecting heaven and earth that reminds us of the rainbow of hope God offered Noah after the Flood. Jacob has a rough passage before him, but he knows for the first time that he will never be alone, that he is indeed special, wanted, and chosen. He knows that he has a purpose and a destination, that his life is more than a series of random acts.

Jacob can't quite absorb this long-awaited blessing. While the ladder in his dream points toward heaven, it remains a fragile stairway, only tenuously planted in the earth. Its top disappears unseen into the future, and nothing holds it up except Jacob's fledgling faith. Though a new sense of confidence and purpose has taken root in him, Jacob still lacks the mature faith of his father, Isaac, and his grandfather, Abraham. It was only a dream, after all. Who knows if a promise made during sleep is enforceable?

Responding in character to God's promise, Jacob answers conditionally. The best he can do is admit the possibility that God will deliver on His promise. *If* God protects him, clothes and feeds him, and leads him safely home again—only then will Jacob accept Him as his God. Jacob isn't ready to fully embrace his spiritual heritage. He doesn't yet feel deserving of his own love, much less God's. But the hope and solace he receives that night, when he needs it most, will sustain Jacob through years of lonely exile.

Dreams of Transcendence, Ladders of Hope

On another level, Jacob's ladder symbolizes his desire to relinquish his boyhood and take control of his adult life. He is cutting the ties to a strong mother and will soon meet his wife and lifelong love. The ladder can be seen as a phallic symbol, expressing Jacob's physical and sexual maturity. God's promise that *"your descendants shall be as the dust of the earth"* is Jacob's wishful fulfillment of his desire for virility and power.

While he is presently at the bottom rung of the ladder, merely beginning his ascent into manhood, Jacob is reaching out to the spiritual heights achieved by the men and women who have preceded him in the family. God reassures Jacob with the same promise he made to Abraham and Isaac: *"All the families of the earth shall bless themselves by you and your descendants."* Jacob's ladder expresses all his yearnings for a spiritual identity that transcends his domestic distress and harmonizes the two opposing poles in his psyche: the mother, represented by the earth, and the father, represented by the heavens.

Jacob teaches us why we must never give up hope or cave in to despair. He answers his fears with the internal command to "Fear not," and whenever he reaches a seeming dead end in his life, he manages to find a way to "Go forth." Jacob is more than merely a self-absorbed neurotic, because he hitches his life to a set of moral and spiritual values that is larger than himself, that transcends the mundane conflicts of his day-to-day existence and imposes meaningful priorities. Like all of us, he is often besieged by self-doubt and anxiety about the future. Yet he is constantly reaching beyond the confines of his daily routine to try to endow his life with larger meaning. Spiritually, Jacob is upwardly mobile.

Like Jacob, we all face difficult passages through life—troubling nights when we are consumed by fears at four in the morning and the dawn seems days away. And like Jacob, we are always standing before the "gateways to heaven," which wait to swing open when we least expect them. But we must first reach out for help and look inward for direction. If we first dispatch emissaries of hope, angels of faith may return to us in kind. Ladders are constantly being lowered into our lives when we have almost despaired of finding an exit. Sometimes they take the form of a teacher or a friend. Other times they appear as personal or professional opportunities. But it falls to us to take the first steps, one rung at a time, beginning at the bottom of whatever ladder we face.

No matter how defeated we feel by the earthly events that swirl around us, we must remember we have a spiritual identity that cannot be diminished or modified by external circumstances. Being created in the image of God means we have the imagination and intelligence—indeed, *the obligation*—to transcend our doubts and emerge from whatever pit of despair we have dug for ourselves. The Talmud reminds us that the conscious exercise of hope is a gift we are obliged not to forsake. Faith in our enduring identity with God is the ladder of hope within each of our grasps.

JACOB MARRIES THE SISTERS: RUNNING HEADLONG INTO DARKNESS

You shall not put an obstacle in the way
of the blind.

—*Leviticus 19:14*

A Buddhist proverb states: "Before enlightenment: chop wood, draw water. After enlightenment: chop wood, draw water." Even after a spiritual insight of searing clarity, we have to go back to our daily routine and try to integrate that transcendent experience into the simplest menial tasks.

It would be wonderful if our lives could be transformed overnight—if our character and destiny could be metamorphosed by the power of a single vision. But it's a lot easier to have a dream of redemption than to actually make a serious course correction in our lives. True change occurs only incrementally, with disciplined work

265

and honest acknowledgment of problems. Even after a midnight moment of transcendent epiphany like Jacob's in Bethel, we must return the next morning to our workaday lives, still encumbered by our unresolved conflicts.

The Bible offers us a starkly realistic description of the two-steps-forward, one-step-backward path of personal transformation. Like so many of us, Jacob is constantly fleeing from darkness into light, and then back toward darkness. There is no finish line in our progress toward peace and fulfillment. There is only the ongoing trial-and-error process of becoming, with all of its attendant anguish and joy.

Having scaled the heights of his celestial dream, Jacob must now continue his journey at ground level, contending as best he can with the potholes and blind turns in the road ahead. His head hangs precariously in the clouds, but a trapdoor is about to open beneath his feet. . . .

Jacob resumed his journey and came to the land of the Easterners.

For seventeen days he had traveled alone on the road to Haran, every step carrying him farther from his home and his family. He had spoken to no strangers along the way, and he'd grown exhausted by the silence of his solitude.

One day he came upon a well in a field. A boulder covered its mouth to protect it from the elements. Three flocks of sheep were waiting to be watered. Only after all the flocks were gathered there at day's end would several shepherds roll the heavy stone back from the mouth of the well.

Jacob hailed the shepherds, "My friends, where are you from?"

And they replied, "We are from Haran."

Jacob's heart quickened at the name. His days of wandering had brought him to the outskirts of the town of his mother's birth. *"Do you know Laban, the son of Nahor?"*

And they said, "Yes, and there is his daughter Rachel, coming with the flock."

Jacob looked up to see Rachel approaching them, herding her flock of sheep before her. Jacob stood and stared at her, straight and graceful against the desert sky. He rushed to the well and grasped the stone in both hands. It was wide and heavy, but in Jacob's arms it felt no larger than his pillow from the night at Bethel. He rolled it from off the mouth of the well, and he watered Rachel's flock, gazing all the while at his cousin. He could see his mother in the corners of Rachel's eyes and in the curve of her neck. She was his heart's destiny, his soul's bride.

Then Jacob kissed Rachel and lifted up his voice and wept. Jacob told Rachel that he was her father's kinsman, that he was Rebekah's son. And she ran and told her father.

On hearing the news of his sister's son Jacob, Laban ran to greet him. He embraced him and kissed him, and took him into his house. Jacob told Laban all that had happened, and Laban said to him, "You are truly my bone and my flesh."

THE WELL AS THE PORTAL OF THE SOUL

A generation after Rebekah's betrothal, a well outside Haran is once again the backdrop for the introduction of a future matriarch. But there are some significant differences between this scene and the one in Chapter 19 between Rebekah and Abraham's servant. The servant had an impressive entourage of camels and gifts for the bride's family. Jacob arrives on foot as a ragged fugitive, with nothing to offer his future father-in-law but the labor of his body. Abraham's servant tests Rebekah's suitability as Isaac's bride by waiting for her to draw water for him and his camels. This time it is Jacob who must prove himself by drawing water for the herd. To do so, he must first perform the physical feat of rolling a huge stone from the mouth of the well.

This display of machismo is a young man's way of showing off in front of a prospective mate. It is also heavy with sexual and psychological symbolism. In the previous episode, the ladder was a phallic image of Jacob's emerging manhood. The well represents Rachel's virgin sexuality, which Jacob unseals by removing the stone, the portal of her body and soul. Psychologically, the well is symbolic of Jacob's unconscious. When he pushes the stone aside, he exposes the dark undercurrents of his wounded psyche. Perhaps it is the power of love that banishes his fear. Or perhaps it is a blind mating urge. But once Jacob draws from this subterranean pool, he is destined to taste its bittersweet waters, with unforeseen consequences.

The moment Rebekah's brother Laban reenters the drama, we are reminded of his keen eye for personal profit when he met Abraham's servant:

> As soon as he saw the nose ring and bracelets upon his sister's wrists, he went up to the man . . . "Come in, O blessed of the Lord. . . . Why do you stand outside, when I have made ready the house and a place for the camels?"

We recognize Laban as a greedy schemer who won't hesitate to exploit Jacob's weakness for his own gain. But Jacob, desperate for the embrace of his family, sees him only as his mother's brother. Playing on Jacob's need to confess his conscience, Laban has likely elicited a detailed rendition of how Jacob had stolen his brother's blessing. Then, exploiting this instant intimacy for all its worth, Laban hails him as a kindred spirit. *Jacob told Laban all that had happened, and Laban said to him, "You are truly my bone and my flesh."*

We may hear a hidden irony in these words, as Laban embraces what he sees as a fellow trickster in the family. But Jacob is deaf to these subtleties and hears only a surrogate father figure embracing him with a directness Isaac never displayed. He lets his guard down altogether, a dangerous posture in the presence of his unscrupulous uncle. Perhaps the writer Benno Jacob best captured Laban's character with this description: "A selfish, greedy, exploiting, suspicious man of wealth who never fails to observe good manners."

Jacob has arrived in Laban's village emotionally vulnerable and overwrought. After his lonely journey, he's overwhelmed with happiness at being reunited with his extended family in this far-off place. So we're hardly surprised to see him breaking into tears and kissing Rachel only moments after they meet. He falls headlong in love with Rachel, the very first woman he encounters in Haran. But love will blind him to the intrigues at work in this strange land.

Now Laban had two daughters. The name of the older one was Leah, and the name of the younger was Rachel. Leah had weak eyes, but Rachel was of beautiful form and fair to look upon. Jacob stayed in Laban's house for a month, keeping watch over his herds and staying close by Rachel's side.

Laban observed all this, and one day asked him, *"Just because you are my kinsman, should you serve me for nothing? Tell me, what shall your wages be?"*

Jacob loved Rachel, so he answered, "I will serve you seven years for your younger daughter Rachel."

And Laban said, "Better that I give her to you than another man. Stay with me."

So Jacob served seven years for Rachel and they seemed to him but a few days because of his love for her.

Then Jacob said to Laban, "Give me my wife, for my time is fulfilled, that I may go in unto her." And Laban gathered all the people of the place and made a feast. He served them all manner of food and wine, and Jacob ate and drank his fill. When the evening's festivities were done, Jacob retired to his wedding chamber where his bride awaited him, veiled by the darkness. Jacob went in unto her, intoxicated by wine and by love. And in the darkness, his seeing hands found their reward. And the labor of seven years was repaid in a single night's embrace.

When morning dawned, there she lay beside him—Leah! Could it be so? Did his eyes now deceive him, as his hands had the night before?

Their gazes met and Leah turned her pale and frightened

face away from him. "Jacob, my husband . . . " she stammered.

But Jacob waved her into silence, pressing his fists against his eyes and then his ears. He was humiliated. He had bared his body and soul to a stranger, had called out in the darkness with passion and with love. Now he saw his bride for what she was: a wretched victim, like himself, of his uncle's treachery. To look at her filled him with contempt. Staggering backward, he fled from his wedding chamber.

Jacob found Laban slumped in a stupor across the banquet table. *"What is this you have done to me? I was in your service for Rachel! Why did you deceive me?"*

Laban wasn't in the least bit apologetic. After wiping his face awake, he assumed a businesslike tone. *"It is not the practice in our place to marry off the younger before the firstborn. Wait until the bridal week of this one is over, and we will give you Rachel too, provided you serve me another seven years."*

Jacob contained his anger, for his desire for Rachel was greater than his desire for vengeance. If he must serve again for Rachel's love, then serve he would. When Jacob's bridal week with Leah was complete, Laban gave him Rachel also as wife, and Jacob went in unto her.

And Jacob loved Rachel more than Leah. And he served Laban another seven years.

WHEN OUR HEARTS LEAD US DOWN A BLIND ALLEY

Why is Jacob so susceptible to Laban's ploy? How can he work seven years to win the hand of his beloved, only to be fooled by a classic bait-and-switch routine? Is Jacob punishing himself for having deceived his father? Has deceit circled back on deceit?

What we learn about ourselves from this story is how easily we can be handicapped by emotional neediness. Jacob is not so much blinded by love as by his *need* for love. So hungry is Jacob for the approval of his surrogate father that he can't see that Laban doesn't care for him, but only wants to take advantage of him. When we need something desperately from someone—love, recognition, money—we often shut our eyes to their true motives for fear of what we might discover.

What is most striking about this story is how Jacob's emotional blindness on his wedding night mirrors Isaac's physical blindness when bestowing his blessing on his son. Both scenes are cloaked in darkness. Both men close their eyes to the deception being worked on them, allowing themselves to be beguiled by their less reliable senses of touch, taste, and smell. Isaac is so in love with the idea of his venison stew that he doesn't realize he's eating goat. Jacob is so intoxicated by the prospect of consummating his passion for Rachel, *of beautiful form and fair to look upon,* that he can't tell her apart from her homely older sister.

We can well understand why Laban works his mischief on Jacob. His less attractive older daughter is a financial liability he wants to be rid of. Laban not only dupes Jacob into marrying both his daughters, he manages to extract fourteen years of free labor in the bargain. No wonder Laban answers Jacob's marriage proposal by replying, *"Better that I give her to you than another man."* But why does Jacob protest so meekly in the face of such a heartless deception? We are told that his first seven years of labor for Rachel *seemed to him but a few days because of his love for her.* But why does he submit so willingly to an additional seven years of labor?

Jacob doesn't stick up for himself because he doesn't feel entitled to fair treatment. His boyhood rejection by his father has been compounded by his guilt over stealing his blessing from Esau. Having deceived his father, Jacob accepts the deception by Laban as his just reward. So when Laban explains his treachery by saying, *"It is not the practice in our place to marry off the younger before the firstborn,"* Jacob doesn't dispute him. Jacob is too conscience-stricken by the parallels to his deception of Isaac. In order to earn Rachel's hand in marriage, Jacob willingly submits to the penance of fourteen years of labor. On the one hand he's able to delay gratification and work toward future happiness. But Jacob also remains indentured to his own low self-esteem. Despite God's blessing during his dream at Bethel, Jacob continues to think of himself as unworthy of love.

This story illustrates how the psychic wounds we suffer in childhood affect our adult self-image and behavior. Until we repair the damage done to our self-esteem in childhood, we are doomed to reenact our personal history of humiliation and failure. Until Jacob feels entitled to the love and affirmation that his father denied him, he is destined to seek acceptance and invite abuse from inappropriate father figures like Laban. I've seen many of my patients subject themselves to years of undeserved emotional abuse. These unresolved feelings of worthlessness are disastrous for intimate relationships, be they friendships or love affairs. When we feel unworthy of love, we often reject those people who care about us most.

There is another way in which we can identify with Jacob. We live in a society of immigrants, where a large segment of the population, like Jacob in Haran, feels uprooted and vulnerable. Even though they have chosen to immigrate, a sense of loss—of family, community, and language—pervades their lives. When any of us is uprooted from our family and familiar surroundings, we become acutely vulnerable to melancholy.

When I first moved to New York from Israel, I remember sitting at lunch counters with tears streaming down my cheeks. I'd stare miserably at mothers and daughters eating their tuna fish salads, deep in conversation and gazing at each other's face. My longing for my own mother and the gaping hole her absence left in my life was overwhelming. Even though I was happily married, I felt terribly alone in a strange land.

Like Jacob, we all experience some kind of separation anxiety during difficult life transitions, whether as little children starting kindergarten, as college students first entering the job market, or as freshly arrived strangers in a new city. We are all at our most vulnerable in these circumstances. By and large, the people who thrive in a new environment are those who arrive with their own culture and values intact. An integrated identity remains our best shield against doubt and insecurity.

RACHEL AND LEAH: COMPETING FOR LOVE, PASSION, AND STATUS

*For love is strong as death, and jealousy as
cruel as the grave.*

—Song of Songs 8:6

Responding to a question asked during a news conference, President John F. Kennedy made the astute observation: "Life is unfair." His own life was a vivid illustration of just how unfairly and unevenly good and ill fortune are distributed among people—and within an individual life. He had all the advantages of a privileged upbringing in a politically powerful family. Yet his life was marked by tragedy.

Kennedy's simple declarative statement, "Life is unfair," endures as a hard truth we must wrestle with. When we look around us at our peers, our friends, and our family, we are reminded of our limitations and of our blessings. It is painful to accept how little control we exert over the forces that affect us most. We cannot choose our gene pool, our parents, our position in our family, or our homeland. Neither can we choose the time or circumstances of our birth and death.

In the juxtaposition of Jacob's wives, Leah and Rachel, the Bible gives us a poignant example of just how unfairly natural gifts can be distributed between siblings. One sister is beautiful, the other homely. One is fertile, one barren. One is loved, while one remains starved for affection. Their story teaches us to look at our lives as a whole, rather than in fragments, and to face our fate with courage and honesty. Whose life, with all its pluses and minuses, would we actually exchange for our own? Who of us, for instance, would want Kennedy's life, with all its fame and fortune, knowing its abrupt and tragic ending? And who among us would barter our unique spiritual identity for the soul of another?

And Jacob loved Rachel more than Leah.

The Lord saw that Leah was unloved and He opened her womb. But Rachel was barren. Leah conceived and bore a son, and named him Reuben, meaning, "Now my husband will love me."

Leah suffered terribly as the undesired wife of Jacob. She hoped in vain that by bearing Jacob a son she would win his love. She continued to bear him children, and with each birth she prayed that she would move closer to his heart, declaring upon Levi's birth, *"This time my husband will be joined unto me, for now I have borne him three sons."* But she continued to dwell on the outskirts of her husband's affections. So after the fourth son, Judah, was born, she decided, *"This time I will praise the Lord."*

When Rachel saw that she had borne Jacob no children, she became envious of her sister. Rachel the beauty, the loved one, was barren. No matter how intensely Jacob loved her, she could not conceive. And with each child Leah bore, Rachel's misery increased. *Rachel said to Jacob, "Give me children, or I shall die."*

Jacob was incensed at Rachel and said, "Can I take the place of God, who has denied you fruit of the womb?"

Jacob was distraught. He desired nothing more than a child with Rachel, the woman he loved. But he knew that the gift of life was God's to confer, not his. But Rachel could not accept her childless state. She resorted, like Jacob's grandmother Sarah, to the desperate tactic of choosing a surrogate mother, saying: *"Here is my maid Bilhah. Consort with her, that she may bear on my knees. Through her I too may have children."*

To console his beloved Rachel, Jacob agreed. And when Bilhah bore him two sons, Rachel declared: *"A fateful contest I waged with my sister, and I have prevailed!"*

Leah was not to be outdone by her rival. She gave *her* maid, Zilpah, to Jacob as a concubine. Jacob had grown weary by now, but to keep peace with Leah, he went in unto her maid, Zilpah, who bore him two more sons.

The sisters became obsessed with their competition for Jacob's attentions. One day while harvesting wheat, Leah's son Reuben came upon some mandrakes and brought them home to his mother. Rachel had heard that the plant was endowed with magical powers to heighten a man's desire. So she asked Leah to share her mandrakes with her, which enraged Leah.

Leah said, "Was it not enough for you to take away my husband, that you would also take my son's mandrakes?"

Rachel replied, "I promise he will lie with you tonight, in return for your son's mandrakes."

When Jacob came home from the field in the evening, Leah went out to meet him and said, "You are to sleep with me, for I have hired you with my son's mandrakes." Jacob was irritated to find himself bartered like a ram between two ewes. But he dared not insert himself between his contentious wives. So he lay with Leah that night. And in time she bore him three more children: two sons, and a daughter, Dinah.

Now God remembered Rachel. She conceived and bore a son. After years of waiting, Rachel finally became a mother. But she still yearned for more children, *so she named him Joseph, meaning, "May the Lord add another son for me."*

WHEN THE MATH OF MARRIAGE DOESN'T ADD UP: A TALE OF TWO WOMEN AND ONE MAN

If we step back and survey the family dynamic constructed around Rachel and Leah—as well as the cultural expectations confronting them—it's clear how they become so hopelessly mired in competition. Their story is another example of Genesis's detailed and vivid portrait of the intricacies of family life. The Bible warns us of the emotional potholes that dot the family pathway, so that we can detour around or repair them as the situation requires.

Rachel and Leah find themselves in an untenable situation, set against each other by their greedy and manipulative father, Laban. He sacrifices his daughters' happiness to gain the indentured service of a son-in-law. Each woman is deprived of what she most desires and tormented by what the other possesses.

Rachel is the princess of the family. *Fair to look upon,* she is adored by her husband. Even as an adult, she is something of a spoiled child, set on a pedestal above her older sister.

Yet Rachel's life is marred by unrequited expectations. Though she was chosen by Jacob as his wife, her wedding bed is usurped by her sister. Not only must she suffer the indignities of sharing her husband, she must bear the shame of failing to become a mother. In a herding and agricultural society, children were a family's most valued asset. Children helped the family tend the flock and raise the crops. And when the parents became aged, their children were expected to take care of them.

Today, the situation is reversed. By the time children become adults, their parents have invested a small fortune in their rearing with no expectation of any direct financial return. Today, parents spend more time worrying about how to finance their children's education than planning their own retirement. And unlike the tribal family of biblical times, when elders were revered and provided for, parents can no longer depend on their children to care for them in their old age. In fact, they are often expected to assist financially dependent children well into adulthood.

Thus Leah's status as the fertile wife gives her a secure and highly respected status in her family. But she's emotionally bereft. All her life, the *weak-eyed* Leah is overshadowed by her beautiful sister. And how could Jacob help but resent her seeming collusion in her father's scheme to dupe him? How can Rachel not be embittered by her sister's "theft" of her bridegroom? Leah is powerless to defy her manipulative father, which only increases Jacob's contempt for her. The more he sees in her what he hates in himself, the more he resents her.

Occupying the third corner in this unhappy triangle, Jacob fares no better than his wives. At face value, he may appear to have an enviable position. As the writer Adin Steinsaltz has observed, Leah is meat and potatoes, while Rachel is dessert. I suppose that relegates their maids, Zilpah and Bilhah, to the status of side dishes. But Jacob pays a heavy price for the lack of harmony in his family. He finds himself caught in the crossfire of a tortured sibling relationship that must strike painfully close to home for him. No matter how fast he runs between the tents of his wives and maids, he will never be able to satisfy all their emotional needs.

THE FREEDOM OF FIDELITY

Perhaps the most profound lesson of this triangular marriage is the most obvious: monogamy, for all its restrictions, works. Polygamy, despite its apparent advantages, doesn't. We may feel far removed from a polygamous society. But our sequential monogamy through multiple marriages and divorces, combined with the prevalence of extramarital affairs, underscores our polygamous leanings. The latest research in evolutionary psychology places us humans about halfway between our most polygamous and most monogamous primate relatives. But the debate over whether our polygamous drives are due to sociology, biology, or psychology is beside the point. What counts is that we acknowledge them and deal with them.

It takes discipline to sustain a monogamous relationship. Sexual intimacy and trust can thrive only between two people. When a third person enters the picture, trust and intimacy are quickly supplanted by jealousy, suspicion, and anger. If we're serious about preserving a relationship, whether inside or outside of marriage, we need to accept that some issues are nonnegotiable. Sexual fidelity is one of them.

Fidelity is a much more complicated proposition now that women are "out of the tent" and in the workplace alongside men. There are fewer dividers today between the sexes. If we accept that we are not monogamous by nature, we have to create boundaries to protect our monogamous relationships.

But if we're not monogamous by nature, how can an exclusive relationship between one woman and one man flourish? It requires maturity, realistic expectations, and a disciplined respect for the exclusivity of the relationship. As one of my male patients once commented, "Fidelity isn't merely a romantic impulse. It's a conscious, ongoing decision."

Being made in the image of God means that we're not enslaved to instinct. Of course, we have strong biological drives. But we can mediate our drives with a commitment to fidelity. This concept of subduing our passions has been blackballed in some quarters as repressive and unhealthy. But it's impossible for us to lead a moral life if we lack the capacity to say "no" when "no" is what needs to be said. Saying "yes" to sexual fidelity means saying "no" in the face of what seems irresistible.

CHASING THE MYTH OF THE "TOTAL WOMAN"

Much has been written about the dilemma facing modern women: how to maximize personal and professional opportunities in formerly male arenas without forfeiting our unique female identity. As the current generation has discovered, trying to do it all—succeed in a fast-track career, raise children, enjoy a romantic and sexually exciting marital relationship—is more a formula for frustration than fulfillment. The competing demands of domestic, professional, and personal roles makes it difficult to succeed in any one of them.

Leah and Rachel offer a fascinating corollary to our contemporary female identity crisis. On one hand they inhabit a realm of gender roles far removed from our own. They don't have to simultaneously measure up to Cindy Crawford and Hillary Rodham Clinton. They garner genuine respect and higher status as mothers and matriarchs than women do today. But in fundamental ways, they grapple with the same dichotomies of female identity. One is beautiful, the other homely. One is fertile, the other barren. One is the archetypal mother, the other the perennial lover. Each is miserable because she covets what the other possesses. Neither feels whole. Neither can appreciate her unique attributes because each is so focused on the other's perceived advantages. Their sibling rivalry, compounded by having to share a husband, is a striking example of how women can become locked in competitive cycles of self-contempt and competition.

One certain recipe for unhappiness, as we learn from Rachel and Leah, is to constantly measure ourselves unfavorably against other women who appear to have it all. When imagining the happiness and contentment levels that other people enjoy, a bit of healthy skepticism is helpful. The story of Leah and Rachel also teaches us that when we typecast ourselves within a relationship, we're asking for trouble. No woman wants to be pigeonholed exclusively as mother or lover, careerist or housewife. Every mistress craves a family of her own, and every matron dreams of a romantic weekend getaway awash in flowers and her mate's undivided attention. Likewise, no man wants to be identified merely as a good provider or simply as a sexual athlete. We all want the flexibility to inhabit a variety of personas.

Beneath the struggle to be everything to all people lies the equally futile desire to be everything to *ourselves*. We women are particularly demanding of ourselves and unforgiving of our limitations. Women feel compelled to prove themselves in all areas simultaneously. Not only must we succeed in our chosen professions, we must also have fat-free, aerobicized bodies. If our children have problems we blame ourselves for neglecting their needs, and if our husband's fancy wanders we assume it's because we aren't attentive or attractive enough.

How can we escape from this perpetual performance anxiety? Our best hope of success lies in pursuing the variety of roles available to us *sequentially*, rather than *simultaneously*—especially today, when most women can expect a long life span. I work with a lot of female patients who are torn between motherhood and careers. I've found that if I can help them to take the long view of life, their anxiety about simultaneous "ticking clocks" recedes. We need to view our lives as a series of time frames in which to explore various aspects of our personal and professional aspirations—not as competing time slots into which we must simultaneously cram all of our ambitions and loves.

Women today have options that Rachel and Leah never dreamed of. The average woman of their day had ten to fifteen children and spent most of her life caring for them. We need to remember to count our blessings for having options to agonize over. We need to take time out to appreciate the unprecedented opportunities that women can take advantage of today—rather than allow them to become the source of unending conflicts and anxieties.

JACOB FLEES
IN THE NIGHT:
RUNNING FROM PAST
AND PRESENT DANGER

My soul also is sorely troubled.

But Thou O Lord—how long?

I am weary with my moaning;

every night I flood my bed with tears.

I drench my couch with my weeping.

—Psalms 6:3–6

Guilt has fallen out of fashion. Everybody wants to rid themselves of the burden of guilt and get on with life. As a psychotherapist, I spend much of my time working with patients to locate the source of their guilt and diffuse its power to cause them pain. But as a Bible teacher, I am obliged to point out the moral value of this troublesome emotion.

A guilty conscience is the evidence that we are human—that we know the difference between right and wrong, and that we care about that difference. When we feel guilt, it's because we've transgressed a moral code that we believe in. We feel remorse for our misdeeds and desire to behave differently the next time.

Experiencing no guilt at all is destructive to both the individual and the community he inhabits. A total immunity from guilt creates remorseless criminals who can commit the most heinous brutalities without the slightest twinge of conscience. We've all seen their expressionless faces staring out from witness boxes at street-crime trials and war-crime tribunals. But when feelings of guilt erode our self-esteem out of proportion to our misdeeds, it can cripple us emotionally. Our goal should be to achieve a balance in our moral and emotional lives, to feel guilt when appropriate and to use it as a behavioral barometer rather than as a weapon against ourselves.

As psychiatrist and author M. Scott Peck describes the two extremes of guilt:

> Neurotics assume too much responsibility; the person with the character disorder not enough. When neurotics are in conflict with the world, they automatically assume that they are at fault. When those with character disorders are in conflict with the world, they automatically assume the world is at fault.

By Peck's definition, Jacob is certainly a neurotic personality. Twenty years after fleeing his home, Jacob is still on the run from his guilty conscience. Though he is now a middle-aged man, he still identifies with the frightened boy trembling beneath goat skins as he steals his father's blessing. He continues to be pursued by his guilt and by the feeling that he's an impostor.

I can't help admiring Jacob for taking full responsibility for his actions. Jacob doesn't indulge in parent-bashing, proclaiming that it was all his family's fault, that he was manipulated by his mother, ignored by his father, or bullied by his older brother. He doesn't invoke his youth or God's will as mitigating circumstances.

In fact, Jacob shoulders so much responsibility for his youthful acts that he loses all sense of proportion. Over the years his feelings of guilt erode his self-esteem. No matter how much Laban manipulates and exploits him, Jacob feels that he has to accept it. He doesn't feel entitled to stand up for himself and demand justice. And when he finally can't cope with Laban's abuse any longer, Jacob's response is to regress to his adolescent pattern of fleeing in the face of conflict. But now that he is laden with wives and livestock—in addition to his residual guilty conscience—Jacob is not nearly so swift in flight.

After Rachel had borne Joseph, Jacob said to Laban, "Give me leave to go back to my own homeland. Give me my wives and my children, for whom I have served you, that I may go. For well you know what services I have rendered you." For twenty years Jacob had tended Laban's flock with no wages. *"When shall I provide for my own house?"* Jacob asked.

But still Laban was reluctant to release his son-in-law. "Continue to reside with me, my son, and I will share with you my flock." Laban agreed to let Jacob have the mongrels of his flock, the speckled and spotted sheep and goats. But God smiled on Jacob and made his flock multiply. As his flock increased, Laban's dwindled. *And Jacob grew exceedingly prosperous and came to own large flocks, maidservants and menservants, camels and asses.*

The sons of Laban whispered against Jacob, complaining that he had prospered at their expense. *Jacob also saw that Laban's manner toward him was not as it had been in the past. Then the Lord said to Jacob, "Return to the land of your fathers where you were born, and I will be with you."*

Jacob worried that Laban would try to prevent him from leaving with all that he owned. He called Rachel and Leah into the field where he tended his flock, and spoke to them in hushed tones, explaining that the Lord had called him back to Canaan. *"As you know, I have served your father with all my might. But your father has cheated me, changing my wages time and again. The moment has arrived to take what we have and depart."*

Rachel and Leah had little loyalty left for their father. "Surely he considers us outsiders now that he has sold us for your labor and can gain no more by us. If God has told you to leave, then let us leave."

Thereupon Jacob put his children and wives on camels. And he carried off all his livestock and all the wealth that he had amassed in Haran, to return to the land of Canaan.

Meanwhile, Laban had gone to shear his sheep, and Rachel stole her father's household idols. Rachel wanted a memento of her father's house, knowing she might never see it again. Perhaps she was also getting back at her father, whom she'd never forgiven for betraying her on what was to have been her wedding night. *Jacob kept Laban in the dark, not telling him he was fleeing. And he fled with all that he had. Soon he was across the Euphrates and heading toward the hill country of Gilead.*

Three days later, Laban heard that Jacob had fled with his wives and his livestock. Outraged at this news, he gathered his kinsmen and together they gave chase for seven days, finally catching up with Jacob in the hill country of Gilead.

Laban overtook Jacob and questioned him angrily, *"What did you mean by outwitting me and carrying off my daughters like captives of the sword? Why did you flee in secrecy and mislead me and not tell me? I would have sent you off with festive music, with mirth and with song. You did not even let me kiss my sons and daughters good-by! It was a foolish thing for you to do."*

Jacob answered Laban, saying, "I was afraid, because I thought you would take your daughters from me by force."

Laban gestured toward his many armed kinsmen, saying, *"I have it in my power to do you harm."* Jacob didn't flinch, though his heart beat faster within his chest. Laban shrugged. *"Very well, you had to leave because you were longing for your father's house. But why did you steal my gods?"*

Now Jacob understood why Laban had pursued him for seven days over hill and desert. Not for his kinsmen, his daughters and his grandchildren, but for the sake of his household idols hewn from wood and stone. Jacob did not know that Rachel had stolen them, so he declared aloud for all to hear, *"Anyone with whom you find your idols shall not remain alive! In the presence of our kinsmen, point out what I have of yours and take it."*

So Laban proceeded to search the camp, tent by tent. Finally he rifled through Jacob's tent and the tents of his two wives' maidservants. But he found nothing. And in Leah's tent he found not his precious idols.

Rachel, meanwhile, had taken the idols and placed them in the camel cushion and sat on them. Laban rummaged through her tent without finding them. For she said to her father, "Let not my lord take it amiss that I cannot rise before you, for the period of women is upon me." Thus he searched, but could not find the household idols.

As he watched his father-in-law roughly turning his camp inside out, Jacob felt his fury building within him. When Laban emerged from Rachel's tent empty-handed, Jacob finally unleashed his rage at his uncle.

Now Jacob became incensed and took up his grievance with Laban. "What is my crime? What is my guilt that you should pursue me? You rummaged through all my things. What have you found of all your household objects? Set it here before my kinsmen and yours."

Laban was taken aback by this outburst. But Jacob was just beginning. *"These twenty years I have spent in your service, your ewes and she-goats never miscarried; nor did I feast on rams from your flock. That which was torn by beasts I never brought to you. I myself made good the loss. You exacted it of me, whether snatched by day or snatched by night. Often, scorching heat ravaged me by day and frost by night, and sleep fled from my eyes. Of the twenty years that I spent in your household, I served you fourteen years for your two daughters, and six years for your flocks, and you changed my wages time and again. Had not the God of my fathers been with me, you would have sent me away empty-handed."*

Laban made a final play at saving face: *"The daughters are my daughters, the children are my children, and the flocks are my flocks. All that you see is mine."* He paused a beat, then relented. *"Yet what can I do? Come, let us make a pact between you and me."*

Together, Laban and Jacob and their men gathered stones

and made a mound of them. And Laban said, "*May the Lord watch between you and me when we are out of sight of each other. If you ill-treat my daughters or take other wives besides my daughters, though no one else be about, remember that God Himself will be witness between you and me.*"

Jacob made a sacrifice on that spot, and all his brethren ate together late into the night. *Early in the morning, Laban kissed his sons and daughters and bade them good-by. Then Laban left on his journey homeward, and Jacob went on his way.*

WHEN PROBLEM-SOLVING CREATES COURAGE

Running away from our past is a short-term solution at best. Eventually it circles around to our present and confronts us head-on. And like Jacob, so long as we run away from conflicts and confrontations, we flee from the opportunity for personal transformation. Only through facing our problems do we grow. As M. Scott Peck explains: "Problems call forth our courage and our wisdom; indeed they create our courage and wisdom."

When we run from conflict, particularly in a clandestine manner, it takes a terrible toll on our self-esteem. It's humiliating to feel that we have to flee from family crises, and it's even more humiliating to be overtaken in flight the way Jacob is. Before finally permitting him to go his way, Laban takes every opportunity to intimidate and infantilize Jacob. He pointedly reminds him that "*the daughters are my daughters, the children are my children, and the flocks are my flocks. All that you see is mine,*" and threatens him with his superior force: "*I have it in my power to do you harm.*"

Jacob's feeling of impotent rage toward his uncle is similar to that of many people who are persecuted by someone who wields emotional or financial control over them—and against whom they have no recourse. The same impotent rage will intensify over years in an abused child, an exploited or sexually harassed employee, or a battered wife. Anger and frustration build up, grudges accumulate.

The repressed anger turns inward, magnifying self-contempt. Eventually this impotent rage finds its voice and bursts forth in a torrent of anger that is difficult to control. In the most extreme cases, the victim lashes out with a knife or a gun, killing a hated employer or maiming a sadistic spouse.

Jacob's anguished outburst when his uncle Laban searches the camp for his stolen gods is a classic example of long-repressed and unleashed rage. Something about the sight of Laban ransacking his tents sets him off. Perhaps it stirs up memories of his earlier cathartic scene in his father's tent. It certainly reminds Jacob of all the other times his trust has been violated by his uncle. Finally Jacob proclaims his outrage and his innocence. *"What is my crime? What is my guilt? Show me the evidence!"*

Jacob's cri de coeur is not simply aimed at his uncle. It is a direct plea to himself for release from his guilty conscience. He's finally broken through to the realization that, back in his father's tent, he was only an innocent boy caught up in the intrigue between adults. But Jacob has never let himself off the hook.

THE REWARDS
OF RECONCILIATION

When Jacob finally stands up to Laban, his archenemy and tormentor is momentarily stunned. He realizes that Jacob is no longer a powerless young refugee, but a man of substance who has accumulated a family and considerable wealth—despite Laban's attempts to keep him dependent. Jacob must be reckoned with, if only because he has married his daughters and fathered his grandchildren. Despite all the bad blood that has flowed between them—all the threats, posturing and recrimination—even these two unlikely adversaries manage a reconciliation of sorts. Or at least an amicable divorce. Jacob will never see his uncle again, and we have every reason to believe that he has buried his guilt and his resentment beneath that pile of stones in the hills of Gilead.

Reconciliation demands tolerance and self-restraint, but not necessarily love and forgiveness. It's important to recognize the distinction between reconciliation and forgiveness. There are practical benefits to reconciling with estranged family members that don't necessarily begin with forgiveness. In fact, holding out for forgiveness is often an impediment to reconciliation. Only when Jacob stops looking for love from his uncle does he summon the courage to stand up to him and demand respect as an equal.

I've found that seeking the more limited goal of reconciliation rather than forgiveness is a very liberating concept for many of my patients who are struggling to make peace with their families. As long as we honestly address the issues and conflicts involved, we can achieve very satisfactory reconciliations. Once we have reconciled ourselves to our past conflicts with a family member or friend, we have renewed a relationship that may deepen and develop with time. We have opened the door to the possibility of love and forgiveness.

What's most important is that we maintain realistic expectations. We shouldn't expect to change someone we've been in conflict with for years. Nor should we expect instant love and mutual understanding. The goal of an authentic reconciliation is twofold: to make peace with a long-time adversary, and to release the corrosive anger and resentment that have burned within us for years.

———

JACOB PREPARES TO MEET HIS TWIN: CONVERTING FEAR INTO ACTION

*A brother offended is harder to be won than a
strong city, and his contentions are like the
bars of a castle.*

—*Proverbs 18:19*

A nimals have powerful homing instincts. Salmon make 2,000-mile journeys from the depths of the oceans to the creeks and rivers of their birth, while arctic terns migrate more than 22,000 miles every year between the Arctic and the Antarctic. For humans, returning home is less a biological than a spiritual journey. But the gravitational attraction to our home base is virtually irresistible at crucial junctures in our lives. Whether we are a child returning home from school, a young man coming back from war, or an estranged family member returning to the nest, home marks our ultimate destination—what Herman Melville called "the final harbor from whence we unmoor no more."

For many mythic heroes, returning home after a long exile is a treacherous passage. In Homer's *Odyssey*, it takes Odysseus ten years to battle his way home from the Trojan War, dueling along the way with an assortment of gods, demigods, and sorceresses. The hurdles in Jacob's path are not jealous gods, but the warring factions within Jacob's own psyche. As he wends his way homeward, Jacob must navigate an obstacle course of competing wives, a rapacious uncle, a wronged brother, and his own guilty conscience. He charts his path by a complex compass of intellectual, emotional, moral, and spiritual bearings. And if he finally succeeds in finding a safe passage home, it will be because he is guided by other reference points than self-interest.

For Jacob, returning to the land of his birth involves a climactic confrontation with unresolved internal conflicts and with his troubled past. Like any of us returning to the scene of a traumatic episode in our youth, Jacob becomes more vulnerable and fearful the closer he gets to home. Though he is now a middle-aged man surrounded by wives, children, servants, and herds, the frightened boy within him is still groping for the courage to face his big brother. But time is running out for Jacob.

Jacob was finally free from his uncle Laban. Free to return to his homeland with his family and his flocks intact. Ready to take up the leadership of his clan and the mantle of the covenant that God and his father had bestowed on him.

Or was he? In his anxiety to escape his uncle's domination, Jacob had almost put his other nemesis out of mind. His twin brother, Esau, now stood in the path of his return. It had been two decades since Jacob's hurried departure from Canaan, and he had heard little news of Esau since. Had the ensuing years soothed his brother's wrath or merely fed it? Would he be waiting for him with open arms or a drawn sword?

To be on the safe side, Jacob decided to dispatch a deferential greeting to his estranged brother. *Jacob sent messengers ahead to his brother Esau in the country of Edom and instructed them as follows: "Thus shall you say, 'To my lord Esau, thus says your servant Jacob: I stayed with Laban and* remained until now. I have acquired cattle, asses, sheep, and servants. I send this message to my lord in the hope that I might find favor in your sight.' " Jacob wanted Esau to know that he had become a man of substance during his years away. He was no longer the barefoot boy who fled before his brother's wrath.

The messengers returned to Jacob, saying, "Your brother Esau is coming to meet you, and there are four hundred men with him."

This was not the response that he had hoped for. *Jacob was greatly afraid and distressed.* After all, he had but a hundred souls with him, none of whom was armed. Knowing his brother Esau, Jacob imagined his four hundred men as ferocious warriors, armed to the teeth with bows, swords, and daggers. Jacob did what little he could to defend his tribe. *He divided the people with him, including the flocks and herds and camels, into two camps, thinking, "If Esau comes to the one camp and attacks it, the other camp may yet escape."*

Since his entreaty to his brother went unanswered, Jacob then turned to prayer. He beseeched the Lord for protection and reminded Him of the promises He had made. *"O Lord, who said to me, 'Return to your native land and I will deal bountifully with you.' Deliver me, I pray, from the hand of my brother Esau. I fear he may come and strike me down, mothers and children alike. Yet You have said, 'I will make your offspring as the sands of the sea, which are far too numerous to count.' "*

After praying, Jacob passed a restless night, fearful of falling asleep lest he be awakened by an attack. The next morning he decided to take one more measure to appease his brother. From among his herds and flocks, Jacob handpicked two hundred she-goats and twenty he-goats, two hundred ewes and twenty rams, thirty camels with their colts, forty cows and ten bulls, twenty she-asses and ten he-asses. Then he sent his servants ahead of him with the herds and instructed them to separate into a succession of droves. And as each drove approached Esau's camp the servants were to announce the animals as gifts from Jacob to his lord Esau, adding, *"Jacob your servant is right behind us."* Thus Jacob hoped to douse whatever anger still smoldered within his brother's heart.

That evening they came to the Jabbok River. Jacob sent his wives, his two maidservants, and all his children across the ford of the river. Then he sent all his possessions across after them. And Jacob remained behind, left alone on the shores of the Jabbok. He needed this night, perhaps his last, to himself. If he was to face his twin in the morning, tonight he wanted to take stock of all that he had gained and lost in his travels.

THE WAGES OF FEAR VERSUS THE REWARDS OF FAITH

The faith that guides Jacob is of a less heroic, more human character than that of his grandfather Abraham. Abraham was endowed with the kind of faith that empowers a person to go forth into totally unexplored terrain, to wait a hundred years before having a vision realized. He asked nothing of God and withheld nothing from Him, even his long-desired son. But Jacob is more like you and me. He hedges. He cajoles. He negotiates with God rather than accepting His blessing outright. He wrestles with the demands of the covenant and doubts his ability to carry on in the face of adversity.

In this episode we see Jacob as the tactical survivor. He trusts that God is with him and will give him the strength to make the right decisions. But he doesn't rely solely on God to protect him and his family. Jacob takes whatever concrete measures he can to improve his chances of survival. First he sends a conciliatory message to get some sense of the reception he can expect from his brother. When his emissaries return with the ominous news that Esau is heading their way accompanied by four hundred men, Jacob is both *afraid and distressed.* But he does not allow his fear to paralyze him. Instead Jacob uses it as a catalyst for action. He knows he can't outrun his brother, or outwit him. Neither can he hope to defeat him in a face-to-face battle. So he executes the defensive maneuver of dividing his camp in two. Next, he prays to God, imploring Him to *"deliver me from the hand of my brother,"* and reminding Him of His promise that *"I will deal bountifully with you."* Finally, borrowing a tactic from his father Isaac's dealings with the Philistines, Jacob tries to appease his adversary. He offers him lavish gifts of livestock. Without actually apologizing or asking forgiveness, he does everything he can to behave submissively and ask for mercy.

Some biblical interpreters have given Jacob a hard time for humbling himself before Esau in this manner, for referring to his brother as "lord" and himself as "his servant." But I've always seen it as evidence of Jacob's wisdom as a leader. After assessing his situation pragmatically, he takes whatever action will preserve his clan—in the same way that Abraham and Sarah made difficult, humbling choices when they were driven by famine into Pharaoh's Egypt. Jacob is committed to survival. I personally have no trouble with his behavior. After all, it isn't only his personal safety that is at stake. His wives and children are certain to share his fate, whether good or ill.

This story is a reminder to us that though God is a source of internal strength, each of us is responsible for making strategic choices in our lives and the lives of our dependents. In the midst of our spiritual journeys, we are also traveling across firm ground where difficult political realities hold sway. If we hope to inhabit both worldly and spiritual realms, we must learn to reach out to both God and man to ensure our safe passage through life.

HOME AS THE BASELINE
OF OUR IDENTITY

A character in a Robert Frost poem defines home as the place where "when you have to go there, they have to take you in." Jacob doesn't have the luxury of assuming that he'll be "taken in." So why does he feel drawn to return to Canaan after all these years? Why are so many of us impelled to return to the home of our youth?

As so many of the patriarchs' and matriarchs' lives demonstrate, we need to leave home to grow up. Though we don't necessarily have to leave home geographically, we seem to need to distance ourselves enough from our parents to make our own mark in the world. But if we leave home to grow up as individuals, we are drawn back home, as if to a refueling station, when our reserves of emotional and spiritual energy run low.

My father grew up in Glasgow, Scotland. As soon as he was old enough to travel on his own, he set off to explore Europe by foot and by rail. He was exhilarated to escape the provincialism of his surroundings and the narrow emotional confines of his parents' household. In the 1920s, while studying in Rome and preparing to assume a teaching position at Glasgow University, he decided to visit Palestine, which was then a British League of Nations mandate. He fell in love with the idealism of this new society, the simplicity of its Mediterranean lifestyle, and the depth of historical richness he saw in the landscape. He met my mother, herself a transplanted Canadian, and they settled in Haifa.

Though he loved and was committed to his life in Israel, my father always felt the need to maintain ties to the culture he had left behind. His subscriptions to *The London Observer*, *The New Statesman*, and *Nation* were renewed annually, and every few years he returned to Scotland, not only to visit family, but to replenish the cultural and sensory wellsprings of his youth.

More than anything, he missed the cold, damp climate of Scotland. During the late autumn in Israel, when the first rains of the season finally arrived, I remember my father running excitedly out onto our balcony, rubbing his arms and luxuriating in the chilly shower. As often as possible, he would retreat on his own to the remote Isle of Skye off the northern coast of Scotland, accompanied only by his manual typewriter. Though he had made a career as an art critic for *The Jerusalem Post*, he felt he did his best and most personal writing when sequestered on that damp, windswept island in the North Atlantic.

Home is the starting point of our identity, the baseline against which we measure our progress in life. Coming home means taking stock of who we are, where we have been, and what we have achieved. That's why it's so important for us to give our children a strong sense of identity while they're growing up. If they take something with them when they go out into the world, they will have something substantive to return to later in life.

Isaac and Rebekah are gone now, buried in the soil of their promised land at the cave of the Machpelah. But they have bequeathed to Jacob a strong family identity and a family destiny that remains to be fulfilled. He's not merely returning to take over a family business or family farm. He's coming home to reclaim his role in his family's covenant with God and to reclaim his place in the promised land.

Beyond the physical manifestations of his covenant with God —the land, the traditions, the rites—Jacob is returning home to carry on and transmit a body of spiritual beliefs. The enduring principles of faith and action, fidelity and trust, privilege and responsibility are the moral magnets drawing Jacob home from his twenty-year exile.

————

JACOB WRESTLES WITH THE ANGEL: PREVAILING OVER THE DEMONS WITHIN

*What is man, that Thou art mindful of him? For
Thou hast made him but little lower than the angels,
and hast crowned him with glory and honor.*

—*Psalms 8:4–5*

When we are alone in the stillness of the night, we face our worst fears and our deepest wishes. It is often at these dark moments that we discover who we really are. When we reach deep within ourselves for guidance, or call out to a higher power for comfort, we find out if we are truly alone or in the company of others—our ancestors, our personal angels, our God.

Jacob has reached the terminus of his homeward journey. He won't uncover the intent of his brother's heart until the next morning. But this night, on the eve of that fateful reckoning, Jacob will take stock of where he has been and what he has become. He is finally ready to face the spirits that haunt his waking and sleeping soul—and he is determined to test the limits of his power to overcome them.

Jacob was alone on the shores of the Jabbok River. Alone, it seemed, for the first time in years. Alone, like the youth who had fled his home with barely a shirt on his back.

He wondered if he had really accomplished anything during all these years away. He had worked hard and prospered. But what of the covenant his grandfather and father had made with God? Was he ready to finally assume responsibility for leading his clan and following Abraham's vision? How could he answer the demands of God's covenant when he could barely cope with the world of men?

Jacob laid his tired body down by the riverbank, but the ground was a harder bed for him at forty than it had been at twenty. The campfires across the river smoldered dimly against the black sky. The silence of the night was broken only by a dog barking plaintively somewhere far off. The moonless dark reminded him of the shadowed places he had stumbled through in his life: his father's blind embrace, the amazing dream of the ladder by the side of the road in Bethel, his unhappy surprise in the wedding chamber. Jacob wondered, in the dark of this night, what mystery awaited him and whether he would face it with fear or with courage. Was he finally ready to emerge from darkness into light, to assume responsibility for leading his clan and fulfilling Abraham's covenant? Or was it death, the final veil of darkness, that awaited him on the far shore of the river?

Jacob was left alone. And a man wrestled with him until the break of dawn.

When he saw that he had not prevailed against him, he wrenched Jacob's hip from its socket. Then he said, "Let me go, for dawn is breaking."

But Jacob answered, "I will not let you go, unless you bless me."

Said the other, "What is your name?"

He replied, "Jacob."

The other said, "Your name shall no longer be Jacob, but Israel, for you have striven with God and men, and have prevailed."

Jacob asked, "Pray tell me your name."

But he said, "You must not ask my name!" And he took leave of him there.

So Jacob named the place Peniel, meaning, "I have seen God face-to-face, yet my life has been preserved."

The sun rose upon him as he passed Peniel, limping on his hip.

WRESTLING WITH PERSONAL ANGELS AND DEMONS

Throughout time, crossing rivers has symbolized the overcoming of an important personal threshold of experience. In Greek mythology the river Styx represented the boundary between life and death. And when Julius Caesar crossed the Rubicon, it marked his ascent to absolute leadership of the Roman Empire. The Jabbok River, where Jacob camps alone the night before he faces Esau, is an eastern tributary of the river Jordan, which marks the boundary between the biblical countries of Sihon and Og. But for Jacob, the Jabbok River is more than a geographic border. It is a spiritual divide between his youth and his adult self, between his doubt and his faith in his own destiny. In Hebrew, the word *jabbok* is closely related to the word meaning "to wrestle." On the banks of this mysterious stream, Jacob is destined to wrestle his personal demons to the ground and leave them behind him on the far shore.

Martin Buber saw Jacob's wrestling match as a metaphor for all of humanity's struggling with life's existential questions. And indeed, this episode raises more questions than it answers:

Who is the "man" who wrestles with Jacob on the riverbank and finally blesses him with a new name? Is he his departed father, Isaac, from whom Jacob had tried to wrest a blessing? Is this "man" his twin brother, Esau, with whom he wrestled in the womb and whom he must confront the next morning? Is he Jacob's shadow self, the darker part of his psyche that doubts and fears—that he must integrate before he can become whole? Could he be an angel of death, Jacob's fear of mortality rising up to greet him on the eve of his brother's revenge? Or is this "man" in fact an angel of God, Jacob's spiritual destiny wrestling with his worldly ambitions for primacy in his soul?

It seems to me that the "man" is all of these. As Jacob wrestles through the night with his personal demons, he subdues each of these incarnations and transforms himself in the process. The withholding father gives way to the contentious brother, who finally yields to the angel of God, a messenger announcing Jacob's new spiritual identity: *"Your name shall no longer be Jacob, but Israel, for you have striven with God and men, and have prevailed."* The *break of dawn* sheds new light on the meaning of the night's dream. Jacob realizes that he has finally scaled the ladder connecting heaven and earth, and indeed his soul has *seen God face-to-face.*

Finally, after decades of humiliation and flight, Jacob wins the blessing he once sought in his father's tent. Self-affirmation was never something he was able to cajole from his father or usurp from his brother. Blessedness could only be claimed as his birthright when he had prevailed over his doubts and fears, when he had wrestled against his darkest demons. Only after enduring a long midnight of despair could Jacob earn the blessing of the dawn's light.

The night when Jacob wrestles with the angel by the riverside proves to be a turning point in his life. Until then he has been a passive player in the drama of his destiny—the mama's boy cowering in his brother's shadow, ignored by his father and humiliated by his uncle, forever scrambling to stay one step ahead of his conscience and his tormentors. But this night he prevails over his past and is rewarded with a vision of his future. Jacob finally stands his ground, rather than running away, and demands that the angel bless him. No longer at war with himself, Jacob is now blessed by the faith of his forefathers, and by God.

In becoming Israel, Jacob leaves his insecure adolescent self behind. He's arrived at a new plateau, finally ready to assume the adult mantle of patriarch along with all its responsibilities to future generations. He is no longer the frightened child defined only by his powerless position in his family. Reborn as an adult with a family of his own, Jacob can now embrace his covenant with God.

Jacob is so transformed by this frontal assault on the dark twin of his soul that he earns a new name and a new identity. As the new day dawns he is no longer Jacob, the "one who grasps" at his brother's gifts and his father's love. He becomes Israel, "the prevailer," who earns his blessing through sheer doggedness, by clinging to his faith with all his might and refusing to let go. Having grappled with man and God, Jacob prevails. Jacob now walks with a limp, but he is no longer running from his past.

Jacob's trials are by no means over. In years to come he will face family crises and heartbreaking separations from those he loves most. But throughout these ordeals Jacob never loses faith in his purpose and his special bond with God. He remains true to his new name, Israel, and prevails over his personal tragedies. He never loses sight of his uniquely dual identity: a great patriarch anointed by God to lead his family into a secure future, and a vulnerable human being hobbled by a limp that will mark his steps for the rest of his days.

Jacob rose up from the bank of the river, his hip still throbbing with pain. He forded the river and rejoined his wives and children on the far side.

Looking up, Jacob saw Esau coming, accompanied by four hundred men. It was time to discover what his dream foretold, whether his new name augured ill or good. *Jacob divided his children among Leah, Rachel and the two maids, putting the maids and their children first, Leah and her children next, and Rachel and Joseph last.* He couldn't help himself from placing his favorite wife and child the farthest from harm's way. *He himself went on ahead and bowed low to the ground seven times until he was near his brother.*

Jacob's hip ached as he raised himself off the ground. His

twin brother loomed before him, his red hair raging, his sword glinting in the sunlight. . . .

Esau ran to greet him. He embraced him and, falling on his neck, he kissed him. And they wept. As Jacob stood weeping in his brother's embrace, he felt the power of those muscular arms and the strong animal smell surround him. For a moment he felt safe and at peace.

Esau asked, "What do you mean by all this company which I have met?"

And Jacob answered, "To gain my lord's favor."

Esau said, "I have enough, my brother. Let what you have remain yours."

But Jacob said, "No, I pray you. If you would do me this favor, accept from me this gift. For to see your face is like seeing the face of God, and you have received me favorably. Please accept my presents, for God has favored me and I have plenty." And when he urged him, Esau accepted.

Esau then offered to escort Jacob back to Esau's homeland in Seir. But Jacob politely declined, urging him to go on ahead and saying he would follow him at a slower pace with the cattle and the children. Both brothers knew that they were destined to dwell apart from each other, each pursuing his own way of life. Though they were reconciled, they would never live side by side. *Jacob journeyed on to Succoth and built a house for himself and made stalls for his cattle.* After so many years wandering abroad and dwelling in tents, he was happy at last to live within four solid walls.

Esau took his wives, his sons and daughters and all that he had acquired in the land of Canaan, and went to another land because of his brother Jacob. For their possessions were too many for them to dwell together, and the land where they sojourned could not support them because of their livestock. So Esau settled in the hill country of Seir in the land of Edom.

THE POWER AND LIMITS OF RECONCILIATION

Daytime talk shows present a fantasy version of how deep-seated family rifts are healed. The alcoholic parent and abused child face off in front of an audience of millions. In the twelve minutes between commercial breaks, the host coaxes his guests through a cathartic cycle of recrimination and forgiveness, culminating in the obligatory tearful hug—all performed to the appreciative applause of the studio audience.

Genesis offers us a more realistic view of the challenges and limitations of family reconciliations. It takes Jacob twenty years to work through his issues of sibling rivalry. His story shows us that reconciliation is not a passive process. Both sides must want it and be prepared for the pain of the process. First we must admit the depth of our hurt. True reconciliation, as Jacob and Esau demonstrate, is a visceral experience. Jacob has to wrestle with his conscience all night, then prostrate himself in front of his brother and beg for forgiveness. Only after years of anguish and painful self-examination could they embrace and weep with relief in each other's arms.

Their fraternal embrace ends the cycle of rivalry begun in the womb. Jacob and Esau go their separate ways, recognizing that they are better off dwelling at a distance from one another. But at least the family is no longer at war with itself, and Jacob and Esau are freed from their childhood trauma to pursue their adult lives without fraternal strife. Their story expresses one of the distinctive strengths of their family: no matter how badly they might hurt or betray one another, there is always the possibility for reconciliation.

THE TENACITY OF FAITH

Finally, Jacob's life teaches us the value of tenacity. Jacob's triumph is that he prevails over every obstacle life lays in his path—not only by virtue of intelligence or righteousness, but by having the faith to endure. Faith in himself, in his destiny, and in his ability to outlast adversity.

This redeeming virtue of endurance is what sets Jacob apart from Esau and marks him as the leader of his family. While Esau is driven by the need for instant gratification, Jacob has the tenacity to persevere. He has to work for fourteen years to earn his beloved Rachel as a wife. Together they wait another five years before being able to conceive a child. Jacob endures a twenty-year exile from his family and homeland, but his patience is rewarded. He waits two decades to secure the blessing he could not win from his father, and on the shores of the Jabbok River he finally earns it.

If there's one truth that Jacob's struggle illustrates, it's that growing up means not expecting any one experience to solve all our problems. Each step forward brings new challenges, only some of which we are equipped to deal with. There are no permanent solutions to life's problems, and certainly no state of ultimate perfection. Even after moments of great spiritual catharsis, Jacob must resume the journey of his life with a limp. There is no tangible finish line in his journey.

Few of us can equal Jacob's fortitude in the face of adversity, but each of us is tested, in ways small or large. "Fear not" means believing that our life has meaning and that we have value as human beings. No matter how terrible our circumstances, others have endured worse and emerged to love life once more. Whether confronted by sickness, ill fortune, or political persecution, human beings have an incredible capacity to endure.

In his darkest hours, with all his senses of hearing, sight, and touch, Jacob apprehends God for a fleeting, searing moment. God's message to him is the same as it was to Abraham and Isaac: "Fear not." But this "God of Abraham, Isaac, and Jacob" is heard with a different inflection by each generation. Each patriarch clears his own path through life and forges his own interactive relationship with God. For Jacob, "Fear not" is not a statement of blind faith, but a precondition of his ability to act decisively, overcome obstacles, and stand up to the vicissitudes of his life.

We despair when confronted by seemingly insuperable obstacles. By refusing to surrender to adversity, Jacob shows us the amazing power of human perseverance. Sheer endurance is often the most heroic act that we humans can perform. Throughout his trials Jacob wrestles with the angel of his soul, demanding the blessing that he tenaciously clings to and claims as his birthright. His triumph proves that for anyone who has the courage to endure life's journey one step at a time, there are ladders pointing the way out of despair, and personal angels waiting to show us the way.

As Elie Wiesel wrote about Jacob's encounter with the angel:

Jacob has just understood a fundamental truth: God is in man, even in suffering, even in misfortune, even in evil. God is everywhere. In every being. God does not wait for man at the end of the road, the termination of exile; He accompanies him there. More than that: He is the road, He is the exile. God holds both ends of the rope, He is present in every extremity, He is every limit. He is part of Jacob as He is part of Esau.

———

THE RAPE OF DINAH: HUMILIATION AND RETALIATION

He who is slow to anger is better than the strong man, and a master of his passions is better than a conqueror of a city.

—*Proverbs 16:32*

This next episode in Genesis is a story of lust, rape, pillage, greed, and bloody vengeance. Most of our Sunday school teachers deleted it from our Bible study. But the biblical authors refused to censor tales that might reflect badly on Jacob's sons, who will become the founders of the twelve tribes of Israel. The authors wanted us to be privy to this brutal tale of violation and revenge and to grapple with the complex issues it raises.

After twenty years of exile, Jacob finally makes peace with the male figures of his youth. He gets out from under his manipulative father-in-law, affirms his father's blessing and love, and reconciles with the older brother he had wronged. Now that he has put his youthful conflicts to rest, Jacob must lead his tribe and contend with the challenges of reining in his large and unruly brood of sons. Like his father and grandfather before him, the new patriarch is soon tested by a confrontation with more powerful and hostile neighbors.

A few years after building his house in the Jordan valley, Jacob moved his flocks and herds to the hill country to the west. *Jacob arrived safe in the city of Shechem, named for its prince, and he encamped before the city. The parcel of land where he pitched his tent he purchased from Hamor, Shechem's father, for a hundred kesitas.*

Now Dinah, the daughter whom Leah had borne to Jacob, went out to visit the daughters of the land. She was a young girl, curious about the customs and the dress of the local women who lived within the walled city. The young prince of the city, Shechem, noticed Dinah strolling through his streets and decided to have his way with her. *He saw her, took her, lay with her, and humiliated her.*

But after he raped Jacob's daughter, Shechem felt tenderly toward the girl. *Being strongly drawn to Dinah and in love with the maiden, Shechem spoke to her heart. Then Shechem said to his father Hamor, "Get me this girl-child as a wife."* Hamor could never find it in his heart to deny his son anything that he desired and agreed to help him acquire Dinah as his wife.

Now Jacob heard that Shechem had defiled his daughter Dinah. He was uncertain how to respond. As he edged into old age, Jacob felt weary in both body and soul. Having just moved to this region, he wasn't eager to pick a fight with a much more powerful and established adversary who occupied a fortified city. How could he recover his daughter without putting his entire tribe at risk? He decided to do nothing until he could confer with his sons about what action to take. *And since his sons were in the field with his cattle, Jacob kept silent until they came home.*

Then Jacob's sons, having heard the news, came in from the field. The men were distressed and very angry, because

Shechem had committed an outrage by lying with Jacob's daughter—a thing not to be done.

Since Hamor had recently done some business with Jacob —selling him the site for his tents—he thought it best to deal directly with the patriarch in order to placate Dinah's clan for the grievous offense his son had committed. Hamor took his son Shechem and went out from the city to speak to Jacob and his sons. *And Hamor spoke to them, saying, "My son Shechem desires your daughter. Please give her to him in marriage. Intermarry with us: give your daughters to us and take our daughters for yourselves. You will dwell among us and the land will be open before you. Settle, move about, and acquire holdings in it."*

Hamor believed that he was making a generous offer. How could these nomads not be pacified by his invitation to become citizens of Shechem? They would prosper, and the town would certainly benefit from the addition of this industrious tribe. Best of all, his son would acquire a woman whom he loved.

Then Shechem said to Dinah's father and brothers, "Do me this favor, and I will pay whatever you tell me. Ask of me a bride price ever so high, as well as gifts, and I will pay what you tell me. Only give me the maiden for a wife."

Jacob and his sons were in a precarious position. They had been invited to join the people of Shechem, and they knew if they intermarried they would soon be absorbed into an alien people and face extinction. But to reject Hamor's offer outright would be to give offense and risk attack. So they devised to name so high a bride price that Shechem would have to refuse.

Jacob's sons answered Shechem and his father Hamor— speaking with guile because he had defiled their sister Dinah— "We cannot do this thing, to give our sister to a man who is uncircumcised, for that is a disgrace among us. Only on this condition will we agree with you: that you will become like us in that every male among you is circumcised. Then we will give our daughters to you and take your daughters to ourselves. And we will dwell among you and become as one kindred. But if you will not listen to us and become circumcised, we will take our daughter and go."

They were bluffing, of course. The prince still held Dinah within the city, so they were not negotiating from a position of strength. And they were, after all, only a small tribe camped outside the gates of a great city. To *"take our daughter and go"* was easier said than done.

But to the surprise of Jacob and his sons, Hamor and Shechem accepted their terms. Shechem himself lost no time in becoming circumcised, because he desired Dinah greatly and wished to persuade the other men of the town to do the same.

So Hamor and his son Shechem went to the public place of their town and spoke to their fellow townsmen, saying, "These people are our friends. Let them settle in the land and move about in it, for the land is large enough for them. We will take their daughters to ourselves as wives and give our daughters to them." They made no mention of Dinah, or of Shechem's infatuation with her, but only stressed the advantages of absorbing Jacob's people. *"Their cattle and substance and all their beasts will be ours, if only we agree to their terms."*

So delighted were the townsmen by the prospect of acquiring the flocks of Jacob that they barely flinched at the terms. *All who went out of the gate of his town heeded Hamor and his son Shechem, and all males of his town were circumcised.*

Now Simeon and Levi were Dinah's brothers and Jacob's sons by Leah. They were furious at the thought of their sister belonging to the man who had defiled her. And because they knew that Jacob had never been in love with their mother, his sons doubted he would go to any great trouble to rescue Dinah. *So on the third day, when the men of the city were still hurting from their circumcision, Simeon and Levi took each his sword, came upon the city unmolested, and slew all the males. They put Hamor and his son Shechem to the sword, took Dinah out of Shechem's house and went away.*

Then the other sons of Jacob came and plundered the town, because their sister had been defiled. They seized their flocks and herds and asses, all that was inside the town and outside—all their wealth, all their children, and their wives, all that was in the houses they took as captives and booty.

Now Jacob was panicked by the news of the mayhem his sons had wrought. His daughter had been rescued, but at what cost? *He said to Simeon and Levi, "You have brought trouble on me, making me odious among the inhabitants of the land. My men are few in number, so that if they unite against me and attack me, I and my house will be destroyed."*

But the sons answered, "Should our sister be treated like a whore?"

To which their father made no response.

The Rights of Self-defense Versus the Limits of Retribution

The vulnerability of this small seminomadic clan to the whims of its neighbors emerges as a problem in each generation of Genesis. Abraham is powerless to prevent Pharaoh from taking Sarah into his harem. Abimelech and the Philistines ruthlessly usurp Isaac's wells as soon as Abraham dies. And Jacob himself has spent his youth in Haran as an alien with no rights and no power. Now he and his sons find themselves caught up in the power politics of Canaan, where the local chieftains have no compunction about exploiting their advantage. This story examines the limits of retribution and the rights of self-defense set against a complex political, psychological, and moral background.

Despite the fact that the sons of Jacob have limited options for rescuing their sister, we are shocked by their bloody revenge and pillage, which seems to us out of all proportion to the offense against Dinah and her family. When the Bible later prescribes *an eye for an eye and a tooth for a tooth* as the standard of permissible retribution, it intends to ensure that the punishment is not disproportionate to the crime.

The scholar Clinton Bailey has pointed out that the desert has always been a brutal environment where the strong systematically prey on the weak, particularly nomads. "To ensure their security, Near-Eastern nomads have resorted to a number of strategies. One is their social organization into clans, or blood revenge groups. All males are obliged to defend and avenge each other." Failure to wreak vengeance is seen as weakness on the part of the clan. "People who are seen as weak or are deemed easy prey," concludes Bailey, "simply cannot go on living in the desert." Viewed in the light of this unwritten law of desert survival, the reaction of Jacob's sons to their sister's rape and abduction may appear more pragmatic than ruthless.

WHEN PARENTS FAIL TO LEAD

But this is far more than a cautionary tale about cruel retribution. Beneath this tragedy lies a strong indictment of parents who forfeit their moral authority as family leaders. Hamor, for one, doesn't seem the least bit concerned that his son has raped a girl and held her captive. He treats the whole incident as an everyday exercise of his private and public power—nothing that can't be made right by a few diplomatic words and an offer of reparation.

But the main focus of our concern is Jacob, not Hamor. For someone who has embraced the mantle of patriarch, he assumes a decidedly passive role in resolving this family crisis. Jacob has not previously dealt with conflicts in a forthright manner, and he's clearly at a loss as to how to respond to the violation and abduction of his only daughter. Certainly his options are limited. Hamor and his son are holding all the cards in their negotiation. But why does Jacob yield all his authority to his sons? Jacob must know that they are hotheaded young men, and that this situation cries out for the measured response of an experienced father.

If, as the story indicates, Jacob disapproves of his son's slaughter of all the men of Shechem, and the pillage that follows, why does he fail to intervene? What does it say about our own reluctance to intercede in the behavior of our adult children?

Sometimes we lack the courage to correct our children when we see them stepping out of bounds. Held hostage by our fears that our children may stop loving us and cut off contact, we turn away from unpleasant confrontations. Not until his deathbed blessing at the end of the Book of Genesis does Jacob express his moral condemnation of his sons' violent acts, saying:

"Simeon and Levi are a pair. Their weapons are tools of lawlessness. Let not my person be included in their council. Let not my being be counted in their assembly. For when angry they slay men. And when pleased they maim oxen. Cursed be their anger so fierce, and their wrath so relentless."

Like many of us, Jacob displays more ambivalence than resolve about controlling his adult children's behavior. We often fail to take a strong hand with our children because our own pasts are not beyond reproach. Does Jacob feel too self-conscious about his own personal history to condemn his sons' deceptive behavior? Perhaps he feels ambivalent about their tactics, not knowing whether to encourage or denounce them. Should he be teaching his sons the survival strategies that have sustained him through his own difficulties? Would he be doing them a disservice to promote an abstract code of morality over pragmatism?

My guess is that both Jacob and his sons are acting partly in response to conflicts buried deep in their relationship. Jacob knows he has distributed his affections unevenly between his two wives and their maids who have borne him sons. Leah, in particular, has gotten less than her fair share of his attention, and Jacob has probably been emotionally stingy with her sons and daughter. Now, when Dinah is raped and held captive, Jacob is paralyzed by guilt and fear. He doesn't feel he has the moral authority to countermand his sons' brutal plot to ambush the town and rescue their sister. Jacob also knows enough about the realpolitik of the desert to fear for his clan's survival in the wake of either option—to attack their larger foe or to show weakness by failing to do so. In light of Jacob's reticence, it's hardly surprising that Dinah's brothers step forward into the vacuum left by their father's inertia.

The Bible is replete with stories of neglected sons acting out their anger toward their powerful fathers. For example, when King David is too absorbed in the affairs of state to pay attention to his son, dire consequences ensue. Absolom sleeps with his father's concubines and sets his fields on fire. Simeon and Levi's bloodthirsty rampage is directed at the men of Shechem, not Jacob. But they surely know that he and the entire clan stand to suffer the consequences of their excesses. As Jacob plaintively cries, *"You have brought trouble on me, making me odious among the inhabitants of the land. My men are few in number, so that if they unite against me and attack me, I and my house will be destroyed."*

But Genesis gives his sons the last word, throwing his self-pity back in his face, when they ask rhetorically, *"Should our sister be treated like a whore?"* they are not only speaking on behalf of their sister, but also for their wronged mother, Leah. Jacob is at a loss to answer their accusation because in his heart he knows they are right. He never fully accepted Leah, and he failed to take action to rescue his only daughter. Dinah is never mentioned again in the biblical narrative, by which we can infer that Shechem's violation has robbed her of a future.

On a political level, the sons are rebuking their father for not taking the steps necessary to defend their family's security. If he stands by passively when his daughter is abducted and raped, what kind of message is he sending to his neighbors about his clan's ability to defend itself?

Unfortunately, Jacob's anguish in fatherhood is just beginning. He might want to limp into a dignified old age, but his sons will not let him go so quietly. They are determined to repay their father for the wrongs done their mothers. And as Simeon and Levi demonstrate, when our children feel wronged, they vent their rage in all directions with little concern for proportion or consequence. And as we learn from Jacob's example, we parents are often powerless to defend ourselves or our families against the wheel of emotional retribution once it is set spinning.

Part Four

Joseph and His Brothers: a Family's Journey from Betrayal to Forgiveness

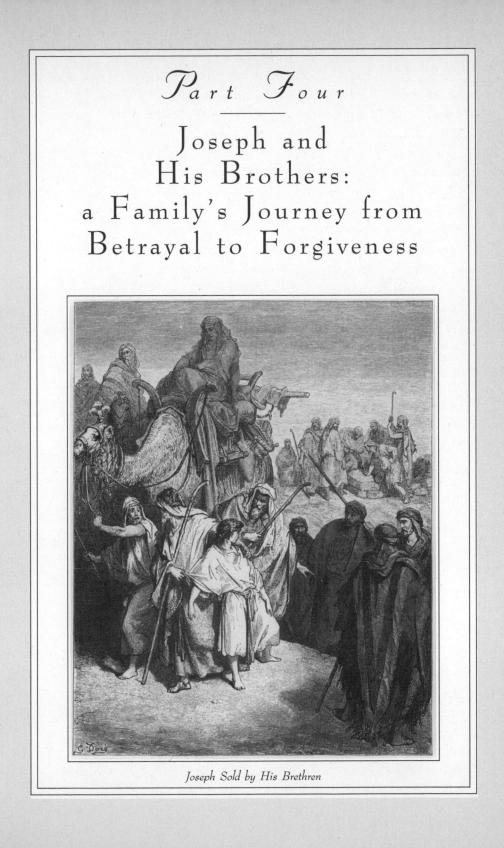

Joseph Sold by His Brethren

The saga of Abraham and Sarah's family now moves from Jacob, the aging patriarch, to young Joseph, the next pivotal character in the family's lineage. Joseph is the historical bridge between the era of the patriarchs in Canaan and the period of slavery in Egypt that is narrated in the Book of Exodus. He will carry the family on the final leg of its multigenerational journey down the length of the fertile crescent —from the Mesopotamian city of Ur to the hill country and deserts of Canaan to the cosmopolitan world of the Egyptian court.

Each character in Abraham's family forges his own unique relationship with God. God communicates with Abraham through visions, with Isaac through blessings, and with Jacob through dreams. Joseph's covenant with God operates on a more secular plane. He goes forth into the glittering Egyptian court of the pharaoh, a society not unlike our own: sophisticated, materialistic, rife with intrigue and power politics. Joseph's fidelity to the faith of his fathers manifests through the choices he makes as he ascends to the pinnacle of power in an alien culture.

Joseph's story is a finely wrought and self-contained novella, describing in vivid detail the development of his character from charismatic and arrogant youth to compassionate middle age. The style of the biblical text in this final section becomes more naturalistic and the pace quickens as the narrative builds to its conclusion. Genesis reaches a melodramatic peak in these climactic last chapters: a riches-to-rags-to-riches tale replete with every human passion—love and hate, ambition and glory, jealousy and fury. Tears of joy and grief are shed. Garments are rent in anguish. It's a gripping saga of treachery and deception, betrayal and forgiveness.

In short, it's the story of a family's survival.

Until now the first family of the Bible has endured famine, war, and the rigors of seminomadic life in a hostile landscape. But the growing pains that afflict this clan present the greatest threat yet to its survival. It will fall to the young Joseph—the dreamer and the man of action—to redeem his family from the sibling rivalry and intergenerational strife that threaten to tear it apart. Only by going forth naked into the world and building his faith from the ground up can the young Joseph hope to rescue his family from the brink of self-destruction.

JOSEPH, THE CHARISMATIC YOUTH: THE PERILS OF SELF-LOVE

Do not boast thyself of tomorrow,
for thou knowest not what the next day will bring.

—*Proverbs 27:1–2*

We've all known a young Joseph. The gifted child, adored and doted upon by his parents, envied and resented by his peers. The charismatic adolescent who charms us with his intelligence and brash self-confidence while alienating us with his self-absorption. It's impossible to remain indifferent to these magnetic personalities. We are either attracted or repelled, forced to love or to hate them. When we befriend them, they beguile and antagonize us in equal measure. Over time, their self-centeredness tends to fray the friendship, and we drift apart. But when a young Joseph emerges within our family and we lack the luxury of terminating the relationship, siblings and parents are forced to take sides—and the enfant terrible becomes the axis around which the family revolves.

Jacob is growing weary with age and the burdens of leadership. After the rape of Dinah and the ensuing mayhem, all he wants is to return to a peaceful life of herding his flocks in Canaan. But another tragedy lies waiting just ahead. . . .

After the bloody incident at Shechem, it was time to flee again. Jacob moved his tents southward, toward Bethel. *As they set out, a terror from God fell on the cities round about, so that they did not pursue the sons of Jacob.* When he reached Bethel—where God had first visited Jacob in a dream as he fled from his brother Esau—God appeared to him again. He blessed Jacob and reaffirmed their covenant.

Then Jacob steered his tribe farther south, toward Mamre and Hebron. Jacob's beloved wife Rachel was heavy with child. Worried for her comfort and safety, Jacob pressed his caravan onward, hoping to at least reach Ephrath before her time arrived.

They set out from Bethel. But when they were still some distance short of Ephrath, Rachel was in childbirth, and she had hard labor.

When her labor was at its hardest, the midwife said to her, "Have no fear, for it is another boy for you." But as she breathed her last, for she was dying, she named him Ben-oni, meaning "son of my suffering." *But his father called him Benjamin,* meaning "son of my old age."*

Thus Rachel died. She was buried on the road to Ephrath —now Bethlehem. Over her grave Jacob set a pillar. It is the pillar at Rachel's grave to this day.

* "Son of my old age" would actually be *ben-yamin* in Hebrew. Others have interpreted *Benjamin* as "son of my right arm."

WHEN DEATH DIVIDES
A COUPLE

The sudden and unexpected death of a spouse is a crushing blow. In addition to shock, deep grief, and numbness, the surviving spouse has to deal with the aftermath emotions of depression, guilt, and loneliness. When our life partner is taken away from us without warning, there is always a haunting feeling of unfinished personal business—plans that will never be realized, endearments left unspoken, emotional conflicts that may never be resolved.

The single most important ingredient in the grieving process is an emotional support network—or at the very least, one person who can lend a patient and sympathetic ear. But Jacob is left totally alone to grieve the loss of his beloved wife. Leah certainly wouldn't want to listen to Jacob mourn her departed rival. Leah's sons, who resented Rachel and the special place she held in their father's heart, would offer little comfort. Rachel's son Joseph is just a boy, and Benjamin a motherless newborn.

We can only imagine what Jacob was feeling and thinking in his solitary sorrow. The things he should have done with Rachel had he known that the end was so near. Had he only listened to her with more patience when she anguished over not being able to conceive. If he had only set out earlier for Hebron, she might have been spared the discomfort of giving birth on the roadside. At the very least, had he not been in transit he could have buried her in the cave of Machpelah, alongside his parents and grandparents. That his beloved Rachel should die so painfully and be buried by the side of the road—it was too agonizing to contemplate.

Bereft of any confidant, Jacob bears his grief alone. Not until his deathbed does he even allude to the tragic event and the sorrow it brought him. Though we don't hear him grieving Rachel's death, Jacob's loss will have profound consequences for his entire family. Like many bereaved spouses, Jacob will transfer his emotional attachment to the most tangible link to his dead wife—her child.

On this somber chord of grief—a mother's life extinguished without warning, a father brokenhearted by the loss of his life's partner—young Joseph enters center stage of the family saga.

Now Jacob was settled in the land where his father had resided, the land of Canaan. At seventeen years of age, Joseph tended the flocks with his brothers, as a helper to them. And Joseph brought bad reports of them to their father.

Now Israel* loved Joseph best of all his sons, for he was the child of his old age. And he had made him an ornamented tunic. And when his brothers saw that their father loved Joseph more than any of his brothers, they hated him so that they could not speak a friendly word to him.

Once Joseph had a dream which he told to his brothers. "Hear this dream which I have dreamed. There we were binding sheaves in the field, when suddenly my sheaf stood up and remained upright. Then your sheaves gathered around and bowed low to my sheaf."

And his brothers answered, "Do you mean to reign over us? Do you mean to rule over us?" And they hated him even more for his talk about his dream.

But Joseph took no notice of their feelings, so full was he of his own visions. He dreamed another dream and told it to his brothers, saying, "Look, I have had another dream: This time the sun, the moon, and the eleven stars were bowing down to me."

And when he told it to his father and brothers, his father berated him. "What is this dream you have dreamed? Are we to come and bow low to you to the ground?" So his brothers were wrought up at him, and his father kept the matter in mind.

One time, when his brothers had gone to pasture their father's flock, Israel called to Joseph. "Go and see how your

---

* Jacob and his new name, Israel, will be used interchangeably throughout the rest of the biblical narrative.

brothers are and how the flocks are faring, and bring me back word." So he sent him from the valley of Hebron.

It was a long journey to where Joseph's brothers were pasturing their father's flock. Wearing the ornamented tunic his father had given him, Joseph walked alone for several days through the valley, away from his father and toward his brothers. *They saw him from afar, and before he came close to them they conspired to kill him.*

They said to one another, "Here comes the dreamer! Come now, let us kill him and throw him into one of the pits, and we can say, 'A savage beast devoured him.' We shall see what comes of his dreams!"

But when Reuben heard it, he tried to save him, saying, "Let us not take his life. Shed no blood! Cast him into the pit out in the wilderness, but do not touch him yourselves"—intending to save him and restore him to his father.

When Joseph came up to his brothers, they stripped him of the ornamented tunic that he was wearing, and took him and cast him into a pit.

Then they sat down to a meal. And while they ate, Joseph sat at the bottom of the pit, which was an old well now dry of water. He kept calling out to his brothers above, but they did not answer his cries.

Looking up, they saw a caravan of Ishmaelites coming from Gilead, their camels bearing gum, balm and ladanum to be taken to Egypt. Then Judah said to his brothers, "What will we gain by killing our brother and covering up his blood? Come, let us sell him to the Ishmaelites, but let us not do away with him ourselves. After all, he is our brother, our own flesh."

His brothers agreed. They pulled Joseph up out of the pit and sold him for twenty pieces of silver to the Ishmaelites who brought Joseph to Egypt.

Then his brothers took Joseph's tunic, slaughtered a kid, and dipped the tunic in the blood. They took the ornamented tunic to their father, and they said, "We found this. Please examine it. Is it your son's tunic or not?"

Jacob recognized it, and said, "My son's tunic! A savage beast devoured him! Joseph was torn by a beast!"

Jacob rent his clothes, put sackcloth on his loins, and observed mourning for his son many days. All his sons and daughters sought to comfort him, but he refused to be comforted, saying, "No, I will go down to the grave to my son in mourning." Thus did Joseph's father bewail him.

WHEN PARENTS SOW THE SEEDS OF THEIR CHILDREN'S DISCORD

Regardless of how familiar this story may be to us, it never fails to shock. How can brothers, no matter how badly provoked, sell their own sibling into slavery? One of my students, a former private school headmaster who had counseled countless fractured families over the years, was taken aback when we read this episode in class. "I know we should respect this first family of the Bible," he said almost sheepishly, "but I can't help being appalled by their behavior. They seem to me to be monsters."

But Jacob's sons are flesh and blood human beings, not monsters. Genesis is much more subtle and complex than a fairy tale, and it reveals hard truths about human nature. If we look closely, we will discover much more than a simple story of evil brothers conspiring against an innocent sibling. As we have seen before, sibling rivalry is often a symptom of deep-seated conflicts that have been germinating for generations. The seeds of contention between Jacob's sons have been sown years before by their parents, and it will be decades before the full cycle of revenge, reconciliation, and forgiveness will be complete.

The troubled dynamics of Jacob's family reflect contemporary domestic issues. Today people don't have two wives simultaneously, but our sequential marriages create a similar set of conflicts: siblings and half siblings competing for parental attention, parents overcompensating for a divorced, absent, or deceased spouse and bribing children or currying favor with expensive gifts.

The chilling lesson of this story is that love and hate are closely related emotions. Nothing better symbolizes this paradox than Joseph's *ornamented tunic,* or "coat of many colors," as it is commonly known. What begins as a symbol of a father's love for a son drives an insuperable wedge between Joseph and his siblings:

Now Israel loved Joseph best of all his sons, for he was the child of his old age. And he had made him an ornamented tunic. And when his brothers saw that their father loved Joseph more than any of his brothers, they hated him so that they could not speak a friendly word to him.

As a victim of his own father's favoritism, Jacob would be expected to be more sensitive to his sons' feelings. He, better than anyone, should understand the destructiveness of loving his sons unequally and then bestowing a special gift of clothing on his favorite. We can only assume that, like many recent widowers, Jacob is too absorbed in his own grief to notice. And people who have not fully acknowledged their childhood conflicts—in Jacob's case, having his father openly prefer his brother—tend to reenact those situations later in life.

When Joseph sets out for the distant pasture, far away from the protection of his father, he inflames an already hostile situation by wearing his ornamented tunic. It's no surprise that when Joseph's brothers see their hated sibling approaching, the tunic becomes the focus of their jealous rage:

They stripped him of the ornamented tunic that he was wearing, and took him and cast him into a pit.

When the brothers then dip the tunic in blood and present it to Jacob as grisly evidence of their brother's demise, they are rubbing their father's face in his own folly, repaying cruelty with cruelty. *"Is it your son's tunic or not?"* they demand. Not "our brother" or "Joseph," but rather "your son." When Jacob exclaims, *"My son's tunic! A savage beast devoured him! Joseph was torn by a beast!"* he could well be referring to the savage beast of sibling rivalry he has fostered among his own children. But Jacob remains blind to the truth of the situation—both his sons' treachery and his own culpability in Joseph's fate.

Like many self-centered people, Joseph remains oblivious to the rage that his arrogant behavior arouses. We're told that he tattles on his brothers, bringing *bad reports of them to their father*. While they toil in the fields, their spoiled younger brother regales them with his dreams, ripe with unconscious sexual bravado: *". . . when suddenly my sheaf stood up and remained upright. Then your sheaves gathered around and bowed low to my sheaf."* Small wonder that *they hated him even more for his talk about his dream*, which clearly portrays his older brothers humbling themselves before him. And in an age when dreams are believed to be prophetic, Joseph's message that he would someday rule over his brothers is doubly enraging. Young Joseph is unarguably a pain in the neck.

None of these extenuating circumstances excuses what the brothers do to Joseph. We can well understand why they feel such murderous rage for their half brother. But it's quite another thing to actually conspire to murder the object of their hatred, and then to sell him into slavery. They show no compassion for the fact that their younger half brother has just suffered the loss of his mother. Their sole concern is how to dispose of him with the least amount of guilt and incriminating evidence. Is it possible that they rationalize to themselves that selling Joseph into slavery is less cruel than leaving him to die in the pit? To me, the most shocking detail of all is their remorseless behavior after they strip Joseph and throw him into a pit: *Then they sat down to a meal.*

HOW SELF-LOVE
BECOMES SELF-DESTRUCTIVE

The question remains: How is it that Joseph is so self-absorbed as to seemingly invite his own destruction? His personality and behavior —from his heedlessly expressed dreams of supremacy to his flaunting of his *ornamented tunic*—are a precise match for the classic textbook description of narcissistic traits:

"A grandiose sense of self-importance or uniqueness; exaggerated tendency to self-dramatization, preoccupation with fantasies of unlimited success and power; an exhibitionistic need for constant attention and admiration; feelings of entitlement and lack of empathy; the behavior masks a fragile self-esteem."

This last trait, "fragile self-esteem," is perhaps the most telling. Joseph's behavior toward his brothers conceals underlying feelings of insecurity and inadequacy. He knows he has his father's love, but he's also aware of his brothers' resentment. At a certain point, parental adoration alone becomes infantilizing. Once we reach adolescence, we all hunger for acceptance and admiration from our peers —in Joseph's case, his older brothers. But because he lacks empathy for their feelings, Joseph's attempts to woo his brothers have the opposite effect.

We can trace much of Joseph's personality to his early development. As a boy, he has the advantage of occupying a favored position with both his parents. He is the long-awaited child of Rachel, who no doubt dotes on him for the first seven years of his life. Growing up in his mother's tent—just as his father Jacob had with his mother Rebekah—Joseph doesn't have to share her affections with any siblings. And we can deduce from Rachel's fierce rivalry with Leah that she would certainly have been grooming her son for leadership of his clan. Psychoanalyst Dorothy Zeligs draws a comparison between Joseph and Sigmund Freud, who once commented about his own childhood: "A man who has been the indisputable favorite of his mother keeps for life the feeling of a conqueror, that confidence of success that often induces real success."

Unlike Jacob, Joseph also enjoys the focused attention of his father. After six or seven years of being reared by his mother, Joseph's care is taken up by Jacob, who is predisposed to favor Joseph as the son of his favorite, and now deceased, wife. Jacob probably hopes to compensate for Jacob's lost mother, and he's determined to lavish on Joseph all the paternal affection he never got from his own father. Joseph certainly reminds Jacob of himself—a younger son and a dreamer. Abraham and Jacob were both visionary leaders who were able to reach out to God for a dream of deliverance whenever they lost their way. In Joseph, Jacob discovers an heir to this tradition.

What Jacob doesn't see—his near-fatal blind spot—is how his undisguised favoritism pits his other sons against Joseph. *And when his brothers saw that their father loved him more than any of his brothers, they hated him so that they could not speak a friendly word to him.* This inability to even speak to Joseph underscores the depth of the brothers' hostility. With all channels of communication severed, there is little hope that they can avoid the violent confrontation to come.

If Jacob had any notion of the depth of sibling resentment he has helped foster, he would never have sent Joseph out alone to check up on his brothers—particularly not cloaked in the ultimate symbol of his father's patronage, the many-colored coat. Perhaps he hopes that having Joseph spend time alone with his brothers will draw his sons closer together. He may even intend to toughen up his soft young son by throwing him into a difficult situation with no protection from his father. Whatever his expectations, they prove wildly misguided, and the many-colored coat is soon dyed red with the blood of a sacrificial goat.

Parental love carries rewards and liabilities for the young Joseph. He inherits leadership qualities from both his father and mother, some of which won't emerge until later in life: he's articulate, self-confident, and intuitive. Most important, the love he receives from his parents in childhood makes him feel like a lovable human being of immense value. This heightened feeling of self-worth will attract people to Joseph wherever he goes in life.

What Joseph lacks is the maturity to understand how his arrogant behavior affects others. His self-absorption almost proves his undoing. But as we will soon see, Joseph has the personal resilience to bounce back from adversity. When tested by circumstances, he will outgrow his narcissism and develop the empathy he needs to earn other people's confidence and trust.

SETTING LIMITS ON SELF-LOVE

In her book *The Psychological Birth of the Human Infant,* Margaret Mahler describes an infant's early ego development:

> From the twelfth to eighteenth month, the world is the junior toddler's oyster. . . . The child seems intoxicated with his own faculties and the greatness of his own world. Narcissism is at its peak! The child's first upright independent steps mark the onset of the practicing period. With substantial widening of his world and of reality testing, the mother needs to be supportive and limit-setting.

Normally, this inflated sense of self fades as the child comes to understand that he is not the center of the universe. But some people, like Joseph, sustain these feelings of grandiosity well into adolescence. As Joseph's story demonstrates, prolonged and exaggerated self-love is not only inappropriate, it's eventually self-destructive.

On the other hand, self-love is closely related to positive attributes such as self-esteem, self-respect, and self-confidence. And as we'll see in Joseph's story, enhanced self-worth is an invaluable asset in later life, particularly for leaders. Living in Washington, DC, I've gotten to know many United States senators and representatives over the years, and I can't think of one of them who would have gotten to Capitol Hill without an extra measure of self-love.

It's a delicate balancing act: giving ourselves enough love to nurture and protect ourselves from rejection, without allowing self-love to become what Oscar Wilde described as "the beginning of a lifelong romance." Voltaire noted that "self-love is the instrument of our preservation; it is necessary, it is dear to us, it gives us pleasure, and we must conceal it." The absence of discretion in conveying his grandiose dreams almost proves to be Joseph's downfall. But without the belief that he is destined for greatness, Joseph will never survive the trials that lie before him. In my practice I become concerned when exaggerated self-love becomes an obstacle to a patient's intimate relationships and a handicap in pursuing his or her work.

The wisest commentary I've ever found on the conundrum of self-love comes from the first-century sage Hillel, who asked:

> If I am not for myself, who will be?
> If I am only for myself, what am I?
> If not now, when?

What does Hillel mean, and how can we integrate the wisdom of his questions into our own lives?

First, we must feel we are valuable human beings who care for and respect ourselves. If we don't love ourselves, how can anyone else?

However, if we love only ourselves and don't extend that caring to others, we are doomed to loneliness and alienation.

When is the time, if not now, to begin putting these words into practice? It is never too early to start down the road to change.

These three consummately existential questions—If I am not for myself, who will be? If I am only for myself, what am I? If not now, when?—could well be reverberating through Joseph's mind as he wends his way toward bondage in Egypt.

JOSEPH IN EXILE: MATURING THROUGH ADVERSITY

Even though I walk through the valley of the
shadow of death, I will fear no evil, for
Thou art with me.

—*Psalms 23:4*

The British dramatist Ben Jonson once wrote, "He knows not his own strength that has not met adversity." None of us is ever really tested until we face obstacles in our life path and grapple with them on our own. Only when we lose a secure job, have our heart broken in love, or have a close relative or friend die, do we really find out what we're made of. We can't help but want to avoid obstacles and spare ourselves unhappiness. Many parents believe they're doing their children a favor by protecting them for as long as possible from the harsh realities of life. But as we find out from Joseph's saga, the learning curve of life ascends most steeply when we face seemingly insurmountable obstacles with nothing but our inner resources to sustain us.

As Jacob's sheltered favorite son, Joseph never really had a chance to discover the outer limits of his character. Now, as a powerless slave in an alien land, Joseph will be tested on both a physical and a spiritual level. Can he survive in a hostile environment and fulfill his dreams of glory? After the cruel betrayal by his brothers, can Joseph recover his faith in both man and God?

As he sat at the bottom of the pit, despair descended on Joseph, the pampered youth crying out to his remorseless brothers while they ate their meal and debated how best to dispose of him. He listened with anguish as they haggled with the passing caravan over his buy price. "He's worth at least twenty pieces of silver. Perfect for a household slave, even if he can't carry his weight in the field." When the transaction was complete and the silver was traded for flesh, not one of his brothers cast a backward glance at Joseph as he was carted off to market.

Throughout the long days of journeying toward Egypt, Joseph sat in silence atop a camel, listening to the Ishmaelites call to each other in their strange tongue. He was alone in the world now. Formerly his father's pet, he was now reduced to merchandise, mere chattel in the slave trade.

The Ishmaelites, meanwhile, sold him in Egypt to Potiphar, a courtier of Pharaoh and his chief steward. Potiphar's was a prominent household with many slaves. Joseph began as a common house servant, doing menial jobs. But as his talent for managing people and property emerged, he rose to a position of great responsibility.

The Lord was with Joseph and he was a successful man, and he stayed in the house of his Egyptian master, who took a liking to Joseph. He made him his personal attendant and put him in charge of his household, placing in his hands all that he owned. He left all that he had in Joseph's hands, and he paid attention to nothing save the food that he ate.

Joseph allowed himself to look ahead with hope toward

his future. Perhaps his master would allow him to buy back his freedom some day. Or even recommend him to Pharaoh's court, where his talents might be welcomed. So long as his master's household prospered under his care, Joseph's status might improve.

Now Joseph was of beautiful form and fair to look upon. After a time, his master's wife cast her eyes upon Joseph and said, "Lie with me."

But he refused. He said to his master's wife, "With me here, my master gives no thought to anything in this house, and all that he owns he has placed in my hands. He wields no more authority in this house than I, and he has withheld nothing from me except yourself, since you are his wife. How then could I do this most wicked thing, and sin before God?"

Potiphar's wife refused to relinquish her hold on her house slave. *But much as she coaxed Joseph, day after day, he did not yield to her request to lie beside her, to be with her.*

One such day, he came into the house to do his work. None of the household being there inside, she caught hold of him by his coat and said, "Lie with me!" But he left his coat in her hands and got away and fled outside.

She called out to her servants and said to them, "This Hebrew came to lie with me, but I screamed aloud. And when he heard me screaming at the top of my voice, he left his coat with me and got away and fled outside."

She kept his coat beside her, until his master came home. She told her husband the same story, that she had been assaulted by the Hebrew slave he had brought into their household and entrusted with the management of their estate. *So Joseph's master had him put in prison, where the king's prisoners were confined.*

SEXUAL HARASSMENT
AND THE ABUSE OF POWER

What could be more contemporary than this tale of sexual harassment in the workplace? This perennial problem, which Anita Hill brought into all of our living rooms, is clearly one that dates back to ancient times. I think it's fascinating that the Bible chooses to highlight this issue by narrating an episode in which a male "employee" is the victim of harassment. I like to believe that this treatment of the story raises the consciousness of male readers about the plight of women who have traditionally been economically dependent on male employers, and therefore vulnerable to sexual coercion.

Today, with more and more women sharing the workplace at all levels of management, the sexual dynamics and pressures are more complex than ever. Working together on an equal footing, traveling together on business, and collaborating intensively on projects, all create feelings of intimacy between men and women. This intimacy often leads to sexual attraction—which may or may not involve elements of coercion or harassment. Women working with men as equals is such a recent phenomenon that we are only now beginning to deal with its ramifications. Social psychologists such as Andrea Bardion and David Eyler have recently formulated a set of behavioral guidelines, a so-called "new sexual etiquette," to help people manage volatile sexual chemistry that, if ignored, can become destructive to their working relationships.

In today's world this biblical tale sends a cautionary message to both women and men. As women continue to ascend the management heirarchy, more and more of them will assume positions of power over men. Only time will tell if women prove more sensitive to the rights of their subordinates than Potiphar's wife was to Joseph's.

We don't know how attractive and tempting Potiphar's wife may have been. What we do know, and what Joseph surely knew, is that she had the power to make or break him. For a slave to spurn the ardent advances of his master's wife was to court disaster. "Hell hath no fury like a woman scorned," William Congreve warned.

After he scorns this powerful woman and *left his coat in her hands*, Joseph's next home is the hellish pit of Pharaoh's prison. With yet another coat stripped from his body, it is as if Joseph is repeatedly shedding his skin as he descends from his father's favor into enslavement in Egypt and finally into imprisonment.

The Bible displays a continual concern with abuse of power. According to the Bible, whoever possesses political, economic, or social power over another person has the responsibility to exercise that power ethically and with compassion. The Book of Deuteronomy sets out detailed rules defining proper behavior toward workmen, servants, and even slaves. While slavery was an established and accepted institution in biblical times, the Bible emphasizes that even a slave is a human being, created in the image of God, and is therefore entitled to certain basic rights—including the offer of freedom after seven years of labor.

THE POWER OF PERSONAL INTEGRITY

Joseph continues to arouse strong feelings in everyone he meets. No one remains indifferent to him. He soon wins his master's trust, and before long, he is managing all of Potiphar's affairs. His master's wife is also interested in Joseph's talents, but in a different realm altogether. We know Joseph to be an ambitious young man, but we now discover that he is also capable of reining in his ambition when it collides with the code of ethics he carried with him into Egypt.

Only after he is stripped of all privileges and sold into slavery does Joseph's strength of character begin to emerge. In light of the sexual promiscuity that was historically prevalent between slaveowners and slaves in Egyptian society, Joseph's self-restraint is especially exemplary. A liaison with Potiphar's wife could well have solidified his position in the household. But at great risk to his own safety, Joseph repeatedly declines her overtures out of loyalty to her husband. It's no wonder that his behavior drives Potiphar's wife wild with rage. Not only does he, a slave and a foreigner, reject her advances—he takes the moral high ground as well, invoking her husband's trust and his covenant with God: *"How then could I do this most wicked thing, and sin before God?"* Considering the woman's accusations against him, Joseph is lucky to be thrown in prison, rather than fed to crocodiles in the Nile—a punishment often prescribed in Egyptian folktales of the day.

For the young Joseph, the self-restraint he exhibits with Potiphar's wife emerges as an important leadership trait—as well as the foundation of personal integrity. In every generation of Genesis, the one who can control his urges wins out over those who are enslaved by their passions. All morality begins with self-restraint and the ability to delay gratification. And all leaders, whether of families or of nations, must learn to plan and to defer. As we will see later in Joseph's career, his ability to plan for the future will prove crucial to his rise to power.

Joseph has not left Canaan empty-handed. An alien with no rights or power, Joseph transcends his enslaved state through his covenant with God. By holding himself accountable only to God— in whose likeness he was created—Joseph cannot be subjugated by man or woman. Though his brothers have betrayed him and Potiphar's wife has accused him falsely, Joseph believes that God will not abandon him no matter how far he descends in the world. As he heads off for an indeterminate stay in Pharaoh's prison, Joseph does not permit despair to overtake him.

So Joseph's master had him put in prison, where the king's prisoners were confined. But even while he was there in prison, the Lord was with Joseph. He disposed the chief jailer favorably toward him. The chief jailer put in Joseph's charge all the prisoners who were in that prison, and he was the one to carry out everything that was done there.

Sometime later, the cupbearer and the baker of the king of Egypt gave offense to their lord the king of Egypt. Pharaoh was angry with his two courtiers, the chief cupbearer and the chief baker, and put them in custody in the same prison where Joseph was confined. The chief steward assigned Joseph to them, and he attended them.

When they had been in custody for some time, both of them—the cupbearer and the baker of the king—dreamed in the same night. When Joseph came to them in the morning, he saw that they were distraught. He asked Pharaoh's courtiers, who were with him in custody in his master's house, saying, "Why do you appear downcast today?" And they said to him, "We had dreams, and there is no one to interpret them." So Joseph said to them, "Surely God can interpret! Tell me [your dreams]."

Then the chief cupbearer told his dream to Joseph. He said to him, "In my dream, there was a vine in front of me. On the vine were three branches. It had barely budded when out came its blossoms and its clusters ripened into grapes. Pharaoh's cup was in my hand, and I took the grapes, pressed them in Pharaoh's cup, and placed the cup in Pharaoh's hand."

Joseph said to him, "This is its interpretation: The three branches are three days. In three days Pharaoh will pardon you and restore you to your post. You will place Pharaoh's cup in his hand, as was your custom, formerly when you were his cupbearer.

But think of me when all is well with you again, and do me the kindness of mentioning me to Pharaoh, so as to free me from this place. For in truth, I was kidnapped from the land of the Hebrews. Nor have I done anything here that they should have put me in the dungeon."

The baker was watching and listening to Joseph all the while. When the chief baker saw how favorably he had interpreted the cupbearer's dream, he urged Joseph to consider his own. *"In my dream there were three openwork baskets on my* head. In the uppermost basket were all kinds of food for Pharaoh that a baker prepares. And the birds were eating it out of the basket above my head."

Joseph answered, "This is its interpretation: The three baskets are three days. In three days Pharaoh will lift off your head and hang you on a tree. And the birds will pick off your flesh."

On the third day—his birthday—Pharaoh made a banquet for all his officials, and he singled out his chief cupbearer and his chief baker from among his officials. He restored the chief cupbearer to his cupbearing, and he placed the cup in Pharaoh's hand. But the chief baker he hung on a tree—just as Joseph had interpreted to them.

Yet the chief cupbearer did not think of Joseph. He forgot him.

EMPATHY, THE PATH TO MATURITY

Antoine de Saint-Exupéry defined despair as "the rejection of God within oneself." If we look at Joseph's experience in exile, it's amazing how resilient he proves. Throughout his trials in Egypt, Joseph refuses to forsake the covenant that his father and mother instilled in him at an early age. Despite the depths to which human treachery consigns him, he doesn't cave in to despair or bitterness. No matter how little control he wields over his fate, Joseph never relinquishes his moral integrity and his right to define his own spiritual identity.

Psychoanalyst Viktor E. Frankl could well have been writing about Joseph when he made the following observation about survivors of wretched imprisonment:

Men can preserve a vestige of spiritual freedom, of independence of mind, even in terrible conditions of psychic and physical stress. Everything can be taken from man but one thing: the last of the human freedoms—to choose one's attitude in any given set of circumstances.

In prison, Joseph's life touches bottom. Even as a slave he had more prospects than as a prisoner. Like the pit his brothers cast him into, Pharaoh's dungeon is closer to a grave than a life. But rather than wallow in depression, Joseph begins to build his own ladder out of his pit. Before long, he once again finds favor with an authority figure—perhaps another surrogate father—in this case, the chief jailer. *The chief jailer put in Joseph's charge all the prisoners who were in that prison, and he was the one to carry out everything that was done there.*

We also see Joseph developing the very characteristics he lacked in his youth: humility and empathy. Instead of taking personal credit for his skills in dream interpretation, he attributes whatever insights he gleans to God, saying, *"Surely God can interpret!"* In Egypt, the interpretation of prophetic dreams was a highly developed discipline. Whole encyclopedias of dream interpretations were compiled and religiously consulted. Joseph and Daniel are the only biblical characters who interpret dreams, and only as exiles in foreign lands where this skill is prized—Joseph in Egypt and Daniel in Mesopotamia. Augury and magic were forbidden in the Israelite tradition because God is the only source of prophecy and miracles; but God endows these men with the skill that they need to survive in an alien culture.

In prison, Joseph develops the empathy and sensitivity to intuit the fears and anxieties that haunt the baker and cupbearer, whose care has been put in his hands. After weeks, and perhaps months, of close observation, Joseph understands his charges well enough to accurately interpret their dreams. He grasps that the cupbearer, who dreams of hand-pressing his grapes into Pharaoh's cup, is probably a conscientious servant who will be restored to his position. But the baker, who negligently leaves his breads open to the birds above, will himself become food for birds of prey.

It would certainly have been safer to grant the baker a more favorable interpretation. Bearing bad news has always been a hazardous occupation. But Joseph trusts his instincts and intuition in interpreting dreams. Even though his penchant for truth-telling has gotten Joseph into trouble in the past, he does not compromise his dream interpretations for the sake of protecting himself from retaliation. I find it very revealing that Joseph stops short of full disclosure when he pleads his innocence to the cupbearer. He still cares too much about the good name of his family to bad-mouth them by revealing how he was sold into slavery and by whom. His claim that *"in truth, I was kidnapped from the land of the Hebrews,"* is not quite the whole truth. Joseph's "white lie" reminds me of the advice my husband's grandmother used to give him: "It's important to tell the truth, but not necessarily the whole truth."

Joseph's plea to the cupbearer—*"think of me when all is well with you again, and do me the kindness of mentioning me to Pharaoh, so as to free me from this place"*—is particularly poignant. Over the course of three decades of living in Washington, DC, I've observed that people rarely want to be reminded of the times in their lives when they were out of power and dependent on the kindness of others. So it doesn't surprise me when the cupbearer puts the Hebrew slave, Joseph, out of mind as soon as he is restored to Pharaoh's court: *Yet the chief cupbearer did not think of Joseph. He forgot him.* The frequent amnesia of people we've once helped is another dose of harsh reality that the Bible doesn't hesitate to warn us of. As Orson Welles, a film director whose career was marked by dramatic peaks and valleys, once wryly observed, "When you are down and out, something always turns up—and it is usually the noses of your friends."

THE COURAGE TO
EMBRACE ADVERSITY

Joseph's personal transformation while enslaved and imprisoned teaches us why so many gifted but immature young people fall by the wayside. Talent alone is not enough to carry us over the inevitable potholes that lie in our life's path. Only character and a strong sense of identity can get us through. The careers of talented young musicians and athletes are rife with sad stories—prodigies waylaid by the temptations of celebrity, or overgrown and overindulged children who fall apart when confronted with the simplest of adult problems. If, as Thomas Edison insisted, "genius is ten percent inspiration and ninety percent perspiration," the period when gifted youth are tested by adversity is critical to both their careers and their personal development.

It's difficult to seek out adversity, or to wish it on those we love, but we intuitively understand that we need adversity in order to grow. Some of us seek structured challenges such as Outward Bound because modern urban life is devoid of the primal survival struggles that transform children into adults.

Parents find it particularly difficult to expose children to adversity, to give them the freedom to deal with their problems on their own, to watch them struggle without rushing to their rescue. Especially when the cultural mythos is built on parents giving children the advantages they never had. At what point do too many advantages become a disadvantage? Too often, the "advantages" of extended education and freedom from any financial constraints only insulate our children from the real life challenges they need to encounter head-on.

Children need to strive, and sometimes fail, in order to grow. But every parent knows how excruciating it can be to put this simple principle into practice. I remember the anguish of watching my youngest son's first Fourth of July sack race. A row of six-year-olds gamely hopped along inside their burlap sacks, falling on their faces and getting up and falling down again. As those boys and girls tumbled clumsily toward the finish line, we adults in the audience cheered them on with our hearts caught in our throats. Even then, it struck me that this child's game was a poignant metaphor for the human "race." Sometimes it seems as if we are all hobbled by invisible sacks that trip us up and mock our desire to sprint through life. If only we could hold on to that six-year-old's brave determination to rise from every fall and continue—no matter how clumsily— along our course.

Joseph's story always reminds me that what we desire and what we need to grow are often entirely different things. My friend Jeffrey once sent me a poem on this theme, written by an anonymous

Civil War soldier wounded in battle, which I've kept taped to my refrigerator door ever since. My favorite lines read:

> I asked for riches, that I might be happy;
> I was given poverty, that I might be wise.
>
> I asked for power, that I might have the praise of men;
> I was given weakness, that I might feel the need of God.
>
> I asked for all things, that I might enjoy life;
> I was given life, that I might enjoy all things.
>
> I am, among all men, most richly blessed.

Chapter Thirty-two

(Genesis 41)

———

JOSEPH'S
METEORIC RISE:
KEEPING IN TOUCH
WITH
OUR ROOTS

Know from where you came, where you are going,
and before whom you will have to give an
account of your life.

—The Talmud

After he's forgotten by the cupbearer, Joseph continues
to languish in Pharaoh's dungeon for years. Yet his
spirit doesn't die. Despite his enslavement and unjust
imprisonment, he continues to believe that *even while he was there
in prison, the Lord was with him.* What is it that allows some people
to endure long imprisonment? How does a Nelson Mandela or a
Natan Sharansky emerge from decades of unjust captivity with
enough strength and courage to lead?

In Bruno Bettelheim's landmark book about concentration
camp inmates, *The Informed Heart,* he concluded that prisoners with

strong identities—whether political convictions or confirmed religious beliefs—had higher survival rates. Bettelheim found that to the degree we can maintain a larger, more comprehensive vision of who we are and why we need to survive, we remain more resilient in the face of persecution.

Viktor Frankl, himself a survivor of the death camps, wrote a penetrating study about why some prisoners endured this ordeal better than others. In *Man's Search for Meaning*, he surmised that "free decision" was a more important survival factor than the particulars of their imprisonment:

> Psychological observations of the prisoners have shown that only the men who allowed their inner hold on their moral or spiritual selves to subside eventually fell victim to the camp's degenerating influences. The question now arises, what could, or should, have constituted this "inner hold"?

Joseph can't sink any lower in the world. But even as a slave and a prisoner in a foreign land, he will not be denied his humanity. His knowledge that he is made in the image of God protects him against misfortune and human treachery. Joseph also feels the obligation to survive in order to carry on the covenant that his forefathers struck with God. Bolstered by his faith in the God of Abraham, Isaac, and Jacob, Joseph keeps despair at bay and sustains himself for the day when he will have a chance to deliver himself from bondage. When he finally emerges from prison, he is no longer a self-absorbed adolescent, but a seasoned adult, self-reliant and self-aware.

One morning two years later, Pharaoh awoke with a start from troubling dreams.

Next morning, his spirit was agitated, and he sent for all of the magicians of Egypt and all its wise men. And Pharaoh told them his dreams, but none could interpret them.

The chief cupbearer then spoke up and said to Pharaoh, "I must make mention today of my offenses." And he told Pharaoh of the Hebrew slave, still imprisoned in his dungeon, who had so accurately interpreted the dreams of Pharaoh's cup-bearer and baker.

Thereupon Pharaoh sent for Joseph, and he was rushed from the dungeon. He had his hair cut and changed clothes, and he appeared before Pharaoh. And Pharaoh said to him, "I have had a dream, but no one can interpret it. Now I have heard it said of you that for you to hear a dream is to tell its meaning."

Joseph answered Pharaoh, saying, "Not I! God will give Pharaoh an answer of peace."

Then Pharaoh said to Joseph, "In my dream, I was standing on the bank of the Nile, when out of the river came seven sturdy and well-formed cows, and they grazed in the reed grass. But presently, seven other cows came up from the Nile close behind them, scrawny, ill-formed and emaciated—never have I seen their likes for ugliness in all the land of Egypt! And the seven lean and ugly cows ate up the first seven cows, the sturdy ones. But when they had consumed them, one could not tell, for they looked just as bad as before. And I awoke.

"In my second dream, I saw seven ears of grain, full and healthy, growing on a single stalk. But close behind them sprouted seven ears, shriveled, thin and scorched by the east wind. And the thin ears swallowed up the seven solid and full ears. I have told my magicians these dreams, but none has an explanation for me."

And Joseph interpreted them. "Pharaoh's dreams are one and the same: God has told Pharaoh what He is about to do. The seven healthy cows are seven years, and the seven healthy ears are seven years. The seven lean and ugly cows and the seven empty ears scorched by the east wind are seven years of *famine. Immediately ahead are seven years of great abundance in all the land of Egypt. After them will come seven years of famine, and all the abundance in the land of Egypt will be forgotten. As the land is ravaged by famine, no trace of the abundance will be left in the land, for the famine will be very severe. As for Pharaoh having had the same dream twice, it means that the matter has been determined by God, and God will soon carry it out."*

As Pharaoh contemplated the meaning of this interpretation, Joseph proceeded to lay out a plan to deliver Egypt from the famine to come.

"Accordingly, let Pharaoh find a man of discernment and wisdom, and set him over the land of Egypt. And let Pharaoh take steps to appoint overseers over the land, and organize the land of Egypt in the seven years of plenty. Let all the food of these good years that are coming be gathered, and let the grain be collected under the Pharaoh's authority as food to be stored in the cities. Let that food be a reserve for the land for the seven years of famine, so that the land of Egypt may not perish in the famine."

The plan pleased Pharaoh and his courtiers. And Pharaoh said to his courtiers, "Could we find another like him, a man in whom is the spirit of God?" So Pharaoh said to Joseph, "Since God has made all this known to you, there is none so discerning and wise as you. You shall be in charge of my court, and by your command shall all my people be directed. Only with respect to the throne shall I be superior to you. I put you in charge of all the land of Egypt."

USING OUR GOD-GIVEN
SURVIVAL SKILLS

Once he emerges from prison, Joseph's latent leadership talents come to the fore. The dreamer has now become the man of action. Not only does he display his intuition in deciphering the meaning of Pharaoh's dream, he has the political acumen to conceive a plan for coping with what the dream portends. Joseph doesn't try to pass himself off as a soothsayer or a magician, but takes care to credit God as the source of his insights. But he uses his God-given talent of persuasion to get himself appointed to carry out his rescue plan.

Another God-given talent that Joseph possesses—and that all of us share in greater or lesser measure—is the ability to read facial and body language. Joseph, as the Bible's first dream "analyst," possessed extraordinary powers of observation. He was probably able to predict the baker's and the cupbearer's fate based largely on his sensitivity to their facial expressions and body language. And the day he is called before Pharaoh, Joseph certainly takes careful note of Pharaoh's agitation and the grave concern etched in his face.

When I listen to patients describe their feelings, whether recounting an event or a dream, I watch closely for nonverbal clues to their underlying state of mind. Does he smile inappropriately when talking about a painful subject? Does she calmly describe an upcoming crisis at work, while her fingers are twisting her handkerchief into knots? Whether we're mothers tuning in to our infant's unspoken needs or lovers evaluating the sincerity of a partner's sweet talk, we all try to read people's minds and moods by decoding their body language and the involuntary movements of their faces. The more sensitive we are to these involuntary clues, the more attuned we become to the nuances of our interpersonal and professional relationships. And if we're adept at picking up the unspoken feelings beneath people's words and actions, we're a lot less likely to be misled.

In addition to his intuitiveness, Joseph displays remarkable intelligence in his dream interpretation and in developing his rationing plan. He may or may not know exactly when famine will come. But his knowledge of Egyptian agricultural cycles and his own life experience doubtless taught Joseph two important truths: that times of plenty are inevitably followed by periods of scarcity, and that humans are reluctant to plan for "rainy days" while the sun still shines. We need look no further than the energy crisis of the 1970s for a contemporary example. And today, instead of stockpiling fuel or conserving energy during oil gluts, we drive more and in larger cars, heedless of yesterday's and tomorrow's inevitable shortfalls. We can't seem to learn to delay gratification for the sake of our future security, to forgo some pleasures now in order to avoid privation later. When Joseph displays both the vision to conceive a plan of grain stockpiling and the political skill to carry it out, we see the value of a leader who can strategize for the future.

We also see that Joseph's performance instincts did not desert him during his years in prison. When he is suddenly *rushed from the dungeon* to appear before Pharaoh, Joseph has the presence of mind to *have his hair cut and change clothes*. He doesn't display any nervousness before Pharaoh, even when predicting a calamitous famine. And before the import of his dark prediction can sink in, Joseph quickly presents a detailed action plan to rescue Egypt from disaster.

We then get a revealing glimpse of the ambitious Joseph thinking quickly on his feet. Others might have been content with escaping prison, but Joseph sees an opportunity for professional advancement. He urges Pharaoh to *find a man of discernment and wisdom, and set him over the land of Egypt*. We well know which *man of discernment and wisdom* Joseph has in mind for this task. But he's tactful enough to describe his own qualifications without explicitly nominating himself.

On multiple occasions he credits God as the source of his insights, implying that he enjoys a special relationship with God. It isn't long before Pharaoh, who acknowledges the existence of multiple gods, makes the self-evident choice: *"Since God has made all this known to you, there is none so discerning and wise as you. You shall be in charge of my court, and by your command shall all my people be directed."* Within the space of an hour, Joseph has persuaded Pharaoh to choose him—a wretched Hebrew slave and prisoner in his dungeon—as his prime minister.

I am reminded of an analogous episode in the recent annals of Washington public life. The country's largest cultural organization, the Smithsonian Institution, was searching for a new director to guide it through the tight financial straits of the nonprofit world. After six months of combing the ranks of prospective candidates, the head of the search committee resigned and entered his own name into nomination for the post. Calling a news conference, he announced that after long consideration, he felt he was the most qualified candidate for the job. A few months later, the board of directors concurred, and he was installed as the new director.

THE WISDOM THAT
COMES WITH MATURITY

There is one other attribute that allows Joseph to so astutely interpret Pharaoh's dream: the wisdom that comes with maturity. He has learned from his own experience that life is dynamic and constantly changing—that emotionally, feast is eventually followed by famine. The wheel of fortune has spun around continually through Joseph's youth. After the joy of his mother's love came the grief of her death. After the exhilaration of his father's focused attention, the despair at his brothers' betrayal. No sooner did he rise in Potiphar's household than he was cast down again into the dungeon.

What we learn from Joseph's experience in prison is that if we can survive life's dry spells—whether emotional, financial, or professional—the wheel of fortune will eventually spin around again. But first we must survive. Joseph accepts his life in its totality, its good times and its bad. Because life has so much meaning for him, Joseph feels responsible for making the right choices, regardless of his circumstances. As long as he believes that what he chooses to do matters—even in prison, in a foreign land far from his family—despair will never overwhelm him.

Famines in Genesis symbolize all the catastrophic life events over which we have no control. During famines our faith and our resourcefulness are tested to the limit. But our character is also tested during periods of plenty. As Joseph learned during his charmed youth—and as he will rediscover now that his star has risen again—success carries its own temptations, its own challenges to our identity and our integrity.

For Joseph, one success followed quickly on another.

Removing his signet ring from his hand, Pharaoh put it in Joseph's hand. And Pharaoh had him dressed in robes of fine linen and put a gold chain about his neck. He had him ride in the chariot of his second-in-command, and they cried before him, "Abrek!" Thus he placed him over all the land of Egypt.

Pharaoh said to Joseph, "I am Pharaoh, yet without you, no one shall lift up hand or foot in all the land of Egypt." Pharaoh then gave Joseph the name Zaphenath-paneah. And he gave him for a wife Asenath, daughter of Poti-phera, priest of On. Thus Joseph emerged in charge of the land of Egypt.

Joseph was thirty years old when he entered the service of Pharaoh, king of Egypt. Leaving Pharaoh's presence, Joseph traveled through all the land of Egypt.

During the seven years of plenty, the land produced in abundance. And he gathered all the grain of the seven years that the land of Egypt was enjoying, and stored the grain in the cities. He put in each city the grain of the fields around it. So Joseph collected produce in very large quantity, like the sands of the sea, until he ceased to measure it, for it could not be measured.

Before the years of famine came, Joseph became the father of two sons whom Asenath bore to him. Joseph named his first-born Manasseh, meaning "God has made me forget completely my hardship and my father's house." And the second he named Ephraim, meaning "God has made me fertile in the land of my affliction."

The seven years of abundance came to an end, and the

seven years of famine set in, just as Joseph had foretold. There was famine in all the lands, but throughout the land of Egypt there was bread. And when all the land of Egypt felt the hunger, the people cried out to Pharaoh for bread. And Pharaoh said to all the Egyptians, "Go to Joseph. Whatever he tells you, you shall do." Accordingly, when the famine became severe in the land, Joseph laid open all that was within and rationed out grain to the Egyptians.

The famine, however, spread over the whole world. So all the world came to Joseph in Egypt to procure rations.

THE SLIPPERY
SLOPE OF ASSIMILATION

Our culture glorifies self-made men and women, people from simple backgrounds who rise to power or wealth by dint of talent and hard work. Immigrants with talent and ambition arrive on American shores in every generation, and some of them, like the Chairman of the Joint Chiefs of Staff, John Shalikashvili, rise to high office in their adopted country. But what becomes of these people's sense of self as they ascend the ladder of status, wealth, and power?

Joseph's story points out to us the dangers of becoming dazzled by the glare of celebrity. When we rise from obscurity to prominence, the trappings of success threaten to supplant the values of our early life—the very values that were instrumental in helping us succeed. We can become so mesmerized by our own power that we lose touch with who we are and where we have come from.

Once launched on his meteoric rise, will Joseph loose touch with his historical, moral, and spiritual roots? As ruler over Egypt at the age of thirty, he seems embarked on the treacherous path of celebrity we so often witness in the newly prominent: the robes of fine linen, the gold chains, the grand chariots, the crowds shouting their adulation. Under Pharaoh's patronage, Joseph takes on a new

Egyptian name and an Egyptian wife—the daughter of the high priest of On, which was the great cultic center of the sun-god Re. And when he is blessed with a child, Joseph gives him an Egyptian name that seems a direct rebuke to his past: *Joseph named his first-born Manasseh, meaning "God has made me forget completely my hardship and my father's house."* Now that he has become a savior to Egypt, providing it with food and sustenance, Joseph seems to have left his boyhood self behind.

Or has he? In *The Power of Myth*, Joseph Campbell draws the important distinction between the celebrity and the hero: one lives for himself while the other acts to redeem society. What sets Joseph apart from merely ambitious men is that he sees himself as a player in a larger historical and spiritual movement. He is always the visionary statesman, never the petty politician. He remains accountable to a vision larger than himself—namely, the covenant with God that his parents transmitted to him in his youth. For Joseph, his new position as viceroy of Egypt represents more than just an expedient path to power and wealth. He feels obliged to use his God-given talents for the benefit of others.

CHERISHING THE BRIDGE THAT BROUGHT US ACROSS

It never occurred to me, until I came to this country, how vigilant one must be to maintain one's identity. I left Israel in the fifties, not long after its War of Independence, during a time of great economic austerity. In retrospect, it would have been so easy to abandon the Spartan ideals I was raised with and embrace the culture of affluent consumerism that surrounded me. I went out of my way to guard against the seductive display windows of Tiffany's, Saks, and Bergdorf's, which beckoned to a way of life that was coming within my reach. As I walked down Fifth Avenue, stealing an occasional glance at the marvelous storefront offerings, I used to hum my old school songs with their Hebrew lyrics about ploughing and protecting the land. With each passing window, I hummed louder and hurried faster down the street.

No matter what our roots are, if we develop an authentic personal identity early on, it will anchor us throughout our life. My mother used to tell me, "Even if you come from Timbuktu, if you know everything there is to know about Timbuktu, you can travel anywhere in the world and never lose your way."

I was very moved recently while reading an interview with the mother of a young football player from a tiny town in Mississippi. Her son had just signed a lucrative contract with an NFL team for "more money than anyone in my family ever dreamed of." But she harbored no fears for her son or her family's identity. "I'll still keep this house. Fix it up, maybe, but this is where we live. None of us will change, because money can't change love. I firmly believe what I've taught all my boys: cherish the bridge that brought you across."

Joseph has every reason to be embittered about his youth. He feels rejected by his family and embraced by the "country of his affliction." But the critical question remains: When his past shows up unexpectedly at his palace door, will Joseph slam it shut, or open it wide in welcome?

Chapter Thirty-three

(Genesis 42–44:17)

The Brothers Reappear: Wrestling with Unresolved Pain

*Can the Ethiopian change his skin, or the
leopard his spots?*

—Jeremiah 13:23

Try as we might to repress painful memories, they inevitably resurface at other times of our lives, when we least expect them. The most extreme examples of this phenomenon are cases of childhood abuse in which the victims repress all memory of the events for decades. The unresolved pain of these incidents, though consciously forgotten, continues to wreak havoc on personal relationships. Pain is not a tidy emotion that we can conveniently tuck away out of sight. Repressed traumas eventually reemerge. When they do, we have an opportunity to resolve the pain and damage done years earlier. But not without courage and hard work.

Joseph's position in his adopted country is now secure, his assimilation nearly complete. The slave has become a prince, and Joseph is doing everything he can to put his past behind him. We see Joseph consciously attempting to bury his painful history, thanking God who *"has made me forget completely my hardship and my father's house."* But we know that this wish, by its very expression, has not been fulfilled. Fate and circumstances, like the workings of our unconscious mind, are largely beyond our control. When Joseph's past comes hurtling toward the present, his Hebrew youth will vie with his Egyptian adulthood for primacy. His hunger for his family's love will contest with his drive for revenge. Will Joseph the Egyptian acknowledge his Hebrew past, or try to extinguish it once and for all? The reappearance of his brothers offers Joseph a fleeting chance to integrate his past with his present. But will he prove equal to the challenge?

This segment of Joseph's story is one of the most finely drawn dramas in the Bible. As the action cuts back and forth between Canaan and Egypt, the tension between Joseph's past and present draws tighter and tighter.

The famine, however, spread over the whole world. So all the world came to Joseph in Egypt to procure rations.

When Jacob saw that there were food rations to be had in Egypt, he said to his sons, "Why do you keep looking at one another? Now I hear that there are rations to be had in Egypt. Go down and procure rations for us there, that we may live and not die."

So ten of Joseph's brothers went down to get grain rations in Egypt. For Jacob did not send Joseph's brother Benjamin with his brothers, since he feared that he might meet with disaster. Ever since Joseph disappeared years earlier, Jacob had become increasingly protective of his only other son by Rachel.

Now Joseph was the Viceroy of the land, and it was he who dispensed rations to all the people of the land. And Joseph's brothers came and bowed low to him, with their faces to the ground. When Joseph saw his brothers, he recognized them. But he acted like a stranger toward them and spoke harshly to them.

"Where do you come from?"

And they said, "From the land of Canaan, to procure food."

Though Joseph recognized his brothers, they did not recognize him. Recalling the dreams he had dreamed about them, Joseph said to them, "You are spies. You have come to see the land in its nakedness."

But they said to him, "No, my lord! Truly, your servants have come to procure food. We are all of us sons of a certain man in Canaan. We are honest men and brothers. The youngest, however, is now with our father, and one is no more."

The ten men cowered before Joseph, their faces pressed against the ground, while he shouted at the top of his voice: "It is just as I have told you: You are spies! By this you shall be put to the test. Unless your youngest brother comes here, by Pharaoh, you shall not depart from this place! Let one of you go and bring your brother, while the rest of you remain confined, that your words may be put to the test whether there is truth in you. Else, by Pharaoh, you are nothing but spies!"

And he confined them in the guardhouse for three days. On the third day Joseph said to them, "If you are honest men, let one of your brothers be held in your place of detention, while the rest of you go and take home rations for your starving households. But you must bring me your youngest brother that your words may be verified and that you may not die."

They said to one another, "Alas, we are being punished on account of our brother, because we looked on at his anguish, yet paid no heed as he pleaded with us. That is why this distress has come upon us."

Then Reuben spoke up and said to them, "Did I not tell you, 'Do no wrong to the boy'? But you paid no heed. Now comes the reckoning for his blood."

They did not know that Joseph understood, for there was an interpreter between him and them. He turned away from them and wept. But he came back to them, and he took Simeon from among them and had him bound before their eyes. They watched with speechless horror as Simeon was led away.

Then Joseph gave orders to his servants to fill his brothers' bags with grain, return each one's money to his sack and give them provisions for the journey. And this was done for them. So they loaded their asses with the rations and departed from there.

As one of them was opening his sack to give feed to his ass at the night's encampment, he saw his money right there at the mouth of his bag. And he said to his brothers, "My money has been returned! It is here in my bag!" Their hearts sank, and trembling, they turned to one another, saying, "What is this that God has done to us?"

Their hearts heavy with foreboding, the brothers returned to their father in the land of Canaan and told him the tale of how Simeon had been taken captive and how they had been sent back to retrieve their youngest brother, Benjamin.

Their father Jacob said to them, "It is always me that you bereave. Joseph is no more and Simeon is no more, and now you would take away Benjamin. My son must not go down with you, for his brother is dead and he alone is left. If he meets with disaster on the journey you are taking, you will send my white head to the grave in grief."

WHEN CONFLICTING EMOTIONS COLLIDE

As happened in Abraham's generation, the ravages of famine now force the tribe of Jacob to look southward to Egypt, the breadbasket of the region, for survival. But this time it is not a faceless Pharaoh who will decide their fate, but their own betrayed brother.

The brothers' arrival in Egypt plunges Joseph into an emotional vortex. The sight of them bowing before him, like the sheaves in his dream, triggers a flood of emotional memories. Anger, revenge, and heartache mix with tender longings to reunite with his father and younger brother, Benjamin. In a reversal of his childhood trauma, Joseph now wields complete power over his brothers' movements, and throughout this episode and those that follow he will manipulate them mercilessly.

Joseph wants his brothers to relive every agony he himself was subjected to: the helplessness, the enslavement and unjust imprisonment. But when he overhears his brothers talking about their lingering guilt, decades after the event, he is deeply moved. *He turned away from them and wept.* After casting them into prison as "spies," Joseph has a change of heart. Much as he may want to repay his brothers' cruelty, he isn't prepared to let his extended family starve. So he sends them on their way with their sacks brimming with food and money.

The brothers' visit raises an intriguing question. Since Joseph immediately recognizes his brothers, why don't they recognize him? Several obvious answers come to mind: Joseph is no longer a boy, but a grown man wearing Egyptian garb. Prostrate before Joseph, *bowed low to him with their faces to the ground*, the brothers probably never look the viceroy of Egypt in the face. He speaks to them only in Egyptian and through an interpreter. Even had they recognized his voice, how could the brothers imagine or believe that the boy they sold into slavery would now be ruler over all of Egypt?

These circumstantial details underlie a more fundamental truth: they don't recognize Joseph because he has transformed himself, both externally and internally. The boastful boy who couldn't resist broadcasting his dreams of glory has become a mature man who is able to hide his strongest emotions. We can well imagine Joseph's feelings of vindication when he sees his brothers bowing down before him, just as his youthful dream had prophesied. How he must have yearned to cry out in self-righteous triumph. But he stifles his desire for instant revenge.

The brothers, on the other hand, have changed very little— which is presumably why Joseph has no trouble recognizing them. They are still quick to snipe at each other, still busy pointing fingers and assigning blame, still struggling to earn their father's confidence.

THE TRAGEDY OF A CHILD'S DEATH

The picture we get of the aging patriarch Jacob is heartbreaking. With Joseph taken from him, he now clings to his youngest son. Benjamin is his last remaining link to his beloved wife Rachel and lost son, Joseph, and he staunchly refuses to risk his safety—even if it means that his older son Simeon will remain indefinitely imprisoned in Egypt. Jacob seems to have surrendered to self-pity, experiencing all his family's woe as a personal assault. *"It is always me that you bereave,"* he cries.

Contrary to what some people believe, suffering doesn't necessarily ennoble us. Even a stalwart personality like Jacob appears to be broken and embittered by his string of misfortune. He never recovers from the triple blow of Dinah's rape, Rachel's death, and Joseph's disappearance.

I learned early on in life that even the strongest people can be bowed low by grief—especially by the anguish of a child's death. Jacob's response to his personal tragedies reminds me of my aunt, who was a formidable person herself. My twenty-year-old cousin Danny fell while defending the Jordan Valley during Israel's 1948 War of Independence. My aunt was crushed by the death of her only child. As far as she was concerned, her life stopped having any meaning for her the day he died. She refused to see her son's old friends or observe the holidays. Despite our protestations that Danny led a full life until the very end and died for a cause he deeply believed in, she never accepted his death and would not allow herself to be consoled. Like Jacob, she *refused to be comforted, saying, "No, I will go down to the grave to my son in mourning."*

Jacob's grief raises another question: Why hasn't Joseph made any attempt to contact his family in the years since his ascent from prison? We can well imagine his reluctance to reunite with his brothers. But what of the father who lovingly reared him? It seems only natural that he would want his father to know he's alive and that his youthful dreams of glory have been fulfilled. But he has continued to leave his father in the dark about his fate. And now he seems intent on punishing Jacob further by making him reenact the loss of a beloved son—this time Benjamin.

As usual, Genesis emphasizes the long, slow journey from hurt to healing, from betrayal to forgiveness. Clearly, Joseph harbors complex and unresolved feelings toward his father. He had years in prison to contemplate his fate and to analyze the family dynamic that landed him there. Joseph no doubt blames his father for feeding his grandiosity and for provoking his brothers with his blatant favoritism. More than anything, the young Joseph wanted to be accepted by his big brothers. But what boy could have resisted a father's unconditional love and his special gifts of elegant clothing? And what brothers could have suppressed their rage at a sibling's favored treatment? As we will see, more tears will have to be shed on both sides before father and son can be reunited. Time is a slow healer, and the detailed description of this phase of Joseph's story reflects his gradual recovery.

Joseph and his brothers are at a standoff. Joseph holds Simeon hostage, while Jacob refuses to relinquish what Joseph wants most: his younger brother Benjamin. Only time and the intractable demands of survival in the face of famine will break the deadlock.

The famine in the land was severe. And when they had eaten up the rations which they had brought from Egypt, their father said to his sons, "Go again and procure some food for us."

But Judah said to him, "The man warned us, 'Do not let me see your faces unless your brother is with you.' If you will let

our brother go with us, we will go down and procure food for
you."

And Israel said, "Why did you serve me so ill as to tell the
man that you had another brother?"

Then Judah said to his father Israel, "Send the boy in my
care, and let us be on our way, that we may live and not die—
you and we and our children. I myself will be surety for him. You
may hold me responsible. If I do not bring him back to you and
set him before you, I shall stand guilty before you forever. We
could have been there and back twice if we had not dawdled."

Then their father Israel said to them, "If it must be so, do
this: take some of the choice products of the land in your baggage, and carry them down as a gift for the man—some balm,
and some honey, gum, ladanum, pistachio nuts, and almonds.
And take with you double money, carrying back with you the
money that was replaced in the mouths of your bags. Perhaps it
was a mistake. Take your brother too, and go back at once to
the man. And may the Lord dispose the man to mercy toward
you, that he may release to you your other brother, as well as
Benjamin. As for me, if I am to be bereaved, I shall be bereaved."

So the men took that gift, as well as Benjamin. They
made their way down to Egypt where they presented themselves
to Joseph.

When Joseph saw Benjamin with them, he said to his
house steward, "Take the men into the house. Slaughter and
prepare an animal, for the men will dine with me at noon."

The man did as Joseph said, and he brought the men into
Joseph's house. But the brothers were frightened at being
brought into Joseph's house. "It must be," they thought, "as a

pretext to attack us and seize us as slaves, with our pack ani-
mals."

They went to the steward of Joseph's house and tried to
explain to him about the money they found in their sack.

The steward replied, "All is well with you. Do not be
afraid." And he brought Simeon out to them.

Then the steward brought the men into Joseph's house. He
gave them water to bathe their feet, and he provided feed for
their asses. They laid out their gifts to await Joseph's arrival at
noon, for they heard that they were to dine there.

When Joseph came home, they presented to him the gifts, bow-
ing low before him to the ground. He greeted them, and he said,
"How is your aged father of whom you spoke? Is he still in good
health?"

They replied, "It is well with your servant our father, he is
still in good health." And they bowed and made obeisance.

Looking about, Joseph saw his brother Benjamin, his
mother's son, and asked, "Is this your youngest brother of
whom you spoke to me? May God be gracious to you, my boy."

With that, Joseph hurried out, for he was overcome with
feeling toward his brother and was on the verge of tears. He
went into a room and wept there. Then he washed his face,
reappeared, and—now in control of himself—gave the order,
"Serve the meal." And they drank their fill with him.

Then Joseph instructed his house steward as follows: "Fill
the men's bags with food, as much as they can carry, and put
each one's money in the mouth of his bag. Put my silver goblet
in the mouth of the bag of the youngest one, together with his
money for the rations." And he did as Joseph told him.

With the first light of morning, the men were sent off with their donkeys. They had just left the city and had not gone far when Joseph's steward overtook them and accused them of stealing the silver goblet. "Why do your repay good with evil? It is the very cup from which my master drinks. It was a wicked thing for you to do!"

And they said to him, "Why does my lord say such things? Far be it from your servant to do anything of the kind! Whichever of your servants it is found with shall die. The rest of us, moreover, shall become slaves to my lord."

The steward replied, "Although what you are proposing is right, only the one with whom it is found shall be my slave. But the rest of you shall go free."

So each one hastened to lower his bag to the ground, and each one opened his bag. The steward searched, beginning with the oldest and ending with the youngest. And the goblet turned up in Benjamin's bag.

At this they rent their clothes. Each reloaded his pack animal, and they returned to the city.

WHEN LOVE WARS
WITH HATRED

As the tension of this drama builds to a breaking point, Benjamin becomes the focal point of this family's tug-of-war. Only when Judah reminds Jacob that the survival of the tribe's children hangs in the balance does the patriarch give in. He has no choice but to surrender his youngest son and resign himself to fate. *"As for me, if I am to be bereaved, I shall be bereaved."* Jacob suggests a course of appeasement, directing his sons to return to Egypt bearing gifts and money.

Because they view the world through their own prism of distrust, the brothers can't quite believe that Joseph will make good on his bargain. Perhaps it is their guilty conscience that makes them fearful that their host will seize them as slaves. Why, after all, would the viceroy of all Egypt want to entertain a ragtag band of starving shepherds? Meanwhile, Joseph is having trouble keeping control of his emotions. On seeing his younger brother Benjamin as a grown man, Joseph is *overcome with feeling toward his brother and . . . on the verge of tears. He went into a room and wept there.*

If Joseph is so drawn to Benjamin, why does he subject him to the ordeal of the silver goblet?

Here, too, we see how deep the hurts of youth can run. Joseph's feelings for Benjamin are apparently divided between love and resentment. Benjamin is his only full brother, an innocent bystander in Joseph's tragedy. But he was also the cause, if unwittingly, of his mother's death. How different Joseph's life would have been if Benjamin had never been conceived. His mother wouldn't have been snatched away from him when he was only seven. His father would not have made him the center of his life and the target of his other sons' wrath. Now Joseph must decide: will Benjamin be his brother in exile or his slave, the bridge back to his family or the instrument of his revenge?

Poets and philosophers have long debated the relative power of love and hate in the human heart. Catullus, a Roman writing in the first century B.C.E., mused:

I hate and love. You ask, perhaps, how can that be?
I know not, but I feel the agony.

Joseph's whole family is now writhing in agony. Jacob waits all alone in Canaan for word about the fate of his youngest. The brothers have rent their clothes in grief over their failed mission. How long will Joseph torment his family and himself? Can he bring himself to acknowledge them as his kin and finally achieve the peace of mind that has for so long eluded him?

THE FAMILY REUNITES: BREAKING DOWN WALLS OF RESISTANCE

*You shall not hate thy brother in thy heart. You
shall not take vengeance or bear a grudge against thy
kinfolk, but you shall love thy neighbor as thyself.*

—Leviticus 19:17–18

Ever since his brothers' appearance in Egypt, Joseph has been struggling to keep a cap on his emotions and maintain control over the flow of information and events. But like most of us, Joseph is frightened to relinquish control over an emotionally explosive situation. He is still torn between the desire for retaliation and a sense of compassion.

It's difficult to identify the exact moment when a person or situation so deeply moves us that we experience a true catharsis. Usually the catalyst for change catches us by surprise, coming at the time and from the person we least expect. An unanticipated word or gesture of kindness can render us momentarily vulnerable. And in that moment, we are suddenly lifted out of ourselves—out of our narrow concern for our own feelings—and into a larger emotional sphere. We feel genuine compassion for someone who, only moments before, we perceived as our adversary. An enormous amount of suppressed emotion is released as the door to closed-off feelings of tenderness and love swings open. Then the process of healing can begin.

A common example of this phenomenon occurs between adult children and their parents. The adult child is playing out an old script with his or her parent, a recurrent pattern of conflict and angry confrontation. Then, in the middle of an argument—the same argument the child and parent have had for decades—something unexpected happens. Perhaps the parent reveals a personal detail that casts him or her in a totally new light. Maybe the parent displays an unaccustomed vulnerability—a hurt expression or a gesture that betrays advancing age. All of a sudden, the child experiences an emotional reversal. The formerly omnipotent parent appears frail and exposed. The child no longer sees this person as an adversary. He no longer wants to vanquish the parent, but instead is overwhelmed with feelings of protectiveness and compassion.

How does this process play out with Joseph and his brothers?

In the climactic scene of Genesis, Judah plays the unwitting catalyst to Joseph's catharsis. In a last-ditch emotional appeal, the very brother who sold him into slavery for twenty pieces of silver now implores Joseph for mercy. One by one he pushes Joseph's emotional "hot buttons"—invoking his "old father," his dead mother, and his youngest brother. What makes this scene so dramatic is that while Judah is consciously trying to evoke the Egyptian viceroy's pity, he has no idea that he is addressing his long-lost brother for whom his words have unbearable associations.

Joseph nervously paced through his house as he awaited the return of his steward and the news he would bring. Had his brothers abandoned their younger sibling to slavery once again and returned to Canaan with their sacks full of food? If so, should he send Benjamin back to his father, or keep his one true brother here in Egypt?

The steward led the brothers inside, brandishing the silver

goblet overhead and pointing to Benjamin as the culprit. *When Judah and his brothers reentered the house of Joseph, they threw themselves on the ground before him.*

Joseph said to them, "*What is this deed that you have done?*"

Judah replied, "*What can we say to my lord? How can we plead, how can we prove our innocence? God has uncovered the crime of your servants. Here we are then, slaves of my lord, the rest of us as much as he in whose possession the goblet was found.*"

But Joseph replied, "*Only he in whose possession the goblet was found shall be my slave. The rest of you go back in peace to your father.*"

Abandoning all caution, Judah rose and approached Joseph, drawing close enough to touch his arm. Speaking in a soft voice, he pleaded, "*Please, my lord, let your servant appeal to my lord. We have an old father, and there is a child of his old age, the youngest. His full brother is dead, so that he alone is left of his mother, and his father dotes on him. My father said to us, 'As you know, my wife bore me two sons. But one is gone from me. Alas, he was torn by a beast! and I have not seen him since. If you take this one from me, too, and he meets with disaster, you will send my white head down to the grave in grief.'*

"*Now, if I return to my father and the boy is not with us —since his own life is so bound up with his—he will die. I have pledged myself for the boy to my father, saying, 'If I do not bring him back to you, I shall stand guilty before my father forever.' Therefore, please let your servant remain as a slave to my lord instead of the boy, and let the boy go back with his brothers. For how can I go back to my father unless the boy is with me? Let me not be witness to the woe that would overtake my father!*"

The image of his bereaved old father, gray-haired and bowed by grief, overwhelmed Joseph with emotion. *He could no longer control himself before all his attendants, and he cried out, "Have everyone withdraw from me!" So there was no one else about when Joseph made himself known to his brothers. His sobs were so loud that the Egyptians could hear, and so the news reached Pharaoh's palace.*

Joseph said to his brothers, "I am Joseph. Is my father still well?"

But his brothers could not answer him, so dumfounded were they on account of him. Then Joseph said to his brothers, "Come forward to me." And when they came forward, he said, "I am your brother Joseph, he whom you sold into Egypt. Now, do not be distressed or reproach yourselves because you sold me hither. It was to save life that God sent me ahead of you. It is now two years that there has been famine in the land, and there are still five years to come in which there shall be no yield from tilling. God has sent me ahead of you to ensure your survival on earth, and to save your lives in an extraordinary deliverance. So, it was not you who sent me here, but God. And He has made me a father to Pharaoh, lord of all his household, and ruler over the whole land of Egypt.

"Now, hurry back to my father and say to him: Thus says your son Joseph, 'God has made me lord of all Egypt. Come down to me without delay. You will dwell in the region of Goshen, where you will be near me—you and your children and your grandchildren, your flocks and herds, and all that is yours. There I will provide for you—for there are yet five years of famine to come—that you and your household and all that is yours may not suffer want.' And you must tell my father everything about my high station in Egypt and all

that you have seen. And bring my father here with all speed."

With that he embraced his brother Benjamin around the neck and wept, and Benjamin wept on his neck. He kissed all his brothers and wept upon them. Only then were his brothers able to talk to him.

WORDS AND ACTS OF REPENTANCE

Before he can forgive his brothers, Joseph needs to discover whether they have repented of their heartless betrayal. Moses Maimonides understood that true repentance is expressed not in words, but in deeds. He defined repentance as refraining from transgressing in the same way one has before. Joseph tests his brothers by making them reenact his own youthful abduction and sale into slavery to see if they have changed. First he forces them to leave Simeon behind to see if they abandon him. And when they return with Benjamin— their father's favorite—Joseph uses his gambit with the silver goblet to find out if they will sacrifice Benjamin the same way they did Joseph.

As the story reveals, his brothers *do* have a conscience. They feel guilt for their past betrayal of Joseph and for the way they grieved their father. And when Joseph threatens to enslave Benjamin, they offer themselves in his place and confess to Joseph's knowing ear their past guilt: *"God has uncovered the crime of your servants. Here we are then, slaves of my lord, the rest of us as much as he in whose possession the goblet was found."*

For the first time in his life, Joseph can identify with his brothers' suffering. Only when they are powerless and vulnerable before him—as he once was before them—is Joseph moved to compassion and forgiveness.

In the midst of Judah's speech, Joseph realizes that by punishing his brothers, he is hurting his father most of all. His family is an interconnected and interdependent organism of children and parents, siblings and spouses. Joseph cannot compartmentalize them, embracing Benjamin while rejecting his other brothers. Joseph finally understands that as long as he remains alive, he will always be connected to this family. His time has arrived to assume the role of patriarch.

STRIVING TO BE A MAN

The Talmud teaches us: "Where there are no men, strive to be a man." With his brothers reduced to starvation and his father debilitated by age and grief, Joseph sees that this is his moment to become a man and his family's next patriarch. Now is the time for him to relinquish his self-centered desire for revenge and to step into the adult's role of providing for his extended family. He stands as a model for any of us struggling to put family hurts behind us and to get beyond the emotional scorekeeping that's so destructive to family harmony. Like Joseph, we truly become adults and leaders in our family when we stop asking: "What has my family—parent, sibling, or child—done for me?" and begin asking: "What can I do for my family?"

When Joseph reveals himself to his brothers, he also reveals himself *to himself.* At this moment of truth, Joseph perceives his life and identity in a whole new context. His youthful dream is realized: his brothers are prostrate before him like so many sheaves of wheat. But he interprets that dream and his personal vision differently now. His brothers and their families—Joseph's entire clan—are totally dependent on him for survival. In this time of famine, he is the one sheaf of wheat still standing. Because of what he has accomplished and the position he has acquired, Joseph has the power and assumes the obligation to preserve his family through the five years of famine still ahead.

The Bible is so wonderfully realistic in showing us that even as he is "striving to be a man," Joseph retains his boyish desire to impress his brothers and father. He repeatedly reminds his brothers that he has become *"ruler over the whole land of Egypt."* And it is with obvious relish that he instructs them: *"And you must tell my father everything about my high station in Egypt and all that you have seen."* Having revealed himself to his brothers, Joseph is now eager to impress his father with his exalted political power. Being human, Joseph can't resist a flash of his old bravado in front of his brothers. But now he has the spiritual perspective to attribute his success to God's plan for the family's *extraordinary deliverance.*

The news reached Pharaoh's palace that Joseph's brothers had come. And Pharaoh said to Joseph, "Take from the land of Egypt wagons for your children and your wives, and bring your father here. I will give you the best of the land of Egypt and you shall live off the fat of the land. And never mind your belongings, for the best of all the land of Egypt shall be yours."

So Joseph gave his brothers wagons as Pharaoh had commanded, and he supplied them with provisions for the journey. To each of them, moreover, he gave a change of clothing, and to his father he sent the following: ten he-asses laden with the best things of Egypt, and ten she-asses laden with grain, bread and provisions for his father on the journey. As he sent his brothers off on their way, he told them, "Do not be quarrelsome on the way."

They went up from Egypt and came to their father Jacob in the land of Canaan. And they told him, "Joseph is still alive. Yes, he is ruler over the whole land of Egypt."

Jacob's heart fainted, for he did not believe them. But when they recounted all that Joseph had said to them, and when he saw the wagons that Joseph had sent to transport him, the spirit of their father Jacob revived. "Enough!" said Israel. "My son Joseph is still alive! I must go and see him before I die."

Jacob's heart was heavy with foreboding at the thought of going down into Egypt. Although he was rejoining his beloved son and escaping the famine, he was afraid to leave the land of Canaan again, now that he was old.

And Israel set out with all that was his, and came to Beersheba where he prayed to the God of his father Isaac. And God called to Israel in a vision by night, and said: "Jacob! Jacob!"

And he answered: "Here am I."

He said: "I am God, the God of thy father. Fear not to go down into Egypt, for I will there make of thee a great nation. I will go down with thee into Egypt, and I will also surely bring thee up again; and Joseph's hand shall close your eyes."

And Jacob set out from Beer-sheba with all his seed: his sons, and his sons' sons, his daughters, and his sons' daughters. The total of Jacob's household who came to Egypt was seventy persons.

And Joseph made ready his chariot, and went up to Goshen to meet his father Israel. He presented himself to him, and embracing him around the neck, he wept on his neck a good while. Then Israel said to Joseph: "Now I can die, having seen for myself that you are still alive."

ESCAPING THE VICTIM TRAP

Why is Jacob so reluctant to go down to Egypt? After all, he has nothing to fear from Joseph, and the news of his high rank in Egypt would seem to guarantee his family's survival for the duration of the famine. But Jacob understands that his family's migration to Egypt has profound historical significance. They are abandoning, at least for a time, the promised land. Although Abraham and Sarah settled in Canaan three generations earlier, his family still has no foothold in the promised land, save for a burial ground at the cave of the Machpelah.

Jacob fears that his family's identity may be too fragile to stand up to the temptations of the cosmopolitan Egyptian culture. He's no doubt haunted by the prophecy God spoke to his grandfather Abraham, *"Know well that your offspring shall be strangers in a land not theirs, and they shall be enslaved and oppressed four hundred years."* Before he leaves the land of Canaan, Jacob calls out to God for reassurance. And as He has at other crossroads in Jacob's life, God visits Jacob in a vision and gives him courage: *"Fear not. . . . I will go down with thee into Egypt, and I will also surely bring thee up again."*

The father-son reunion is narrated very laconically. It's as if words cannot communicate the emotional intensity of their meeting. Any grudges Joseph may have borne against his father melt away as soon as he catches sight of him. *Embracing him around the neck, he wept on his neck a good while.*

Joseph finally appreciates the depth of his father's grief and is able to forgive him for having incited jealousy in his brothers. As a father himself by now, Joseph understands how hard it is to be a wise parent. It is the adult in Joseph, rather than the child, that rises to the occasion and rejoices in his family's reunion.

> *Then Joseph came and reported to Pharaoh, saying, "My father and my brethren, and their flocks, and their herds, and all that they have, are come out of the land of Canaan and are now in the region of Goshen." And Joseph brought in Jacob his father, and presented him to Pharaoh. And Jacob blessed Pharaoh.*
>
> *Pharaoh said unto Jacob: "How many are the days of the years of thy life?"*
>
> *And Jacob answered Pharaoh: "The years of my sojourn on earth are a hundred and thirty. Few and hard have been the years of my life, nor do they come up to the life spans of my fathers during their sojourns." Then Jacob blessed Pharaoh and left his presence.*
>
> *So Joseph settled his father and his brothers, giving them*

holdings in the choicest part of the land of Egypt, in the region of Ramses, as Pharaoh had commanded. Joseph sustained his father, and his brethren, and all his father's household with bread, down to their little ones.

Now that his past, present, and future are finally wedded, Joseph is no longer a lonely stranger in a strange land.

THE FINAL FREEDOM: TO INTERPRET ONE'S OWN SUFFERING

Emboldened by his family's reunion, Joseph now has the self-confidence to reveal himself to all of Egypt. Though he was known to be a Hebrew, he has long since taken on the trappings of Egyptian life. Now his worldly success and emotional maturity give Joseph the courage to acknowledge his past, both in private and public life.

Aliens were looked down upon by Egyptians, but Joseph makes no attempt to play down his Hebrew roots and presents his father proudly to Pharaoh. Though Joseph's family may have been prosperous in the context of Canaanite tribes, these tent-dwelling shepherds are hardly a glittering addition to the court of Pharaoh—the Versailles of its day. But Pharaoh welcomes Joseph's family warmly and offers them *"the best of the land of Egypt and you shall live off the fat of the land."* The land of Goshen, in the northeastern part of the Nile delta near the Egyptian capital of Avaris, is an ideal region in which Jacob's tribe can settle. In Goshen they will enjoy close proximity to and protection from Pharaoh, as well as fertile land on which to graze their livestock. And by settling together in one place, they are less likely to be absorbed by the surrounding Egyptian culture.

The scene between Jacob and Pharaoh is touching in two regards. First, I've always appreciated how respectfully Pharaoh receives his Hebrew visitor. Out of deference to Jacob's age and position as the family patriarch, Pharaoh greets him as an equal, and he graciously accepts the older man's blessing. Secondly, when Pharaoh asks Jacob his age, Jacob's response is very revealing. Though he is one hundred thirty years old, he replies: *"Few and hard have been the years of my life, nor do they come up to the life spans of my fathers during their sojourns."* Despite all his accomplishments and his close relationship with God, he views his life as a painful passage. Ever since losing out to Esau at birth, he has suffered from a chronic sense of inadequacy—particularly when measured against his father and grandfather.

This telling exchange highlights the difference between Jacob and his son. Objectively, Joseph's life has been more tragic than his father's. Yet he never gives in to bitterness. Despite spending his entire adult life as an exile bereft of family, Joseph sees his suffering in the context of a broader framework. Throughout his trials Joseph believes that God is guiding him toward an intended destination. By the time his family is reunited in Egypt, Joseph understands his role in the family's destiny as the "advance man" who descended into Egypt to provide for their survival.

Joseph embodies one of the most important lessons of Genesis: when we feel that our suffering has little meaning—as Jacob does— we become embittered victims. But when we can attach meaning to the adversity we experience, that understanding can be a source of growth and transformation.

For example, Allied soldiers in World War II believed that they were rescuing Europe from fascism. The casualties they incurred, while tragic, were perceived as necessary sacrifices toward a higher goal of resisting tyranny and saving democracy. Some Vietnam veterans, on the other hand, have had a much harder time making sense of lost lives and limbs. Their relatively high rates of alcoholism, drug addiction, and suicide following the war reflect the society's ambivalence toward our mission in Southeast Asia.

Joseph's ability to see his life as a link in an ongoing historical process is what distinguishes him as the patriarch of his generation. He is able to transform something ghastly—his brothers' betrayal— into a positive opportunity. *"God has sent me ahead of you to ensure your survival on earth, and to save your lives in an extraordinary deliverance. So, it was not you who sent me here, but God."* Joseph sees himself not as a passive victim, but as an active player in a larger plan to which he is indispensable. Joseph demonstrates that no matter how dire or exalted our circumstances, we always retain the autonomy to interpret our lives for ourselves. We can forfeit that freedom, but no one can take it away from us.

A good friend of mine, Kitty, spent two years of her early childhood hiding from the Nazis in a windowless attic in a small village in Slovakia. Recently, on a beautiful fall day, she and I were taking a walk and talking about the future. When I asked her if she shared my concerns about financial planning for retirement, she answered, "Naomi, I honestly don't worry about the future. During all the time I spent hiding, I never believed life could be this good, that I could be so fortunate and have such a fulfilling life with as many choices as I have."

She went on to explain and she said, "My mother was the realistic one who got us to escape and found us the hiding place. But it was my father who carried us through. He kept repeating over and over that evil could not win in the long run, that our family would eventually find safety, and that we would be able to rebuild our lives. And you know something? He was right."

My friend Kitty, like Joseph, was able to avoid becoming embittered by her childhood hardship because she believed that she was part of a larger historical process of good prevailing over evil.

THE POWER TO OVERCOME, THE COURAGE TO HEAL

Despite the constant discord in Jacob's generation, Genesis remains staunchly optimistic about our human capacity to overcome family conflicts. Virtually any transgression can be accepted and forgiven within a strong family. William Blake wrote: "It is easier to forgive an enemy than to forgive a friend." A brother's betrayal is even more difficult to forgive than a friend's. But when Judah offers his own life in place of Benjamin's, Joseph is ready to relinquish his desire for revenge and seize the chance for reconciliation.

As we have seen in every generation since Cain and Abel's, family relationships—between siblings, between spouses, and between parents and children—carry within them the seeds of contention. It's not that humans are inherently evil, but that human relationships inevitably have conflict built into them. Rather than see this truth as an insoluble problem, Genesis views it as an opportunity for us to express the best that is in us. Being made in the image of God, we are all endowed with the tools to repair this human predicament. With our uniquely human attributes of patience, trust, and courage, we have the potential to harmonize the conflicts inherent in family relationships. Relationships are one of the domains where God is dependent upon our partnership to repair and renew His creation.

The human family is in a constant state of becoming. Every generation marks a new beginning, a new chance for healing and renewal. In 1960, a delegation of 130 Jewish leaders visited Pope John XXIII in the Vatican. Their mission was to address the Catholic Church's historical hostility toward Judaism, stretching back over two thousand years. On their arrival, the visitors were greeted by the Pope—whose baptismal name was Joseph—with the words: "I am your brother Joseph."

THE BLESSING OF THE PATRIARCH: CLOSING THE CIRCLE OF CONTENTION

Only be strong, and of good courage.

—*Joshua 1:18*

The most enduring legacy we can bequeath to our children is a clear articulation of who we are and what we stand for. We can leave them financial assets, but those can lose their value. A family business can go bankrupt. A family home can burn down. But if we can make clear to our children who we are, where we have come from, and what we value, then they can begin to build their own personal identity based on a solid foundation.

We can't assume they'll absorb our values through osmosis. We need to spell them out explicitly. Once we've discharged this responsibility, it's up to our children to decide what to accept or reject.

My mother died over twenty years ago, but the life lessons she shared with me still guide me on a daily basis. She was not religiously observant, but she held firmly to beliefs about how to live and how to treat people—all of which she practiced in her own life. She was so open and forthcoming about expressing her values and beliefs to me that by the time she died, I felt I had absorbed her entirely into myself.

My father, on the other hand, was very reserved and rarely discussed his feelings with me. Most of what I learned about him I picked up indirectly by listening to conversations between him and my mother. It's taken me decades since his death to understand him fully and to appreciate how profoundly he influenced my thinking and identity.

Children also need to know about their grandparents and great-grandparents, about their aunts, uncles, and cousins. The more varied and specific the family coordinates we can provide for our children—by sharing memories and photographs, telling stories, reading old letters, or even leaving videotaped testaments—the more readily they can locate themselves on the family tree and in life.

Jacob lived seventeen years in the land of Egypt, so the span of Jacob's life came to one hundred and forty-seven years. And when the time approached for Israel to die, he summoned his son Joseph, and said to him: "Do me this favor: place your hand under my thigh as a pledge of your steadfast loyalty: please do not bury me in Egypt. When I lie down with my fathers, carry me out of Egypt and bury me in their burying-place."

And Joseph swore to him. Then Israel bowed down upon the head of the bed.

Some time afterward, Joseph was told, "Your father is ill." So he took with him his two sons, Manasseh and Ephraim.

When Jacob was told, "Your son Joseph has come to see you," Israel summoned his strength and sat up in bed.

Now that his time to die was near, Jacob's thoughts drifted back to the mother of his youngest sons. He spoke to Joseph about her for the first time since her death. *"Rachel died, to my sorrow, while I was journeying in the land of Canaan, when still some distance short of Ephrath. And I buried her there on the road to Ephrath."* She alone among the matriarchs had not been buried at the cave of Machpelah. She would remain alone forever in her roadside grave just short of Ephrath, which is now Bethlehem.

Noticing Joseph's sons, Israel said, "Bring them up to me that I may bless them." Now Israel's eyes were dim with age. He could not see. So Joseph brought them close to him, and he kissed them and embraced them. And Israel said to Joseph, "I had not thought to see your face again, and here God has let me see your children as well."

And Joseph brought them out from between his knees and bowed low with his face to the ground. And Israel stretched out his right hand, and laid it on Ephraim's head, though he was the younger, and his left hand upon Manasseh's head—thus crossing his hands—although Manasseh was the firstborn. And he blessed Joseph's sons, saying,

"The God in whose ways my fathers Abraham and Isaac walked,

The God who has been my shepherd all my life long to this day,

The angel who has redeemed me from all harm,
Bless the lads.
In them let my name be recalled,
And the names of my fathers Abraham and Isaac.
And may they be teeming multitudes upon the earth."

When Joseph saw that his father had placed his right hand on his younger son's head, he tried to correct him. The old man, his mind meandering but his will still strong, insisted that his order be kept—that the younger son be blessed ahead of the older, as it had been in his own father's tent so many years ago.

Then Jacob repeated the promise of the covenant that God had made to him and his fathers. *"The Lord appeared to me at Luz in the land of Canaan, and He blessed me and said to me, 'I will make you fertile and numerous, making of you a community of peoples. And I will give this land to your offspring to come for an everlasting possession.' "*

Then Israel said to Joseph, "I am about to die. But God will be with you and bring you back to the land of your fathers."

Now Jacob's other eleven sons filed into his bedchamber for a final farewell. *Then Jacob called his sons and said, "Come together that I may tell you what is to befall you in days to come." All these were the tribes of Israel, twelve in number, and this is what their father said to them as he bade them farewell, addressing to each a parting word appropriate to him.*

To each of his twelve sons, Jacob gave a final testament. He took note of their achievements and their shortcomings, the deeds of their past and their prospects for the future. Jacob censured Reuben, his firstborn, for forsaking his birthright and mounting his own father's couch to sleep with his handmaid Bilhah. And he rebuked Simeon and Levi for their wanton destruction of Shechem after the rape of Dinah.

Judah was singled out for special notice, his father prophesying that his would emerge as the leading tribe among his sons:

"The scepter shall not depart from Judah
Nor the ruler's staff from between his feet."

But Jacob's most treasured blessing was reserved for Joseph:

"Joseph is a fruitful vine,
A fruitful vine by a fountain;

Its branches run over the wall.
The archers have dealt bitterly with him,
And shot at him and hated him.
Yet his bow stayed taut,
And his arms were made firm
With the blessings of heaven above,
Blessings of the deep that couches below,
Blessings of the breast and the womb.
The blessings of your father
Surpass the blessings of my ancestors,
To the utmost bounds of the eternal hills.
May they rest on the head of Joseph,
On the brow of the elect of his brothers."

Then he instructed his sons, saying, "I am about to be gathered to my kin. Bury me with my fathers in the cave which is in the field that Abraham bought from Ephron the Hittite for a burial site—there Abraham and his wife Sarah were buried, there Isaac and his wife Rebekah were buried, and there I buried Leah."

Jacob's Last Testament

Jacob, like Abraham before him, accepts the approach of death as a fact of life. Before he dies, he tends to his last remaining tasks: to bless his progeny, make arrangements for his own burial, and pass the mantle of the covenant on to the next generation.

For all his failings as a father, Jacob never wavers in clearly communicating his faith to his children. His personal relationships have generally been a source of woe. But in the spiritual domain, Jacob remains focused and steadfast to the end. Despite his tendency toward self-pity when personal tragedy strikes, Jacob provides his children with an unfaltering connection to their covenant with *"the God in whose ways my fathers Abraham and Isaac walked."* The greatest blessing Jacob can bestow on his sons is the guidance and protection of *"the God who has been my shepherd all my life long to this day, the angel who has redeemed me from all harm."*

Though his family has prospered in Egypt, Jacob reminds his sons that their sojourn in this alien land is only a bridge back to the land of promise. He makes them swear to return his body to Canaan for burial so that the next generation won't forget where they have come from and where they are destined to return. All roads lead into the promised future, and Jacob understands who will be traveling there once he is gone. His family's covenant with God and the land is only three generations old. But already they have created a sense of tradition, history, and destiny. Jacob invokes each generation by name in order to reinforce his children's grasp of the unfolding history of their covenant, as well as their indispensable role in its future.

When Jacob finished his instructions to his sons, he drew his feet into the bed and, breathing his last, he was gathered to his people.

Joseph flung himself upon his father's face and wept over him and kissed him. Then Joseph ordered the physicians in his service to embalm his father. It required forty days, for such is the full period of embalming. And the Egyptians bewailed him for seventy days.

Then Joseph asked Pharaoh that he be allowed to return to Canaan to bury his father. *And Pharaoh said, "Go up and bury your father, as he made you promise on oath."*

So Joseph went up to bury his father, and with him went up all the officials of Pharaoh, the senior members of his court, and all of Egypt's dignitaries, together with all of Joseph's household, his brothers and his father's household. Chariots, too, and horsemen went up with him. It was a very large troop.

Thus his sons did for him as he had instructed them. His sons carried him to the land of Canaan and buried him in the cave of the field of Machpelah. After burying his father, Joseph returned to Egypt, he and his brothers and all who had gone up with him to bury his father.

With the death of their father, the brothers became anxious for their safety, wondering, *"What if Joseph still bears a grudge against us and pays us back for all the wrong that we did him!"*

So they sent this message to Joseph, "Before his death your father left this instruction: So shall you say to Joseph, 'Forgive, I urge you, the offense and the guilt of your brothers who treated you so harshly.' Therefore, please forgive the offense of the servants of the God of your father."

And Joseph wept when they spoke unto him.

And his brethren also went and fell down before his face. And they said: "Behold, we are prepared to be your slaves." But Joseph said to them, "Fear not. Am I a substitute for God? Besides, although you intended me harm, God intended it for good, so as to bring about the present result—the survival of many people. And so, fear not. I will sustain you, and your little ones." Thus he reassured them and spoke kindly to them.

DEALING WITH SKELETONS IN THE FAMILY CLOSET

This last scene between Joseph and his brothers raises some intriguing questions. Did Jacob ever leave this "instruction"? Did he ever find out what his sons had done to Joseph? Or are the brothers merely invoking the patriarch's authority after his death to cloak themselves in the protection of his name?

Apparently the brothers don't believe that Joseph has truly forgiven them. Perhaps because they still feel guilty, they can't conceive of their brother's capacity for forgiveness. They assume that he has been withholding his retaliation only until after their father's death. Only after Jacob is gone, when they fear for their lives, do the brothers finally break down and ask for Joseph's forgiveness. And even then they fall back on the questionable story that their father had instructed them to do so just before he died.

I think we may assume that Jacob suspected the truth about what his sons did to Joseph, but never probed for details. Once Joseph turned up alive in Egypt, he must have deduced that the brothers' story about Joseph being "torn by a beast" was a fabrication. But from what we know of Jacob, he probably couldn't bear the unvarnished truth, and so never sought it out. Had he learned that his sons had sold Joseph into slavery, the emotional consequences would have been devastating.

And did Jacob ever leave instructions to the brothers that they ask Joseph for forgiveness? I like to think that Jacob's last thoughts were for the future harmony of his tribe, that his final wishes were for his sons to make up and put the past to rest. Of course, Jacob could have given Joseph this message directly. But he may have realized that his sons needed to seek Joseph's forgiveness themselves.

After so many years of silence, of *not being able to speak a word to each other,* the brothers finally find forgiveness by asking for it directly. Once again, Genesis drives home this crucial lesson: words without deeds are meaningless, but speaking directly to each other—communicating—is a vital part of the healing and growing process in a family. We need to tell each other, face-to-face, about our love, about our resentments. We need to talk about our beliefs, our values, our histories, our visions of the future. Unless we trust enough to reveal ourselves to each other, we will remain at contentious arm's length from the very people we want to be closest to.

FINDING THE RIGHTEOUS
AND COMPASSIONATE PATH

Joseph's final triumph is not over his brothers, but over the circumstances of his life. He had every reason to disown his brothers and resent his father, to distrust women and his fellowman. But he refuses to cave in to bitterness. Instead of repudiating his brothers, he embraces them. In doing so, Joseph delivers himself from his lifetime of alienation and reclaims his birthright of belonging.

Some rabbinical interpreters have called Joseph *Ha-tzadik*, "the righteous and compassionate one." This title is hard-won by Joseph, the end point of a lifelong process of becoming. By forgiving his brothers and promising to care for their children, Joseph finally becomes a *Tzadik*, a righteous man. Joseph's story teaches us, as Elie Wiesel points out, "That one is not born a *Tzadik*, one must strive to become one. And having become a *Tzadik*, one must strive to remain one."

What sets Joseph apart as a *Tzadik* is his ability to remain accountable to a higher moral and spiritual force. Like Jacob, Joseph never forgets *in whose path he walks* or before whom he stands. He doesn't allow betrayal and treachery to destroy his sense of self-worth, or success to erode his fundamental values. Though he is ruler over all Egypt, Joseph views his lofty status as a responsibility, not a privilege.

Pharaoh may be worshipped as a god in Egypt, but Joseph asks his brothers, *"Am I a substitute for God?"* Though created in the image of God, Joseph knows that no man may wield the power of life and death over another. Joseph's words of reassurance to his brothers convey the same message that has sustained him and his forefathers throughout their trials: *"Fear not!"*

So Joseph and his father's household remained in Egypt. Joseph lived to see children of the third generation of Ephraim. At length, Joseph said to his brothers, "I am about to die.

God will surely take notice of you and bring you up from this land to the land which he promised on oath to Abraham, to Isaac, and to Jacob." So Joseph made the sons of Israel swear, saying, "When God has taken notice of you, you shall carry up my bones from here."

Joseph died at the age of a hundred and ten years. And he was embalmed and placed in a coffin in Egypt.

THE END OF THE BEGINNING

So ends the Book of Genesis. But as its name implies, Genesis is merely the beginning of a much longer story that extends over thirty-nine books of the Hebrew Bible—and over all the intervening generations connecting Abraham's family to our own. So long as life continues on this planet, the human drama will renew itself in every generation. So long as we persist in beginning, the creation continues. In the words of Isaac Bashevis Singer: "God is not finished. His highest divine attribute is His creativeness and that which is creative exists always in the beginning stage. God is eternally in Genesis."

GO FORTH AND FEAR NOT

There are two powerful and interdependent calls that resound throughout Genesis: "Go forth" and "Fear not."

"Go forth" addresses the active dimension of our lives. "Fear not" addresses our spiritual dimension.

If we take away nothing from our reading of Genesis but these two directives, our lives will be emboldened and enriched. If we learn to go forth and fear not, we can follow in the footsteps of Abraham, Sarah, Isaac, Rebekah, Jacob, Leah, Rachel, and Joseph.

Go forth.

Go forth into life. Go forth on your journey and discover your personal destiny, your life's destination. Do not wait for life to come to you, to rescue you. Go forth and find a mate, build a family. Repair your community.

Fear not.

Go forth into life and fear not its vagaries. Fear not its struggles. Fear not the doubt that besieges all faith. Fear not the pain that comes with love and the hurt that comes with compassion. Fear not the unknown. Bless life, and seize the day.

Go forth and fear not. But how? By always reminding ourselves that we are created in God's image, that we are endowed with intellect and free will, compassion and responsibility, conscience and creativity. That what we do matters. That our life, and all life, is infinitely precious.

Go forth and fear not.

• • •

Four hundred years after the end of Genesis, Moses leads the children of Israel to *the land which God promised on oath to Abraham, to Isaac, and to Jacob.* And as Joseph requested on his deathbed:

> Moses took the bones of Joseph with him for Joseph had surely sworn to the children of Israel, saying: God will surely remember you, and you shall carry my bones away with you.
>
> —Exodus 13:19

And the story begins again.

Suggestions for Further Reading

Bettelheim, Bruno. *Freud and Man's Soul.* New York: Vintage Books, 1984.

Buber, Martin. *Between Man & Man.* New York: MacMillan, 1947.

Chase, Mary Ellen. *The Bible and the Common Reader.* New York: MacMillan, 1958.

Erikson, Erik H. *Childhood and Society.* New York: W.W. Norton, 1963.

Frankl, Viktor E. *Man's Search for Meaning.* New York: Simon & Schuster, 1984.

Freud, Sigmund. *Civilization and Its Discontents.* New York: W.W. Norton, 1961.

Fromm, Erich. *You Shall Be as Gods.* New York: Henry Holt, 1966.

Gaylin, Willard. *On Being and Becoming Human.* New York: Penguin Books, 1990.

Johnson, Paul. *A History of the Jews.* New York: Harper & Row, 1987.

Leibowitz, Nehama. *Studies in Genesis.* Jerusalem: World Zionist Organization, 1972.

Mann, Thomas. *Joseph and His Brothers.* New York: Alfred A. Knopf, 1934.

Pagels, Elaine. *Adam, Eve, and the Serpent.* New York: Vintage Books, 1989.

Peli, Pinchas, H. *Torah Today.* Washington, DC: B'nai B'rith Books, 1987.

Pritchard, Richard, ed. *The Ancient Near East.* Princeton: Princeton University Press, 1958.

Sarna, Nahum M. *Understanding Genesis.* New York: Schocken Books, 1966.

Steinsaltz, Adin. *Biblical Images.* New York: Basic Books, 1984.

Wiesel, Elie. *Messengers of God.* New York: Summit Books, 1976.

Zeligs, Dorothy. *Psychoanalysis and the Bible.* New York: Bloch Publishing, 1974.

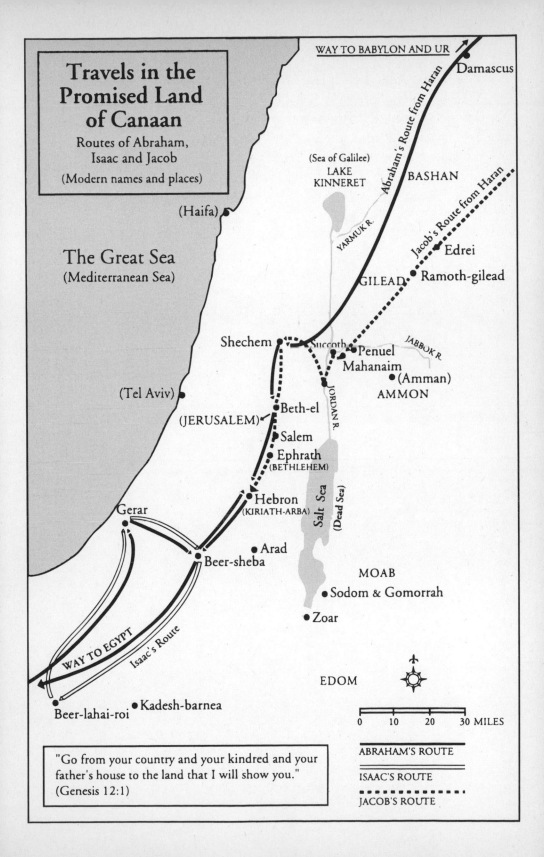

Travels in the Promised Land of Canaan

Routes of Abraham, Isaac and Jacob

(Modern names and places)

WAY TO BABYLON AND UR

Damascus

(Sea of Galilee)
LAKE KINNERET

Abraham's Route from Haran

BASHAN

(Haifa)

YARMUK R.

Jacob's Route from Haran

Edrei

The Great Sea
(Mediterranean Sea)

GILEAD

Ramoth-gilead

Shechem

Succoth

JABBOK R.

Penuel

Mahanaim

(Amman)

AMMON

(Tel Aviv)

JORDAN R.

Beth-el

(JERUSALEM)

Salem

Ephrath
(BETHLEHEM)

Salt Sea

(Dead Sea)

Hebron
(KIRIATH-ARBA)

Gerar

Arad

Beer-sheba

MOAB

Sodom & Gomorrah

Zoar

WAY TO EGYPT

Isaac's Route

EDOM

Beer-lahai-roi

Kadesh-barnea

0   10   20   30 MILES

"Go from your country and your kindred and your
father's house to the land that I will show you."
(Genesis 12:1)

ABRAHAM'S ROUTE

ISAAC'S ROUTE

JACOB'S ROUTE